AGED CARE

To my mother and my father

AGED CARE

Old Policies, New Problems

DIANE GIBSON

PUBLISHED BY THE PRESS SYNDICATE OF THE UNIVERSITY OF CAMBRIDGE
The Pitt Building, Trumpington Street, Cambridge CB2 1RP, United Kingdom

CAMBRIDGE UNIVERSITY PRESS
The Edinburgh Building, Cambridge CB2 2RU, United Kingdom
40 West 20th Street, New York, NY 10011–4211, USA
10 Stamford Road, Oakleigh, Melbourne 3166, Australia

First published 1998

Printed in Singapore by Kin Keong

Typeset in Baskerville 10/12 pt

National Library of Australia Cataloguing in Publication data

Gibson, D. M. (Diane M.)
Aged care: old policies, new problems.
Bibliography.
Includes index.
ISBN 0 521 55957 X (pbk).
ISBN 0 521 55068 8.
1. Aged – Care – Australia. 2. Aged – Care – Standards –
Australia. 3. Aged – Australia – Social conditions.
I. Title
362.60994

Library of Congress Cataloguing in Publication data

Gibson, Diane, 1954–
Aged care: old policies, new problems / Diane Gibson.
p.   cm.
Includes bibliographical references and index.
ISBN 0-521-55068-8 (hardcover) – ISBN 0-521-55957-X (pbk.)
1. Aged – Care – Government policy. 2. Aged – Care – Government
policy – Australia. I. Title.
HV1451.G52 1997
362.6'0994–dc21   97–23196

A catalogue record for this book is available from the British Library

Contents

Tables

Figures

Preface

We are rightly accustomed to seeing social problems as (variously) demographically driven; socially constructed; politically exacerbated. All that is true in trumps of the problem of ageing, as these chapters will show. What is equally true, however, is that *policy makes problems social*. My focus here, most broadly conceived, is on the ways in which personal troubles become public issues – and on the particular, often peculiar, construction put on those problems in their passage from the personal to the social.

Policy responses highlight some aspects of a problem, those to which they are particularly suited, while eclipsing others. The eclipsed aspects remain problematic, but those problems are then seen as the personal province of individuals and families concerned. Consider the themes introduced in Chapter 1, around which the book as a whole is organised: deinstitutionalisation, targeting, regulation, rights, dependency, feminisation. All of these themes point to particular ways of constructing issues raised by an ageing population, as well as to particular policy responses for dealing with them. But those policy responses, in doing what they do well, push back into the realm of 'personal troubles' those aspects of the problems with which those policies cannot cope well. In this process additional personal troubles may emerge; 'personal' problems which are socially constructed as part of a public solution to a 'social' problem.

No policy can do everything at once. Much though it may do in some dimensions, there are inevitably other dimensions along which it leaves much undone. Aaron Wildavsky (1979) used to talk of 'policy as its own cause', March and Olsen (1976) of policy-making as a 'garbage can' in which solutions look for problems at the same time as problems are looking for solutions. The peculiarity about policy areas like aged care is the way in which this process is interrupted, the way in which a residual category of 'personal troubles' soaks up aspects of the problems that constructions of social policy define as outside their own remit. In cases such as these, feedback processes are interrupted. Sociological circuit-breakers serve to interrupt ordinary processes of policy formation and reformation. The 'status quo' of existing policy can continue on its journey, critically appraised in its own terms, but with its destination largely unremarked. Policy is prevented from serving as its own cause.

Policy analysis, of the sort practised in Parts I and II of this book, is a necessary first step. The constructions which policy puts on social problems, the extent to which policy serves its self-defined tasks well or badly, are clearly important considerations. But theoretical reflection on aspects of the problem that those policies inevitably eclipse is an equally necessary next step, as Part III of this book goes on to show.

Any piece of social research must be properly situated. This one is firmly rooted in Australian experience. Throughout Parts I and II, I hope to speak both to Australians about their own aged care system and to bring the experience of Australia (a world leader in several respects, laggard in a few) to the attention of international and comparative analysts of social policy. Interesting though the peculiarities of Australian experiences may be, both to Australians and to comparativists, what is perhaps more striking is the commonality of perspectives on these problems and the commonality of policy responses across virtually all the developed and much of the developing world. Having been led to the broader theoretical reflections of Part III by reflection on Australian problems and practices, those reflections nonetheless apply with equal force to present ways of thinking about problems of ageing internationally.

Acknowledgments

This book is the culmination of work on these topics spanning two decades. Although none of this book literally reprints any previous published work, my first and largest debt is inevitably to my many collaborators, co-authors and co-workers with whom I have worked on these ideas over the years. I ought to single out for particular tribute in this regard: Judith Allen, Fran Boyle, John Braithwaite, Valerie Braithwaite, Dorothy Broom, Warwick Bruen, Stephen Duckett, Ching Choi, Robert Goodin, Coralie Kingston, Zhibin Liu and Don Rowland. A more global vote of thanks will have to serve for the many more people who have influenced my thinking during our time together in the Department of Anthropology and Sociology at the University of Queensland, in the School of Humanities at Griffith University and in the Ageing and the Family Project at the Research School of Social Sciences of the Australian National University.

I should also express my appreciation for the generous funding of a range of consultancies and research projects which have helped towards the development of many of the arguments presented here. The federal Department of Family Services and Health has, despite a bewildering series of name changes, been a consistent supporter of applied health and welfare research in Australia over the past two decades; without their funding of my own and others' work we would simply not have the national data and analysis so necessary to good policy development. While too many to name, I am grateful to many officers of that department for stimulating discussion, critical comment and various forms of assistance with tracking down necessary national data.

This is in no sense an official report from the Australian Institute of Health and Welfare; on the contrary, all the views expressed are insistently my own, and ought not be attributed to them as my present employers. Still, past and present members of my Aged Care Unit there – particularly Anne Jenkins, Sushma Mathur and Debra Rickwood – have contributed ideas and insights which have inevitably found their way into this book. For policy updates in Australian aged care, I would refer the reader to the 'Aged Care' chapter in the biennial report of the Institute, *Australia's Welfare* (Canberra: AIHW 1993, 1995 *et seq.*).

Earlier versions of some of these chapters have been discussed at various professional meetings, among them: the Research Committee on Ageing of the International Sociological Association, the Political Studies Association of the United Kingdom, The Australian Sociological Association and the Australian Association of Gerontology, and various seminars and conferences run by the Social Policy Research Centre of the University of New South Wales. I am grateful to all the commentators and questioners on all those occasions for helping me to sharpen my arguments.

After dozens and dozens of articles, book chapters and research reports, it was a rude shock to find oneself writing one's first single-authored book. Tim Barton, Rudolf Klein, Robin Means, Sid Sax, and various anonymous referees have all helped me to see the shape of the book. Phillipa McGuinness has been patient and persistent, a model editor. My partner, Bob Goodin, has been impatient and insistent (absent that, it would never have been written). I am grateful to them all.

Some of these chapters draw on previously published materials. I am grateful to Judith Allen for permission to reuse material from our jointly authored article 'Phallocentrism and Parasitism: Social Provision for the Aged', and to the following copyright holders:

Kluwer Academic Publishers for material in Chapter 4 from Diane Gibson and Judith Allen (1993) 'Phallocentrism and Parasitism: Social Provision for the Aged', *Policy Sciences*, Vol. 26, No. 2, pp. 79–98.

Blackwell for material in Chapter 9 from Diane Gibson (1995) 'User Rights and the Frail Aged' *Journal of Applied Philosophy*, Vol. 12, No. 1, pp. 1–11.

Sage Publications for material in Chapter 7 from Diane Gibson (1996) 'Broken Down by Age and Gender: The "Problem" of Old Women Redefined' *Gender and Society*, Vol. 10, No. 4, pp. 433–448.

Commonwealth of Australia (AGPS) for material in Tables 3.3, 3.4, 3.5, 5.1 and 5.2 and Figure 3.1 from Diane Gibson *et al.* (1995) 'Aged Care' in Australian Institute of Health and Welfare *Australia's Welfare 1995: Services and Assistance*, AGPS: Canberra.

University of Chicago Press for material presented in Table 1.4 from Walter Korpi 'The Position of the Elderly in the Welfare State: Comparative Perspectives on Old-Age Care in Sweden' in *Social Service Review* June 1995, pp. 242–273.

Abbreviations

AIHW   Australian Institute of Health and Welfare
DCS   Department of Community Services
HACC   Home and Community Care
HFS   Department of Health and Family Services
HHCS   Department of Health, Housing and Community Services
HHLGS   Department of Health, Housing, Local Government and
        Community Services
RCI   Resident Classification Instrument

PART ONE

What's the Problem?

CHAPTER 1

The Issues

Introduction

The distinction between personal troubles and public issues, first articulated by C. Wright Mills in 1959, is a familiar one within sociology. It usefully identifies fit subject matter for a discipline which is inherently disorderly and resistant to definitional encapsulation. But that distinction has never been a particularly clear one. Furthermore, we need to direct at least as much attention to the process by which personal problems come to be recast as public issues.

In many ways, that too has long been clear. From the difficulties confronting bored and lonely suburban housewives, Betty Friedan (1963) drew the 'problem which had no name'. She, in conjunction with writers such as Gloria Steinem, Germaine Greer and Shulamith Firestone, provided the literary basis for the second wave of the feminist movement. In the 1980s there came gay liberation and in the 1990s the disability rights movement. While each of these political movements has close connections to and interactions with academic programs (women's studies, disability studies, queer theory), in all those cases it has typically been political action rather than sociological thought which allowed areas of human life previously deemed to be 'personal troubles' to re-emerge as 'public issues'.

The process of getting a particular personal trouble recognised as a public issue can be a difficult one, particularly for those groups lacking resources and status. Michael Oliver (1990) makes this argument cogently with regard to disability and the disability movement. The challenge here is to have disability recognised as a problem for society because of the way in which society is structured, rather than a problem of the individual because of a perceived personal failing, whether physical or intellectual.

3

If that proposition is not immediately apparent to those not touched
by disability or the disability movement, consider feminists' analogous
claim that 'traditional' structures – traditional marital sex roles, workplace norms, lack of relevant leave provisions and so on – discriminated both overtly and covertly against women. Recall the similar
difficulties which feminists encountered in convincing a disbelieving
society of those propositions. Recall, too, how various shifts in our
understanding of the way in which society works have contributed to
making such claims broadly accepted today. The journey from 'the
problem which had no name' to affirmative action legislation was a long
one, underpinned by significant social change. The parallel example
of evolving thought about the appropriate social place of blacks in
the American deep south (Myrdal 1944) may provide the necessary
intellectual leverage for those who still remain unconvinced of the
malleability of personal troubles into social issues.

It is my contention, then, that what constitutes a public issue rather
than a personal trouble is not intellectually stable ground. Examples
such as women's liberation, black rights, gay rights and disability rights
all point to the importance of political movements in successfully establishing an oppositional discourse: one which locates a particular kind
of disadvantage as socially structured, rather than as an individual
trait. This in turn emerges as a fit area for sociological study. This
process in its turn serves as a useful reminder that 'oppositional discourses' are required because the existing perception is the perception
of a dominant group: male, white, heterosexual, able-bodied, or – in
the case which forms the basis for this book – non-aged.

Yet the emergence of ageing as a public issue rather than a personal
trouble does not fall neatly within the political-activist tradition
described above. True, in the USA there is the example of the Grey
Panthers and other such political pressure groups. In other countries,
however – including Australia, the United Kingdom and much of
mainland Europe – such an argument is much less compelling. There
the emergence of ageing as a social problem seems to have occurred,
not at the urging of older people themselves, but rather from that
sector of society which is charged with providing their care. It gained
centre stage, not as an oppositional discourse built by the aged in reaction to dominant societal norms failing to take account of their particular and peculiar circumstances in contemporary society, but rather by
that dominant group itself.

Concern has escalated as the numbers of people reaching old age
have increased. The yet-to-occur movement of the baby boom generation into old age appears to arouse particular excitement in popu-
larised versions of analyses of population ageing. It is, of course, by

and large the baby boom generation itself which is undertaking these analyses. These baby boomers are seemingly preoccupied with the twin problems of how to pay for the support of burgeoning numbers of older people in the present and yet have sufficient resources available to ensure that they are themselves appropriately cared for in the future.

Several points of relevance to this book emerge from this. First, ageing may have emerged as a public issue rather than a personal trouble. But it has done so in the hands not of the disadvantaged group themselves but rather in that section of society on which they are likely to be reliant for care; that is, as a dominant rather than oppositional discourse. Second, this construction of ageing as a public issue or social problem has an intrinsic component: a concern with how such a level of need can be met – the fear of a future society burdened by the weight of 'elder care'. This is quite a different preoccupation, for example, from that evident in the demands of the disability rights movement to gain recognition for disability as a public issue and one deserving of a fair share of societal resources. Third, much of the work done in aged care research and policy development is premised on the knowledge and understanding developed within that dominant social paradigm. Consequently, problems and their solutions are cast in ways consistent with the views and interests of middle-aged, mid-career social scientists and policy-makers. It is this latter observation which underlies many of the theoretical reflections which comprise the third part of this book.

In any case, regardless of how it was achieved, ageing has attained the status of a public issue rather than merely a private trouble. It is, moreover, a public issue with a remarkably consistent international face. A number of recurrent themes reverberate throughout the international literature on aged care. These are central both to the policy analysis work in Part II of this book and to the conceptual analyses in Part III.

The 'ageing of the population' – under which I include actual, projected and perceived population ageing – has brought with it a number of changes in aged care and in the ways that we think about aged care issues, not all of which are immediately apparent. The most commonly discussed issues include the increased numbers of highly dependent aged persons, the increased demand for aged care services, the associated escalating cost to the public sector, and the likely consequences for the existing system of financing both income support and long-term care.

Less overtly discussed as a consequence of the ageing of the population, but none the less associated with it, are the shifts which are occurring in the way in which aged care services are provided, with implications for both the formal and the informal sectors. These include:

• a probable increasing demand for and reliance on family care;
• the progressive deinstitutionalisation of aged care services;
• closer targeting and rationing of services;
• greater concern with quality of care and regulatory issues; and
• an emphasis on consumer and user rights.

There has also been a growing awareness, at least among a minority of analysts, that the preponderance of old women is more than a demographic oddity and has significant social and policy implications.

Not all of these trends and shifts in emphasis have been equally manifest in developed nations. But interestingly it is consistency rather than difference which appears to dominate the international literature. It is more in the implementation and the structure of existing systems, rather than at the level of explicit or even implicit policy aims and trends, where cross-national variations are evident.

There are also other broader trends at work throughout national health and welfare systems which are not specific responses to population ageing, but nonetheless impact on the ways in which aged care services are provided. While they are neither specifically ageing-related nor quite so consistently evident in an international context, they constitute a salient counterpoint in a number of countries and thereby modify the delivery and funding of aged care services. These include:

• a focus on equity and access;
• moves to better define appropriate outcomes for services; and
• the privatisation of service delivery systems.

This book explores the changing face of aged care in Australia, but it does so with an eye to this international context. It is not a comparative volume, as such. Rather it is one which takes the Australian aged care system as an object of study in its own right, but which also locates it as a social laboratory for ageing policies – an instance where the ageing of the population occurred later than in Europe, but with considerable rapidity. The Australian policy response could thus be informed by experience elsewhere, but at the same time the modifications to that received wisdom put in place in Australia have often been at the forefront of international developments. The remainder of this introductory chapter is devoted to outlining the commonalities in contemporary aged care policy at the international level.

Growing demand

Population ageing is a defining characteristic of all developed and many developing nations in the latter part of the twentieth century, and one which will continue into the twenty-first. In 1950 between 8 and 9 per cent of the population in North America, Europe, Australia and New Zealand were aged 65 and over. Today that figure has increased substantially everywhere. However, regional variation in the rates of increase over that period has resulted in a situation where, by 1990, 13.4 per cent of Europeans were 65 or older, compared to 12.5 per cent in North America and 10.9 per cent in Australia and New Zealand (United Nations 1993b: 25).

My concern here, however, is with the more recent demographic trends which are of relevance to the shape of current and emerging aged care policies. While the magnitude of percentage increases over five- to ten-year periods may lack the drama of a 40-year series, they have the advantage of immediacy, capturing more accurately the changing levels of demand with which public policy is actually confronted.

The Australian population is relatively young among developed nations. The 14-country comparison in Table 1.1 reveals three tiers in terms of population structure. The oldest tier includes most of the European countries, with between 14.5 per cent (France) and 17.7 per cent (Sweden) aged 65 and over. The second tier is a more eclectic cultural mix, but comprises a recognisably 'younger' set of countries, with between 11.5 per cent (New Zealand) and 13.1 per cent (Japan) aged 65 and over. Australia ranks close to the bottom of this group, with 11.7 per cent of its population aged 65 and over. The third comprises a single example, China, representing the so-called 'late initiation' countries, in which the decline in fertility which precedes population ageing did not occur until much later than in the developed nations (United Nations 1993b: 9–11, 20).

The proportion of the population aged 65 and over, while a useful indicator with regard to income support, is a relatively poor measure of the likely need for care among frail and disabled aged persons. While disability levels are the most direct measure, they are not readily available for the purposes of international comparisons. A useful surrogate measure may be found in the proportion of people aged 80 and over, as it is among this group that service use tends to be most heavily concentrated. Hence, it is this segment of the aged population which most directly drives the need for aged care services.

In general, those countries with the largest proportions of people aged 65 and over also have higher proportions of persons aged 80 and

Table 1.1   Aged population in 14 countries (1992 and 1993)

Per cent 65+ in the population		Per cent 80+ in the population		Per cent aged+ in the 65+ population	
Sweden	17.7	Sweden	4.5	France	27.2
Norway	16.2	France	4.0	Sweden	25.4
United Kingdom	15.8	Austria	3.9	Austria	25.3
Denmark	15.6	Norway	3.9	Germany	25.1
Austria	15.2	Denmark	3.8	Denmark	24.6
Germany	15.0	United Kingdom	3.8	United Kingdom	24.3
France	14.5	Germany	3.8	Norway	23.7
Japan	13.1	Netherlands	3.0	United States	23.3
Netherlands	13.0	United States	3.0	Netherlands	22.8
United States	12.7	Japan	2.7	Canada	21.3
Canada	11.8	Canada	2.5	New Zealand	21.1
Australia	11.7	Australia	2.4	Australia	20.7
New Zealand	11.5	New Zealand	2.4	Japan	20.5
China	5.6	China	0.7	China	12.2

Note: This table gives population data for either 1992 or 1993, with the exception of China where the data are for 1990.
Source: Calculated from United Nations (1995) and ABS (1993a).

over. Thus, the countries in the second tier of the table (Japan, Netherlands, USA, Canada, Australia and New Zealand) also have somewhat lower proportions of people aged 80 and over than do those in the first tier. Nonetheless, the two measures do not exactly track each other, owing to variations in both cohort size and longevity patterns. The third column in Table 1.1 (the percentage of people aged over 80 in the 65+ population) illustrates the degree of variation. Thus, when this aspect of the age structure of the older population in the United Kingdom is examined, it is closer to the Unites States than it is, for example, to France, despite the greater similarity of the United Kingdom and France on the other two measures. The Australian population, on the other hand, retains its position as a comparatively young country, regardless of the section of the population examined.

The Australian population has, however, been ageing comparatively quickly in recent years, and the rate of increase is strongest among the very old. Table 1.2 ranks the 14 countries according to the recent annual growth rates of their aged populations, showing a roughly inverse picture to that presented in the preceding table. Here, Japan and China lead the field, followed by Australia, Canada and New Zealand – regardless of whether one examines the rate of growth in the over 65 or the over 80 population. In recent years, all of the countries

Table 1.2   Recent annual growth rates (1985 to 1995)

Annual % increase 65 and over		Annual % increase 80 and over	
Japan	4.4	Japan	7.3
China	3.5	China	6.5
Canada	3.3	Australia	5.0
Australia	3.1	Canada	4.6
New Zealand	2.5	New Zealand	4.5
France	2.2	Germany	3.9
Netherlands	1.7	Austria	3.7
United States	1.7	France	3.4
Austria	1.6	United Kingdom	3.4
Germany	0.9	United States	3.3
United Kingdom	0.9	Denmark	2.7
Norway	0.8	Netherlands	2.7
Denmark	0.5	Norway	2.6
Sweden	0.1	Sweden	2.0

Source: Calculated from United Nations (1993a).

in this table have experienced a rate of growth in their 80 and over population between one and a half times and twice that for the aged population as a whole.

The rate of growth among the very old has been particularly high in the countries with a younger demographic profile. Australia, New Zealand, Canada and Japan all have comparatively young demographic profiles, but have experienced a recent, rapid increase in the size of their very old populations. The United States and the Netherlands, who also have somewhat younger demographic profiles than most of Europe, have experienced more modest rates of growth in their very old populations. Most European countries, although characterised by a larger proportion of very old people, have had comparatively slow rates of growth in the 80 and over population in recent years.

The next decade will, in broad terms, see a continuation of these trends. Australia, like Canada, will experience quite high rates of growth in the very old population, around 3 to 4 per cent per year. Japan (4.3 per cent) and China (4.9 per cent) will experience the most rapid increases in the proportion of very old people over this period, while many of the European countries have projected rates of increase for the 80 and over population of less than 1 per cent.

The high rates of growth in the very old population over the decade just past and the decade to come have placed the Australian aged care

Table 1.3   Projected annual growth rates (1995 to 2005)

Annual % increase 65 and over		Annual % increase 80 and over	
Japan	3.4	China	4.9
China	3.1	Japan	4.3
Germany	1.9	Canada	3.6
Canada	1.8	Australia	3.3
Australia	1.4	New Zealand	2.3
Netherlands	1.2	United States	2.2
France	1.0	Netherlands	2.1
New Zealand	0.9	Norway	1.8
United States	0.6	Sweden	1.3
Austria	0.6	France	1.0
Denmark	0.1	Denmark	0.9
United Kingdom	0.1	United Kingdom	0.8
Sweden	−0.2	Austria	0.6
Norway	−0.5	Germany	−0.1

Source: Calculated from United Nations (1993a).

system under particular stress as it attempts to respond to a rapid change in the demand for aged care services. While the proportion of the population likely to be in need of such assistance remains smaller than in most European countries, the rate of adjustment required of the Australian system has been more dramatic, and will continue to be so. It is thus not surprising that the Australian aged care system has been so thoroughly overhauled during this period, although students of social policy know that changing social circumstances are not in themselves sufficient to ensure commensurate changes in policy systems.

Deinstitutionalisation

Although varying definitions of institutional care can make international comparisons somewhat difficult, available evidence suggests significant cross-national diversity in the proportion of the aged population who are accommodated in nursing homes, aged care homes, or long-stay geriatric institutions, and in the proportion who are accessing home-based care. Nonetheless, in broad terms, it is possible to observe an increasing co-incidence of policy directions towards home-based care, and away from systems heavily reliant on institutional provision.

Table 1.4 gives the percentage of the aged population who were receiving home help services or who were in residential care in the

Table 1.4 Percentage of the aged population receiving home help services
and institutional care

% 65+ receiving home help		% 65+ in residential care	
Denmark	17	Netherlands	10
Sweden	17	Denmark	6
Netherlands	13	Sweden	6
United Kingdom	8	Australia	6
Australia	7	France	6
France	7	United Kingdom	5
United States	0–8	United States	5
Ireland	3	Ireland	5
Germany	3	Germany	5
Italy	<1	Italy	<2
Spain	<1	Spain	<2
Japan	<1	Japan	<2

Note: The data reported here refer to 1990 or 1991. The United States data
are, however, from the early to mid-1980s. The home help percentage
reported for the United States varies state by state.
Sources: Compiled from AIHW (1993); Korpi (1995: 254); Rivlin and Wiener
(1988: 13); Sundström (1994: 41).

early 1990s. While various authorities differ somewhat on the exact
level of home care services available (see, for example, Korpi 1995;
Sundström 1994: 41; Walker and Warren 1996: 8–10), it seems clear
that there are broadly identifiable bands of service provision within
which these countries fall. Denmark, Sweden and the Netherlands can
readily be identified as high providers of home help services, while the
United Kingdom, Australia and France form a moderate provider
group. The remaining countries could be typified as low providers
overall (although within the United States some states range well into
the moderate provider class). Looking at residential care, the Netherlands stands alone with 10 per cent of people aged 65 and over in residential care, followed by more moderate levels of provision (5 to 6 per
cent) in most north European countries, as well as in Australia and the
United States.

Three interesting points emerge from this table. First, there is quite
a substantial range in the levels of both residential and home-based
provision, and these levels do not co-vary with the likely level of
demand for such services in the population, as indicated by Table 1.1.
In other words, France, Denmark and Sweden, each with much higher
proportions of very old people in its population than Australia, have
very similar levels of residential care, and levels of home care services

which are either equal (in the case of France) or higher (in the cases of Denmark and Sweden). Moreover, the Netherlands – with one of the younger demographic profiles in Europe – has the highest level of residential provision, and one of the higher levels of home help as well. Denmark and Sweden – whose demographic profiles are very similar to Germany – have similar levels of residential provision, but much higher levels of home help services.

Second, given the current explicit policy in Australia to increase the level of home-based care and decrease the level of residential provision, one might expect countries to be similarly oriented towards either residential care or home-based care. This does not seem to be the case. Countries which are high on institutional provision do not, by and large, appear to be low on home-based care; in fact if anything levels of provision for one appear to be positively correlated with levels of provision on the other.

Third, a level of 5 or 6 per cent of the population aged 65 and over in residential care appears to provide a 'baseline' of provision below which few countries with reasonably developed social welfare systems fall. Provision levels for home help are much more variable. While the explanation for this greater variability in community-based care is undoubtedly multifaceted, having largely to do with idiosyncratic policy histories in particular countries, it is interesting to speculate on the role of capital in the apparently more stable residential care field. It may well be that institutional provision is not only more stable on a cross-national basis but also more stable over time. Once residential care facilities have been built, there is an institutional (in the other sense) incentive to retain them – the closure of a nursing home or a hospital wing attracts more attention than a 10 per cent reduction in real terms in funding to a community care facility. Residential care structures are at once more visible and are likely to represent a capital commitment – sometimes by the state alone, but often by the state in some collaborative venture with the private-for-profit or voluntary sectors.

Explaining international variations in patterns of aged care is certainly beyond the scope of this book. What is certain is that existing patterns of care are driven by a complex amalgam of historically antecedent events. While factors such as control over the level of supply and rigorous means testing of prospective residents may be useful strategies in reducing institutionalisation levels (Doty, cited in Laing 1993: 81), they do little to explain the trend itself. Indeed, the very acceptability and apparent universality of the trend towards developing home-based care rather than residential care makes it an interesting subject for critical scrutiny.

It has certainly become broadly accepted that most elderly people prefer to stay in their own homes. Walker and Warren (1996) cite results from a Eurobarometer survey that indicate a large majority of people across Europe believe frail people ought to be helped to remain in their own homes, and this finding has been convincingly echoed by older people themselves (Davison *et al*. 1993). Indeed, Tinker asserts that the preference to remain in their own home is the 'one clear message' which we may take from research on older people's housing needs and preferences (1994: 58).[1]

The preferences of older people themselves may well be a driving force in this policy shift. A more sceptical policy analyst, however, might take the position that this preference seems likely to have been the case for some time, and it is not at all clear why the last decade has seen such an upsurge of government interest in policies which facilitate that preference.

Nonetheless, the widespread existence of policy objectives expressed in terms of 'ageing in place', 'staying put' and 'staying at home' is evidence that that preference has been translated into policy terms. Tinker cites a Danish policy statement that the objective is no longer 'in one's home for as long as possible' but 'permanently in one's own home' (1994: 58). Reviewing current trends in the European Union countries, Walker and Warren comment on the policies put forward by all governments in favour of home-based care as opposed to residential or hospital care (1996: 9). The policy direction is a long-established one in some countries, more recent in others, but the consistency of the trend is unquestioned. These and other trends concerning the development of home care services in Europe have recently been charted in the collections edited by Hutten and Kerkstra (1996) and Jamieson (1991).

Since 1985, Australia too has been vigorously pursuing a policy of deinstitutionalisation in aged care. Not only was the Australian system at that time faced with a rapid increase in potential demand, it was also a system which was heavily reliant on expensive forms of residential care. While there was a dual system of delivery, including the less intensive hostel level of care alongside the more intensive nursing home system, it was the latter that predominated, and the home-based care system was both small and poorly co-ordinated. The need to reduce the reliance of the system on residential provision was thus readily apparent, and as will become evident in chapters 2 and 3, the process of change has been quite a rapid one.

In Sweden, Korpi (1995) documents an increasing provision of

---

[1] For a description of these and other housing-related trends among older people see also Pynos and Liebig (1995) whose edited collection contains detailed case studies on nine countries.

home-based care from a much earlier period – the 1950s – with growth rates higher than those in the aged population throughout the 1960s. While absolute growth continued through the 1970s, the proportion of older people receiving home help, and eventually even the absolute numbers receiving care, have begun to decline. The clients themselves have become older and have more severe problems, requiring more hours of service per client. The level of nursing home care (including long-term hospital care and geriatric care) reached a maximum in the mid-1980s, with an absolute as well as a relative decline in supply since then. While the rise of home care has a long history in Sweden, the reduction in residential provision is a more recent phenomenon.

The United Kingdom shows quite a different pattern. Long viewed as one of the shining examples of a system of aged care which emphasised home-based services and provided relatively low levels of residential care (Kendig and Rowland 1983), a revamping of social security entitlements led to an unanticipated and unintended growth in residential and nursing home care. From 1980 to 1991, for example, there was almost a four-fold increase in nursing home beds, and a 57 per cent increase in residential care places (Wistow *et al.* 1994: 44–8). The stage was obviously set for reining in such growth and the re-emergence of an emphasis on home-based care. In a detailed account of subsequent community care implementation in five local authorities, Lewis and Glennerster eloquently conclude that the reforms were 'driven by the need to stop the haemorrhage in the social security budget and to do so in a way that would minimise political outcry' (1996: 8).

Five major reports from 1985 culminated in the influential Griffiths report *Community Care: Agenda for Action* (1988). The Griffiths Report emphasised as one of three key objectives the need to promote non-institutional support services – care was to be delivered in the domestic environment and in community settings in order to allow people to remain in their own homes. It was to be some 18 months before the White Paper (*Caring for People – Community Care in the Next Decade and Beyond*) was released, but it did contain many of Griffiths' proposals, albeit in somewhat more modest forms (Wistow *et al.* 1994: 6–12).

Despite (or perhaps because of) the universality of the trend, it is difficult to establish exactly why it has occurred. To go further, one might ask the even more difficult question of why the trend towards care of the frail aged in the community has come to be regarded as 'a good thing' – and indeed whether it is? After all, the move away from large-scale orphanages occurred at the very start of the century, and that from mental asylums and homes for the disabled in the 1960s. Why aged care in the 1980s?

In general social policy terms the two most common explanations of policy shifts can be summarised under the broad headings of the 'enlightenment theory of social welfare' and the 'necessity theory' of social welfare. The first suggests that as a modern society we progressively improve our ways of doing things, and that the trend to community care for the aged is just such an improvement. The second more fiscally driven explanation, not inconsistent with the first, underlines the expensive nature of institutions, and the fact that we can no longer afford such a model of provision with an ageing population structure.

Specific explanations from the aged care literature are generally offered either in terms of the preferences of the elderly or in terms of cost containment. While the preferences of the elderly provide a straightforward rationale, it is not clear that this represents a sudden shift in the views of older people themselves. Certainly, it seems doubtful that prior generations of elderly people leapt with positive enthusiasm at the opportunity of moving into nursing homes.

The cost containment argument has a certain hard edge in policy terms, and it is clearly a driving force in providing care to growing numbers of highly dependent older people, by virtue of resort to what is generally held to be a substantially cheaper form of care. Moreover, the problem is one being universally encountered by developed countries, and the solution is also a universally applicable one. Not only is the containment of costs in recurrent funding terms a positive advantage associated with home care, so too are the capital savings in the absence of the need to build, maintain and refurbish large numbers of residential aged care facilities.

There are other supporting arguments and explanations. Walker and Warren (1996: 16) suggest that the feminist critique (loosely summarised, the argument that 'community care was care by the family, and care by the family was care by women') of the late 1970s and 1980s was also a factor in forcing governments to recognise the need to support the large amount of care provided by the informal care network. They also suggest that the independent living movement mounted by people with disabilities in the late 1980s and 1990s contributed to the push for an expansion of home-based care services. The latter is, however, a largely British phenomenon, and the former too commenced earlier and entered the public domain more strongly in Britain than in many other countries. Even in Australia, home to the femocrats and with an active feminist social policy network, these arguments were not as salient as they have been in Britain.

Another influence which may well be at work is the changing nature of family life. Family members were very influential in securing the development of services for intellectually handicapped children, and, at least in Australia, we are seeing a similar pattern with regard to acquired brain injury. The emergence of carers' advocacy and support groups, well advanced in Australia, appears to be an increasingly internationally evident phenomenon.

The movement of women into paid work, and the projected reduction in the availability of a 'pool' of informal carers as the demographic profile of the population changes, has also been linked to explanations of the emerging emphasis on home-based care. While such shifts could certainly explain a demand for more formal services, it is not immediately obvious that these should be home-based rather than residential care options.

The family, and its willingness and capacity to provide care, must be of some relevance to broad policy directions in aged care. But family needs, demands and preferences in the real world may involve quite complex trade-offs, and the nature of the trade-offs may change significantly (and quite rapidly) over time. They also differ across cultures. Key issues are likely to be the acceptability and costs of residential care, as well as the emotional, physical and financial burdens involved in caring at home. Family members may variously demand improved residential care, or more and better community-based care, depending on their own circumstances and the needs of the people for whom they care. The family is not necessarily a driving force for deinstitutionalisation in modern society.

Targeting and rationing

In aged care 'targeting' is generally taken to refer to the targeting of services and assistance to those most in need, defined in terms of physical or mental frailty. Yet this is not the interpretation generally associated with the concept in wider social policy circles, where targeting is taken to be synonymous with some form of means testing. While there are inevitably some correlations between the two, key debates in the means testing arena (such as those pertaining to universalism and selectivity) are not directly translatable or even necessarily pertinent, when the discussion turns to targeting on the basis of intellectual or physical disabilities.

In many ways targeting in this latter sense has been a more generally accepted component of social policy than targeting based on means or assets. The decision to provide or not provide a service on the basis of income has been a hotly debated topic in social policy literature, whereas the question of providing aged care services to those with low levels of physical or intellectual problems has been less so. Yet targeting remains in both senses a strategy for rationing, and rationing inevitably means that some people who would like and may even need services will not receive them. Indeed, if this were not to be the case, there would be no need to invoke rationing or targeting principles in the first place.

However, even if the need for some form of rationing is accepted we are left with a key normative issue concerning the adequacy of provision. In simple terms, when does appropriate targeting of resources become an inadequate level of provision? The more stringently services are targeted, the more emotionally difficult become decisions about boundary cases, and the more dire the consequences for those who fall outside the boundary. Decisions about the level of neediness which can or should be met, and the levels of assistance which even those who meet the criteria can expect to receive, become increasingly fraught decisions in periods of scarcity.[2]

Rationing occurs as part of the supply side of the equation. The total resources available are pre-determined, as is the proportion of demand which will be met. Targeting, if appropriately implemented, assures us that those most in need will receive assistance. It does not guarantee, however, that all those genuinely in need of assistance will have that need met.

Targeting has become an explicit part of the Australian aged care policy system. So too has rationing, as will become evident from the policy history to be presented in Chapter 2. In particular, the level of residential care provided in relation to the size of the aged population has been reduced as an explicit policy. The United Kingdom has followed a similar trajectory, although one more couched in terms of the expansion of home-based care than of the explicit reduction of residential provisions. Here, rationing occurs in terms of the amounts allocated to local authorities; it is they who must decide not only who will receive assistance, but also what services (residential versus home-based) will be available to them.

It is certainly the case that the move towards less expensive home-based care, combined with the targeting of available resources on those most in need, offers considerable efficiencies within the aged care system. The point at which the efficiencies to be gained are outweighed by the inadequacy of total available resources remains both contentious and unidentified. Walker and Warren, for example, speak of a generalised 'care gap' in all countries in the European Union, save Denmark

---

[2] The more stringently the lines are drawn the greater the cost to the person being denied the service. At the same time, the mix of errors necessarily shifts – the more stringent the criteria the greater the proportion of false negatives (not giving a service to someone who is in serious need) to false positives (giving a service to someone who is not in serious need). See, for an elaboration of this argument Goodin (1985a).

and Sweden (1996: 17). In Australia, the House of Representatives Standing Committee on Community Affairs undertook an extensive process of community and expert consultation – its final report stressed the need to expand significantly community care services (1994). This tension between maximising efficiency and maintaining adequacy of provision was memorably summed up by Griffiths (1988: iii), commenting on the British situation in the late 1980s:

> The Audit Commission on the one hand were satisfied that better value could be obtained from existing resources. On the other hand, many social service departments and voluntary groups grappling with the problems at local level certainly felt that the Israelites faced with the requirement to make bricks without straw had a comparatively routine and possible task.

There is, finally, a need to consider the role of discretion in a highly targeted and flexible system. While there are indeed advantages to such a system, the example of the changing circumstances of poor frail aged persons in Britain in recent years is a salutary one. Walker and Warren (1996: 20) comment that what the NHS and Community Care Act of 1990 (expanded home care, better targeting of available resources and so on) meant for poor frail aged people in reality was that the previous right of access to private residential care was replaced by home care available at the discretion of the service provider. Targeting, by definition, involves decisions about the 'real' needs of clients being made by professionals and services providers. If not necessarily an oppositional discourse to that of user empowerment, targeting and discretionary provision are certainly not consistent with it.

In Australia aged care assessment teams have assumed the central gatekeeping functions for residential care, and this role seems set to become increasingly important with regard to home-based care as the targeting of these services emerges as a policy issue. As control over access becomes increasingly centralised, there will be a need to more closely scrutinise the performance and impact of assessment procedures. Issues such as national standards, the comparability of assessment procedures and decisions, service quality and the protection of the rights of individual clients all become increasingly important.

Regulation, quality and outcomes

As governments increasingly reduce their roles in direct service provision, their interest and involvement in regulation and accountability undergo a corresponding expansion. While some attention has focused on internal management practices and efficiency audits (Power 1994), there has been a rapidly growing preoccupation with outcome measures and program regulation. The difficulties inherent in establishing agreed outcome measures are familiar to anyone experienced in program evaluation in the health and welfare sectors. From the social indicators debates of the early 1970s, through the focus on outcome evaluation in the early 1980s, to the emergence now of the outcome (or performance) indicators movement within the health and welfare services systems, the search for appropriate and easily measurable indicators in complex fields goes on.

In aged care programs the difficulties facing the evaluator or bureaucrat in search of outcome indicators are compounded by the very nature of the client population, and the kinds of assistance which they require. Care of the frail or disabled aged generally requires some composite of medical, personal care, social, psychological and accommodation services. The clientele often have multiple physical and/or mental health problems, involving a complex amalgam of chronic, episodic and acute conditions. Disease trajectories are, not surprisingly, highly individual, unpredictable, variable on a daily basis, and not infrequently degenerative.

The development of outcome measures as a way of appraising quality of care in residential or home-based services for the aged is, therefore, arguably one of the 'worst case' scenarios facing the program evaluator. One cannot use measures associated with recovery, cure, discharge or exit, as these are all relatively infrequent events. Similarly, death or degeneration are often inappropriate indicators of adverse outcomes, as these are not necessarily uncommon or unexpected experiences in long-term care facilities. Sentinel health events, too, can be problematic; either the event is common in the 'at risk' population, or else it is so infrequent as to be an unreliable indicator of poor quality care.

If the task at hand is the design of a regulatory program, and not one of 'mere' program evaluation, then these conceptual difficulties are further compounded by practical problems of implementation. The designers of regulatory programs have to face the political difficulties associated with gaining agreement among the key players – the industry organisations, the professional associations and unions, as well as in a federal system the support of both federal and state bureaucracies, and the governments of the day. Small wonder if such agreements are long in coming, and if regulatory arrangements in many countries are limited to input measures such as basic cleanliness, fire safety and staffing ratios.

The designers of contemporary systems will also doubtless be expected to come up with a scheme which incorporates into the quality appraisal and regulatory process the perspectives of clients, family members, staff and local managers, while maintaining some kind of independent status. National consistency will also be an issue, as will the costs involved in implementing the regulatory program.

Current shifts towards privatisation and various forms of contracting out have brought regulation and quality appraisal into sharper focus in countries such as the United Kingdom and Australia. Traditionally, the vast majority of Australian nursing home services have, since their inception, been provided by the private-for-profit and voluntary sectors, funded by the federal government. In many ways, this system of government-guaranteed funding presaged the modern purchaser–provider split; with the federal government purchasing the service on behalf of the resident from the private-for-profit or voluntary sector service provider. The inception in recent years of 'contracting out' home-based care services in several states (Victoria, and more recently the Australian Capital Territory) has generated an even greater concern to establish outcome and quality appraisal mechanisms.

To date, progress has been limited in developing quality appraisal processes for home care services, although in Australia a national project to develop such a methodology is currently being funded by the federal Department of Health and Family Services. The Australian systems of regulation for nursing homes and hostels are, however, both long established and at the forefront of international regulatory regimes for aged care services (Braithwaite *et al.* 1993). The systems are outcome based, with outcome being largely defined in terms of the subjectively perceived impact on residents.

This approach (a detailed analysis is presented in Chapter 5) differs quite markedly from the equally well-developed system in place in the United States. Although systems vary from state to state, the emphasis is generally on a large number of specific, objectively determined measures (for example, drug passes, whereby the exact number of errors in the administration of medication are counted, and scored either acceptable or unacceptable). This contrasts with the broadly based, subjectively determined Australian measures – although interestingly the Australian method does well in international comparisons measuring reliability and validity (Braithwaite and Braithwaite 1995).

In the United Kingdom the government has recently announced a decision to review the present system of nursing home regulation. In a recent appraisal of the existing system, Day *et al.* (1996) note a general shift in focus away from inputs (size of rooms, number of staff etc.) to what they refer to as 'quality of care issues' such as privacy, dignity and residents' rights. While recognising the desirability of looking at outcomes, Day and her colleagues offer something of a minority voice in this literature, pointing to the dangers of an over-reliance on the views of residents. They comment:

> Homes tend to shape the expectations of their residents: low standards produce low expectations (1996: v).

Basing the Australian residential regulatory system (billed as an 'outcome standards monitoring system') on the perceived acceptability of the outcomes of care as experienced by residents raises questions as to what actually constitutes an outcome measure. In terms favoured by American gerontologists, and indeed by many evaluators, outcome indicators are conceived as objective and specific measures of program performance (Kane and Kane 1987). From this perspective, 'Management of the nursing home is attempting to create and maintain a home-like environment' would not be classified as an outcome standard. Yet in the Australian nursing home monitoring program from which this example is drawn, the outcome orientation would be held to be less to do with the wording of the standard than with the process by which the standards monitoring team determines whether or not the standard was met. This issue and related questions are taken up in further detail in Chapters 5 and 8.

Rights and independence

In an international context Australia has in some ways lagged behind, and in others sprinted ahead, with regard to user rights developments in aged care services. In comparison to the United States, for example, Australia was certainly a late entry to the field.

The first American nursing home ombudsman services were established in 1972, as part of a response by the Nixon administration to continuing reports of unacceptable conditions in nursing homes. From their base as demonstration projects the ombudsman programs were elevated to statutory requirements under the 1978 Amendments to the Older Americans Act, and expanded to include all long-term care facilities in 1981. The ombudsman programs, together with a range of locally organised resident advocacy services, have thus been part of American long-term care arrangements for almost a quarter of a century.

Yet while the ombudsman programs were seen as 'a product of the 1970s, a decade of heightened and zealous concern with patients' rights' (Monk *et al.* 1984: 8), the legislature did not at that time explicitly identify the nature of those rights. Actual incorporation of residents' rights into national legislation did not take place until 1987, when Congress enacted Nursing Home Reform Amendments laying down regulations on residents' rights for all nursing homes participating in Medicare or Medicaid. The regulations (which took effect from 1990) specified rights to self-determination, personal and privacy rights, rights regarding abuse and restraints, rights to information, rights to visits, transfer and discharge rights, and protection of personal funds, as well as offering protection against Medicaid discrimination.

The rights specified in the 1987 amendments in the US bear many similarities to those introduced under the Australian government's outcome standards program for nursing homes in 1987, and to the various statements of rights and responsibilities and supporting innovations in service systems which followed over the ensuing five years. The incorporation of these residents' rights models into a more broadly defined 'user rights strategy' occurred almost simultaneously, with their application being explored in relation not only to home-based care but also to a range of other welfare services. From a position of laggard in the mid-1980s, Australia had established quite comprehensive user rights mechanisms by 1990, surpassing some, although certainly not all, of the United States' achievements.

In Britain the language has tended to be that of 'user empowerment', rather than 'user rights', but the emphasis and concern are remarkably similar. The policy focus is somewhat more recent than in Australia and the United States, being closely linked to the community care reforms, and in particular to the emergence of purchaser–provider splits. For Clarke and Stewart, empowerment is 'a theme for the 1990s' (1992). Means and Smith (1994: 71) note the importance of such issues in the 1989 White Paper on community care and the subsequently issued practitioner guidelines, citing from the latter the statement that 'the rationale for this re-organisation is the empowerment of users and carers'.[3]

Key distinctions have been made and debated in the British literature concerning the relative roles of exit, voice and rights in empowering consumers. While the debates remain pertinent in Australia it is useful to recognise that the 'user rights' terminology in the Australian context is roughly equivalent to 'empowerment' in the British context,

[3] Note that in contemporary British literature on the social services the term 'community care' is increasingly used to incorporate both residential and domiciliary services. The community care reforms put forward in the 1989 White Paper on community care and the subsequent National Health Service and Community Care Act of 1990 thus subsume both residential and home-based assistance to frail and disabled older people. For an account of these reforms see Means and Smith (1994).

certainly incorporating some elements of 'voice', as well as the more narrowly defined 'rights' and some elements of 'exit'.

In the narrower context of legislatively defined rights, provisions remain limited in the United Kingdom. They have been described as oriented more towards procedural justice, such as the right to representation and consultation provided under the Disabled Persons Act of 1986, than to substantive rights (Means and Smith 1994). The NHS and Community Care Act 1990 did establish mandatory complaints procedures, however, and strengthened the individual's right to an assessment of need.

In the broader sense, the British NHS and Community Care Act 1990 required local community consultation by local authorities prior to the completion of a community care plan. Moreover, notions of empowerment through exit and voice are intrinsic aspects of the 'managed competition' which characterises quasi-market models, although the feasibility of achieving user empowerment through such strategies remains the subject of ongoing debate.[4]

Rights, and especially 'rights talk', has been a key element in debates about quality of care and, at least in Australia, forms a coherent part of the overall regulatory strategy. Yet the capacity of those who are very dependent on the care of others to assert such rights is at best subject to serious question. The capacity of the powerless and poorly resourced to assert rights and to attract the attention of governments is always limited, but for the very frail aged perhaps more so. In the words of one administrator – 'We don't have many riots in nursing homes'. Similarly, not too many residents are in a position to 'take up their beds and walk'. Street marches, riots, or even peaceful protests are not the kind of political activity we associate with older people in advanced stages of frailty or disability.

This is nowhere more evident than in the relationship between service providers and service recipients. Increasingly commentators recognise the power imbalance which is almost intrinsic to that relationship, although some (Walker and Warren 1996: 18–20) continue to place some faith in models of empowerment (user involvement) while others place their faith in the benefits of a cash-for-service nexus (Lakey 1994).

Traditional wisdom demands the involvement of the user in the planning and management of services, not merely involvement in their own plan of care. In both Australia and the United States, residents' committees in nursing homes and other residential facilities emerged

---

[4] See, for example, Le Grand and Bartlett (1993); Beresford and Croft (1993) and Walker and Warren (1996).

in response to such beliefs. In the United Kingdom various models of home-based care have attempted to achieve full community consultation and involvement. In this book the attempts to implement user rights strategies in Australian nursing homes are subjected to critical scrutiny (in Chapter 6), as are the theoretical underpinnings of a rights-based approach and its appropriateness to aged care services (in Chapter 9).

The feminisation of ageing

While the last two decades saw an upsurge of interest among politicians, bureaucrats and academics in the ageing of the population, feminist analyses of social provisions for the aged lagged noticeably behind, and even today the field remains fragmented and uneven. This book focuses on issues pertaining to the care of the frail aged; it thus has an intrinsic 'social problems' orientation. Not surprisingly, this is characteristic of many other dominant strands in social gerontology: income support, social networks, quality of life and so forth. What is surprising, perhaps, is that the social problems approach inherent in much applied social gerontology did not meet and blend more easily with the social problems focus of much of the feminist analysis of earlier decades.

Others may well argue that the failure of traditional social gerontology to engage more fully with feminist discourse is only to be expected. Certainly, social gerontology is not the only field wherein the engagement between feminism and academic disciplines has been uneven. Stacey and Thorne, for example, made precisely this point in discussing the 'missing feminist revolution' in sociology in 1985. More generally, Grosz (1987) identified a series of epistemological problems which partially obstructed the emergence of feminist analyses across the social sciences.

It should have been self-evident that ageing was a sexed issue. Women are the majority of the aged population, the majority of informal carers, the majority of service providers and the majority of recipients of formal care. The practical ramifications of women's life-long oppression are likely to be manifested, rather than dissipated, in old age. At the same time, in old age the structural constraints imposed by the divergent public- and private-sphere responsibilities characteristic of the reproductive phase of the life cycle have ceased to exist, making this group an ideal 'case study' for an analytic model which was heavily organised around the implications and consequences of the public/private split.

Yet traditional gerontology continued to accord sex the status of a descriptive variable, rather than that of a central category of analysis and explanation, and for its own part feminism remained largely pre-occupied with the first 40 years of the female cycle. This is not to sug-gest that the lack of feminist engagement with ageing went entirely unremarked, first by older women themselves, and later in academic journals.[5]

Early contributions to the field were generally a direct response to the androcentrism underlying much gerontological work, taking as their starting point the tendency to ignore old women (most com-monly), or else regard them only as of interest in so far as they differed from the (dominant) male pattern. Sex was certainly employed as an independent variable in empirical work, but even that was by no means commonplace, as Payne and Whittington (1976) made clear in an early analysis of the popular stereotypes, and the available data, concerning older women. What was certainly absent was a coherent recognition of the way in which sex and gender, in terms of both biological bases and social constructions, inflected the experience and the institution of old age.

So, in *The Coming of Age*, Simone de Beauvoir could simultaneously call on her readers to join her in breaking the conspiracy of silence sur-rounding old age, and confidently assert that the problem of old age was predominantly a male problem; the central problem of old age, she argued, was a struggle for power, which necessarily concerned only the stronger sex (1972: 7, 89). She thus moved beyond one dominant social and intellectual paradigm (that old age was a fit subject for pity, but not interest), only to remain captured by another – a male domi-nated intellectual tradition defining what was, and what was not, a relevant and central issue for social analysis.

De Beauvoir was not alone in this view that ageing was predomi-nantly a male problem, as Beeson's (1975) review of the positions held by several leading gerontologists demonstrates. It is hardly surprising, then, that authors such as Sommers (1978) and Sontag (1975) should have sought to draw attention to the 'compounding impact of age on sex' and the 'double standard of aging'. Feminist analyses in the 1960s and 1970s were more generally preoccupied with the problems of inequality that confronted women in comparison to men – whether it be in schools, in the workplace or within the family. The co-incidence of this feminist preoccupation with gender-based disadvantage, and social gerontologists' focus on ageing-as-a-social-problem, led almost

---

[5] The invisibility of older women in the feminist movement was highlighted by Macdonald and Rich (1985). The virtual absence of feminist analyses of ageing has been noted in two identically titled articles by Allen (1988) and Russell (1987); see also Reinharz (1986).

inevitably to the emergence of the 'double jeopardy' approach to the analysis of being old and female.

In Chapter 4 existing social provisions for the aged are subjected to a feminist critique, with an emphasis on Australian systems but taking into account the now quite substantial international literature on this topic. The result is a detailed piece of feminist policy analysis. In Chapter 7, however, 'the problem of old women' – and with it, some of the conceptual premises on which the dominant perspective in this largely feminist literature have been built – are themselves subjected to critical analysis. The result is a reconceptualisation of the problem and a reorientation of the search for solutions.

Dependency: construction and reconstruction

In the early 1980s the social construction of dependency among aged persons became a 'hot' issue. The way in which compulsory retirement structured economic dependency lay at its heart (Townsend 1981; Walker 1980; 1982), but it was also argued that particular systems of service provision unnecessarily exacerbated the dependency experienced as a result of physical and mental frailty (Gibson 1985). One element was the lack of flexibility; for example, in a system dominated by residential care, individuals may have had to go into residential care simply because the more modest services which they had required were not available in their own homes. Another factor was the lack of power or control experienced by service recipients in their dealings with service providers.

Promoting or maximising the independence of the frail aged has become a catchcry in the intervening years. The rise of home-based care, the need for better assessment, more flexible services, user rights strategies, consumer empowerment – all have been gilded by their association with the proposed maximisation of independence. Exactly what independence means, however, in the context of advanced mental and physical frailty remains unclear.

To some, it is as simple as remaining in their own home, and managing on their own:

> I have considered (a retirement village or hostel) . . . but I don't want to go until I've got to . . . You know, because . . . I am self-sufficient. I can do my own cooking. I don't even need Meals on Wheels. With the hot summer, who needs a cooked meal? So I manage with salads . . . I prefer to stay here and live my life alone as long as I can manage . . . Another thing that puts me off is that they take your bankbook. A lady I was talking to told me they do, and a bankbook is your last independence item. I'd hate that to be taken from me. I couldn't stand it . . . (Russell 1995: 98–98).

To others, it is not having to be dependent on and answerable to their family:

> A widow of eighty-three who lived alone said, 'I can go to bed when I like and come back when I like. There's no-one to say "where've you been?"' She slapped the table with laughter at the thought of this reversal of role between mother and child (Townsend 1963: 36).

To some, it is the capacity to manage on their own.

> Elderly single man explaining why he does not want any help: 'You let that sort in . . . they start out by making up your bed . . . they end up by making up your mind' (Montague 1982).

To others, it was not having to manage on their own:

> They set these goals for you which they called 'independent living skills' but which were all about doing physical things for yourself. But really it's a total waste of time, I didn't want to spend hours putting my socks on when I could be at my computer or nattering to my mates. That wasn't my idea of independence (Morris 1993a: 61).

What do we really mean by maintaining independence for the very frail or those with severe disabilities? What do we mean by dependency in this context? What is it that makes dependency in those with severe disabilities undesirable? And what can social policies do about it? I return to these questions in the concluding chapter of the book.

CHAPTER 2

The Australian Policy Response

Introduction

The previous chapter was principally concerned with locating Australian aged care issues in an international context, and in particular with identifying the commonalties among the problems and solutions associated with population ageing in a variety of countries. This chapter provides a more detailed account of the specifically Australian response to the broad policy issues and trends described in the previous chapter.

In Australia, as elsewhere in the world, services for the ongoing care of frail and disabled older people are provided in both residential and community contexts. Residential care is offered by nursing homes (higher dependency residents) and hostels (lower dependency residents). Home-based care is also provided for clients of varying levels of dependency, although here the link between particular programs and higher and lower dependency clients is less clear-cut.

The funding and service delivery arrangements are complex. In part, this is a consequence of a federal system, but it is also a historical legacy of a pattern of development which relied heavily on the non-government sector. The result is a system of services for frail and disabled older people provided by a complicated interaction of federal, state and local governments, the voluntary or charitable sector, and the private-for-profit sector, underpinned by a substantial reliance on the unpaid labour of family and friends.

Historically, services for frail and destitute elderly people without family support were the province of charitable agencies; the federal government did not enter the field until 1954. Policy developments in the following three decades were oriented towards residential rather than home-based services, resulting in a system characterised by a chronic over-reliance on nursing home beds and an inadequately developed community care sector. The situation was compounded by the multiplicity of service providers (state governments, local councils, and a variety of for-profit and not-for-profit organisations), the absence of a firm policy direction, major inequities between the states and territories, inadequate regional planning, fragmentation and poor co-ordination.

These problems did not go unremarked, and from the 1970s a range of government inquiries and reviews probed the effectiveness and efficiency of services for frail and disabled older people. In 1975, for example, the Committee of Inquiry into Aged Persons Housing expressed concerns about the continued dominance of institutional care, the inadequate supply of home and community-based services, the lack of co-ordination, the inefficiency, and the unequal distribution of services by geographical area (Social Welfare Commission, 1975). Subsequent committees and reviews returned repeatedly to these issues, but it was not until the mid-1980s that a substantial and sorely needed overhaul – the Aged Care Reform Strategy – was implemented. While changes since that time have been considerable they cannot properly be understood without some knowledge of the processes shaping Australian aged care over the preceding 30 years. What follows, then, is a brief divergence into history.

A brief policy history (1954–1984)

The first federal government foray into aged care was the *Aged Persons Homes Act 1954*, which allowed for a capital subsidy to approved voluntary (not-for-profit) organisations to provide essentially self-contained and hostel-type accommodation. Nursing home beds were initially included only incidentally, providing nursing care if it was required by existing residents.

Although the Act intended to increase the housing available to poorer aged people, the effect over subsequent decades proved to be the over-supply of nursing home beds and the under-development of home and community care services. The Act itself remained virtually unchanged. There were, however, progressive and incremental shifts in the focus of the program which, over time, essentially eroded its two central objectives.

First, the declared emphasis on financially needy older people was largely subverted by the emergence of 'founder/donor' arrangements which required incoming residents to provide a substantial capital 'donation' in order to secure accommodation. These monies were a major source of capital funds for voluntary sector organisations operating under the Act, enabling the take-up of additional federal subsidies and, hence, the subsequent further expansion of accommodation holdings. Inevitably, the practice reduced the access of poor older people – the group that the program had been established to assist.

Second, the initial focus on housing (that is, on self-contained and hostel-type accommodation) was progressively eroded in favour of nursing home beds. In 1963 the federal government began paying benefits on behalf of persons in 'infirmaries' (nursing home beds) associated with aged persons homes, but such beds initially did not attract any capital subsidy. In 1966, partly in response to the 'ageing' of residents in these homes, the capital subsidy was extended to incorporate nursing home beds as well as self-contained and hostel accommodation, subject only to limitations on the proportion of beds so allocated by each organisation.

This meant that nursing home beds developed by the voluntary sector would attract both capital and recurrent subsidies, making them a not unattractive financial proposition. The proportion of nursing home beds approved under the Act immediately began to increase, from an average of 4 per cent during the years prior to 1966, to 15 per cent in the five-year period immediately following, and subsequently to 55 per cent over the five years from 1976–77 to 1980–81.

Unlike the capital subsidy, eligibility for the recurrent subsidy was not limited to the voluntary sector, it applied as well to nursing home beds in the private-for-profit sector. The implementation of the recurrent subsidy stimulated quite substantial interest in the private-for-profit sector, astutely described by one social policy historian as 'a belief among certain investors that nursing homes were low risk, high profit financial ventures' (Kewley 1980: 154). The consequences were indeed dramatic – a rapid increase in nursing home beds from 25 500 prior to the benefit's inception in 1963 to 51 300 in 1972 (the last year before controls on growth were implemented) (McLeay 1982: 124).[1]

However, in 1969 the recurrent subsidies were extended to hostels – payable only on behalf of more dependent residents.[2] This so-called

---

[1] A further component in the growth of nursing home beds arose indirectly from Australia's federal system, and, more specifically, from a traditional division of funding responsibilities between state and federal governments. The 1960s and early 1970s saw a change in state government policy which led to the movement of large numbers of dementia patients out of state-funded mental hospitals (and hence reductions in expenditure for state governments) and into federally funded nursing homes.

[2] Initially targeted on residents aged 80 and over, the focus was later narrowed to specify more dependent residents in terms of physical and mental capacities. Under current assessment procedures, hostel residents receiving personal care subsidies are those who require some assistance with activities of daily living.

'personal care' subsidy provided the first financial incentive to expand the range of services offered by hostels, and to encourage hostels to cater for residents who would previously have been regarded as requiring a nursing home level of care. At the same time, significant capital incentives were offered to the voluntary sector to increase their hostel bed provisions (the *Aged Persons Hostels Act 1972*). Hostels built under this Act had the further requirement that access was to be on the basis of need – contributions by incoming residents were specifically disallowed.

The increased emphasis on hostels in the early 1970s was partially fuelled by a growing recognition of the escalating costs associated with nursing home care, and partly by a belief (by no means universal) that there was an over-supply of nursing home beds, and a significant level of inappropriate admissions. Hostels were thus seen as both a more appropriate form of care for less dependent frail older people, and a more economical one. Hostels had less stringent regulations concerning staffing ratios (particularly those concerning fully qualified nursing staff), which resulted in substantially lower salary and staffing costs than those incurred by nursing homes.

Most nursing home beds were located in the voluntary and private-for-profit sectors, with a minority being in the state government sector. In 1973 various strategies aimed at controlling growth in the private-for-profit and voluntary sectors were implemented, including control over admissions, control over the growth of new beds and controls over fees. From 1974, however, in a seemingly contradictory move, the government introduced deficit financing for voluntary sector homes – a system which provided a subsidy equal to the annual operating deficit of such homes.

The potential for advantage to voluntary sector homes is obvious, and the subsequent disproportionate rate of growth in those homes was predictable. The extent of the impact was, however, impressive. In the five years from 1975 to 1980, there was a 47 per cent increase in voluntary sector nursing home beds, compared to 18 per cent in government nursing homes and 7 per cent in for-profit homes. The growth of nursing home beds in absolute terms had not been halted, although in bed-to-population terms supply was held at around 47 beds per thousand persons aged 65 and over.[3]

While the major policy developments over the 30 years prior to 1984 occurred in residential care, there were some attempts to establish

---

[3] There were 47.5 nursing home beds per 1000 people aged 65 and over in 1972 (Kewley 1980: 154) and 46.7 per 1000 aged 65 and over in 1981 (Nursing Homes and Hostels Review, 1986: 25).

home-based services. The first of these was the introduction in 1956 of a subsidy to voluntary sector home nursing organisations. It was to be some years before further federal government action occurred, but in 1969 two States Grants Acts were passed providing funding to the states for home care services, the establishment and development of senior citizens centres, the employment of welfare officers for those centres, and paramedical services (physiotherapy, chiropody etc.) for older people in their homes. These developments were followed by the *Delivered Meals Subsidy Act 1970*.

In Australia, services to provide care for frail older people at home have traditionally been scanty and poorly co-ordinated. While the problem was well recognised, little was achieved prior to the 1980s. In 1982 the inadequacy of home-based services was forcefully documented and criticised in a report to the House of Representatives Standing Committee on Expenditure – the influential McLeay Report. The report noted a number of reasons for the divergent patterns of development which had characterised residential and community care services.

The relative generosity of federal financial provisions for the construction and operation of nursing homes compared to community care services was one such factor. The community care field lacked the potential for capital accumulation and for profit which was such an obvious dynamic in the expansion of residential care, making it an attractive field of endeavour for both the voluntary and for-profit sectors. In addition, and perhaps partly as a consequence, community-based services were less well organised and certainly less successful lobbyists. This was evidenced by the notable absence of any national or umbrella organisation representing home care services equivalent to the several such organisations representing (often vociferously) the interests of nursing homes.

There was also a financial disincentive for state and territory governments to involve themselves in the development of home-based care services. The federal government was the responsible body for both the capital and recurrent funding of residential care facilities.[4] Community-based services, on the other hand, were provided on a cost shared basis between the two levels of government. So, for example, the federal government provided a dollar-for-dollar subsidy to state and territory governments for home care assistance from 1970 to 1973, at which point it was increased to $2 for every $1 provided by the states. The exact ratios have varied substantially and frequently over

---

[4] Excluding state government nursing homes (a minority) which attract funding from both state and federal governments.

time, and across service types. Whatever the federal/state funding ratio, however, expanding home-based care necessitated increased expenditure by state and territory governments, whereas expansion of the residential sector did not.

Reforming the system

It is hardly surprising in this context that four major reviews and inquiries into aged care services were conducted during the early 1980s. The year 1980 saw the establishment by the House of Representatives Standing Committee on Expenditure of a Sub-committee on Accommodation and Home Care for the Aged, 1981 the establishment of a Senate Select Committee on Private Hospitals and Nursing Homes, 1984 the establishment of a Joint Review of Hostel Care Subsidy Arrangements and 1985 the Joint Review of Nursing Homes and Hostels.

The system that had come into being was the consequence of a series of apparently unrelated changes made with little recognition of the interrelationships between different sectors of provision. The growth of nursing homes was an unplanned consequence of the responsiveness of the voluntary and private-for-profit sectors to financial incentives. Similarly, financial disincentives underpinned the failure by both state governments and the voluntary sector to adequately develop community care services. It was not until the major reforms of the mid to late 1980s that financial incentives and disincentives were used as a tool for intentional policy change, rather than as a determinant of unintended consequences. While such effects appear obvious in retrospect, it is inappropriate to dismiss them as the product of an earlier, more naive era of social planning – as events surrounding the expansion of the British nursing home system in the late 1980s illustrate (Lewis and Glennerster 1996; Wistow *et al.* 1994).

A number of changes began to be implemented from 1983, which by the mid to late 1980s came to be referred to with increasing frequency as the Aged Care Reform Strategy. Its major objectives were the reform of both home-based care and residential care, and the implementation of appropriate assessment strategies to establish links between the various sectors of provision. These reforms were advocated in the broader context of the federal Labor government's Social Justice Strategy, which emphasised improved access, equity and participation across a wide range of policy areas. In essence, the period from 1985 saw the virtual restructuring of residential care in Australia, and the emergence of a viable array of home and community care services.

The incoherence of the existing system was, of course, not the only dynamic at work; the ageing of the Australian population was emerging in both public and political consciousness as a phenomenon of some importance. Leaving more hysterical concerns about the 'capacity' of society in general to cope with the 'burden' of an ageing population to one side, the early 1980s marked the onset of a particularly rapid increase in the proportion of the population aged 70 and over, with this growth rate continuing over the 15 years from 1981 to 1996.

What was perhaps less recognised at that time was the quite rapid change which was about to occur in the structure of that aged population itself, thereby compounding the predicted growth in demand for aged care services. Increasingly, most Australian projections concerning the supply and demand for aged care services were being based on the numbers aged 70 and over, rather than the previous planning figure of those aged 65 and over. This shift in the planning base was proposed on the grounds that it provided better targeting on that proportion of the aged population likely to be in need of aged care services. It is also true that given the burgeoning numbers in the 65 to 70 age group, planning in terms of a '70 and over' population was a more comfortable activity for a government faced with escalating welfare expenditure (and the 1983 recession). This use of the 70 and over age group as a planning base continues in Australia to the present day, although elsewhere and for international comparative purposes the population aged 65 and over is more commonly used.

Nonetheless, in predicting likely need for services, the changing age structure of the Australian aged population was, or should have been, an important factor. As was shown in Chapter 1, when these policy directions were emerging (in the early 1980s) Australia was about to enter a period not only of quite rapid population ageing, but also of the ageing of the aged population itself. In 1981 those people aged 80 and over made up 28 per cent of the population aged 70 and over. By 2001, after a mere twenty years, it will be 39 per cent (ABS 1987; ABS 1994). Given that severe disability rates and hence the potential demand for aged care services increase dramatically with age, these shifts in the structure of the aged population profile were of considerable policy relevance.

The stage was thus set for a substantial overhaul to the existing system in the face of a pattern of substantial and sustained growth in demand for aged care services which was expected to continue well into the next century. The key elements in this process were deinstitutionalisation, targeting and rationing of services, equity, regulation of quality and service outcomes, and an emphasis on user rights. A timeline and summary of the Australian aged care service system has been included in the Appendix to this book.

Deinstitutionalisation

The deinstitutionalisation of the Australian aged care system proceeded at two different levels. One, the more familiar version, involved the expansion of the home care sector and the reduction of residential care.[5] The other can be loosely described as a process of 'deinstitutionalisation' within the residential care sector itself. This was characterised by a move away from more intensive levels of residential care (nursing homes) towards the less intensive levels of care provided by the hostel sector. At the same time, steps were taken to make temporary residential care more accessible to people who were essentially home-based, through various respite care provisions. The aim there was to increase the permeability of the boundary between residential and home-based care.

Residential care

The government controls over the creation of new nursing home beds which had been in place since the early 1970s were now invoked with a vengeance. New nursing home approvals were virtually interdicted for a period from 1983. Aged Care Advisory Committees were subsequently established in each state, and in the years to come the very limited numbers of new beds which were approved by the federal government were distributed on the advice of these committees.

Under the previous regime of essentially unconstrained growth, bed numbers had doubled over a mere nine-year period, reaching 51 300 by 1972. The introduction of controls in the early seventies had slowed the rate of growth, but a further 20 200 beds were nonetheless added to the existing stock by 1985. From 1985 to 1994, however, only 2800 additional beds were created – a far cry from the pattern of growth in preceding decades.

By 1986 the declared policy objective was to maintain the existing national ratio of 100 residential beds per 1000 persons aged 70 and over, but to reduce the proportion of nursing home beds relative to hostel beds. For nursing homes the goal was set at 40 beds per thousand persons aged 70 and over. In 1985 there were 67 nursing home beds per 1000 persons aged 70 and over – by 1994 it had been reduced to 52 (see Table 2.1). While absolute bed numbers remained fairly static, the concurrent growth in the numbers of aged persons meant a

---

[5] Individual residents were not literally moved out of residential care as was the case with the deinstitutionalisation of mental health and disability services. In the case of aged care the same effect can be quite readily achieved by a process of natural attrition. This and related issues are discussed in more detail in Chapter 3.

Table 2.1   The changing supply of residential care in Australia (1985 to 1994)

| | Places per thousand persons aged 70 and over | | |
	Nursing homes	Hostels	Nursing homes and hostels
1985	67	32	99
1994	52	40	92
Change 1985–1994	−15	+8	−7
Policy target	40	50	90

decrease in the availability of nursing home beds of some 22 per cent, or 15 beds per thousand persons aged 70 and over.[6]

While planning strategies were successful in controlling the growth of nursing home beds, the expansion of the hostel sector was somewhat less than intended. In 1985 there had been 32 hostel places per thousand persons aged 70 and over, with the planning goal set at 60 such places by around 2001. By 1994 the level of supply had increased, but only to 40 places per thousand persons aged 70 and over. In a series of incremental changes over the intervening years the planning ratio for hostel places was reduced to 50 places per thousand persons aged 70 and over, to be reached by around 2011.

In 1990 several strategies were announced to encourage the desired expansion of hostel beds; private-for-profit organisations were made eligible for recurrent subsidies for the first time (although not for capital funding), and the capital funding already available to the voluntary sector was increased. In recognition of the growing dependency of many hostel residents there were progressive real increases in the level of recurrent funding paid on behalf of residents by the government. In 1992 the Personal Care Subsidy was split into three separate levels of payment, a further attempt to more adequately reflect the care needs of these residents. The changes appeared to meet with some success; hostel provision ratios increased more rapidly from 1991.[7] In absolute numbers, of course, growth rates in hostel places were substantial, from 34 900 in 1985 to 57 100 by 1994.

Between 1985 and 1994 the net effect of these changes on residential care (taking nursing homes and hostels together) was a reduction of

---

[6] Data used in these discussions of residential care places are drawn from detailed tabulations published by the Australian Institute of Health and Welfare (AIHW 1993; 1995).

[7] The annual increase in hostel provision ratios was constant at 0.7 per thousand persons aged 70 and over per annum for some years. In 1992, 1993 and 1994 the provision ratio increased by 1.6, 1.3, and 0.5 respectively.

seven places per thousand persons aged 70 and over (from 99 to 92). The proportion of nursing home beds dropped from 68 per cent of the total residential care sector to 57 per cent. Hostel places correspondingly increased. Over the same period the official planning target for residential care was itself reduced from 100 to 90 places (40 nursing home beds and 50 hostel places) per thousand persons aged 70 and over. The policy changes introduced under the Aged Care Reform Strategy thus brought about a significant reduction in the total level of provision of residential care services in Australia.

A corollary, of course, was that a larger proportion of highly dependent older people were now remaining in the community. Although a large proportion had always stayed at home, dependent on home-based services and, more commonly, informal care, the reduction in the supply of nursing home beds in particular and residential care in general meant an increase in the proportion, as well as the absolute numbers, remaining at home. This shift in emphasis was occurring in a context where population ageing was driving an increase not only in the number of aged persons, but in the numbers of highly dependent aged persons.

Home-based care

Not surprisingly, extensive changes were also being wrought in the Australian system of home-based care. These services were expanded significantly with the creation of the Home and Community Care program (HACC) in 1984–85, a program which brought together under one financial and administrative umbrella an array of pre-existing fragmented services. Combined federal and state government expenditure increased from $192.2 million in 1985–86 to $619.6 million in 1993–94 – in real terms a 134 per cent increase. As a proportion of the total aged care budget, the Home and Community Care program increased its share of expenditure from 15 per cent to 22 per cent over the same period.

Not only was the level of funding increased, but the range of services offered was expanded. In addition to the traditional major service areas of home nursing, home help and delivered meals, there was a particular expansion of personal care services, respite care (at home and in day centres) and transport. Gardening services and home handyman assistance, which had been largely unavailable in most states and territories, were developed.

Steps were also taken to make home care services a more viable option for more highly dependent clients. The first of these were the community options projects, introduced in 1987, and explicitly aimed at older people who were in danger of premature admission to nursing home care. Here, for the first time, carers as well as service recipients were officially considered clients of the program. These projects operate on a brokerage model, with a case manager organising a package of services appropriate to the particular clients and their circumstances, emphasising flexibility and responsiveness to individual client needs. Community options brokers hold funds which may be used to purchase additional services on behalf of their clients, over and above those for which they are eligible under the Home and Community Care program.[8]

A related innovation was that of hostel options projects, commenced in 1991, which allowed hostels to deliver personal care services to persons living at home up to a maximum cost equivalent to the Personal Care Subsidy. These were the forerunners of what are now referred to as community aged care packages, a program which is assuming an increasingly important role in the Australian aged care system.

The target population for such services are those with high dependency levels and complex care needs assessed as likely to need admission to residential care, although funding remains tied to the lowest of the three Personal Care Subsidy levels payable in hostels ($25.30 per day in 1994). A recent further innovation, as yet still in the pilot stages, is nursing home options, aimed at maintaining even more dependent older people in their own homes.

Informal care

Since the first Australian national data on the care of frail and disabled older people in the community became available in 1981, it has been well accepted that most home-based care is provided by family members.[9] Yet these activities have never been strongly supported by public systems of provision in Australia.

The Carer's pension provides basic pension eligibility for persons engaged in caring for those who would otherwise require nursing home care. This is a flat rate, means-tested payment (not an earnings replacement provision), roughly equivalent to 25 per cent of the average weekly wage. The Domiciliary Nursing Care Benefit is an ancillary

---

[8] For a national evaluation of the implementation of the community options projects in Australia, see Department of Health, Housing and Community Services (HHCS), 1992.

[9] The Australian Bureau of Statistics has now conducted three national surveys in this area, in 1981, 1988 and 1993. See in particular ABS 1993a; 1993b. For analyses of these data pertaining to the predominance of family care see Gibson and Rowland (1984) and AIHW (1993).

non-means-tested payment intended as partial compensation for the costs associated with caring; in 1995 it was $55 per week. Recent years have seen modest increases in the amounts payable and the liberalisation of eligibility requirements under these schemes.

The expansion of home-based care in general, and in-home, centre-based and residential respite care services in particular, has been an important development for carers. Between 1988–89 and 1993–94, for example, the hours of home-based respite services being provided per 1000 severely disabled persons more than doubled. The proportion of admissions to nursing homes that were for respite care tripled over that period, and in hostels, respite admissions reached half the total admissions. Changes to previous policies allowed more flexible use of vacant beds for respite purposes, and a higher level of payment for respite residents in nursing homes increased the attractiveness of this client group to service providers (Gibson *et al.* 1996).

These developments occurred as part of the carer support strategy announced in 1992, and included the development of 'carers' kits' to disseminate information on available forms of services and assistance. The role played by carers has been increasingly recognised, and carers' advocacy and lobby groups are becoming increasingly active.

There is little by way of national data concerning the adequacy, appropriateness and availability of assistance for carers of highly dependent older people. The national Respite Review, announced in the 1995–96 Budget as part of the carer-related policy initiatives, identified as one of its major terms of reference the task of identifying the need for respite care in the community.[10] While the expansion of home-based care is of obvious benefit, the adequacy of existing provision remains uncertain. In 1994 the House of Representatives Standing Committee on Community Affairs (1994) was deluged with demands for the further expansion of home-based care, and the National Carers' Association continues to lobby for further expansion. Finally, the potential 'flow-on' effects of the more stringent rationing of residential care on both highly dependent older people and their carers remain to be fully identified, as the system continues to feel the impact of ongoing reductions in the supply of nursing home beds.

For the last ten years, then, increasing levels of demand have occurred in the context of a changing balance of care between the nursing home, hostel and home-based care sectors. The supply of nursing home care in another decade is intended to be at a substantially lower level than at present, but will be serving an older (and

---

[10] Several publications emerged from the national Respite Review, among them Gibson *et al.* (1996).

hence more frail) aged population. While simultaneous increases in hostel and home-based care are envisaged, the adequacy of this form of provision remains uncertain. A key question is the extent to which increased targeting of more intensive services on those most in need can be used to contain growth in the residential sector before overall adequacy of provision is seriously compromised.

Targeting and rationing

Targeting and financial circumstances

As already discussed in Chapter 1, targeting and rationing of aged care services can involve a focus on those in most financial need of assistance (targeting by means testing), as well as on those in most need due to their high level of dependency. To date, the Australian system has placed most emphasis on the latter; there is, however, evidence of an escalating trend towards means testing in the Australian aged care service system.

One of the unusual aspects of the Australian residential care system has been its accessibility in financial terms. Resident contributions to nursing homes and hostels have been set at a maximum level of 87.5 per cent of the full aged pension plus the associated federally funded rent assistance – in 1993 about $166 per week. Thus, even older people whose only income is the pension can afford the necessary resident contribution to the cost of nursing home or hostel care. While the aged pension itself (a flat rate non-contributory pension set at roughly 25 per cent of the average weekly wage) is subject to a means and assets test, there had traditionally been no means testing of the federal government payments made on behalf of each resident to nursing homes and hostels.

This changed in 1991, when the lowest payment category (the so-called 'Hostel Care' subsidy) was made subject to a means test for the first time. In 1993 a further targeting element was introduced, to increase access to hostel care for the financially disadvantaged. An entry payment (partially refundable) for aged persons with assets and income above a certain level became mandatory.[11] In the 1996–97 federal budget the government announced its intention to introduce similar payments into the nursing home system, although the details of

---

[11] After paying the entry contribution a resident must be left with a minimum of 2.5 times the annual maximum aged pension in assets ($20 500 in September 1993). The hostel may retain a maximum of between $600 and $1200 (subject to the size of the entry payment) for each six-month period up to a maximum of five years. A recent survey reports that the majority of hostels (69 per cent) have charged entry contributions, receiving them on average from 54 per cent of their residents (Gregory 1994: Chapter 8).

this policy shift remain the subject of considerable debate and contention. In a related move the government has also announced its intention to means test all payments made on behalf of nursing home and hostel residents from July 1997.

Home-based care has historically been subject to means tests of various kinds and of various degrees of formality. The exact details vary enormously, sometimes involving sliding fee scales, sometimes a set fee-for-service and on other occasions they are 'donation' based. Of course, the amount of service available is often strictly rationed, requiring even those clients eligible for public provision to obtain supplementary assistance from informal carers, or on the private market.

Targeting and dependency

Targeting on the basis of dependency, as distinct from financial circumstances, has long been evident in both the home-based and residential care sectors. Indeed, targeting on the basis of dependency is generally regarded as a legitimate criterion for determining access to aged care services. The differences which have emerged in recent years have been to do with formalising systems of assessment, with the intent of gaining a more equitable and appropriate distribution of available services.

The shift in the balance of care between more intensive nursing home and less intensive hostel services, taken together with the overall reduction in supply, might have been viewed as a straightforward rationing of the quantum of services which would progressively lead to a more targeted system of provision as available services were concentrated on those at higher levels of need. Yet while constraint in the supply of services is an effective rationing device, it does not of itself ensure targeting on those most in need.

Given that the past decade has been characterised by a reduction in the supply of nursing home beds, it is hardly surprising to find that modifications to the system were initially aimed at this sector of the aged care system. The modified system actually consisted of two distinct strategies to facilitate the process of targeting expensive nursing home care on those most in need. One involved the manipulation of demand – a new assessment process was implemented which determined eligibility for entry to the system. The other modified the financial incentives operating on service providers – making the admission of more dependent clients a more lucrative prospect for nursing home proprietors.

Eligibility for entry to nursing homes had previously been determined by both general practitioners and government medical officers, with the result that the process lacked both rigour and consistency. In 1985 a pilot scheme was developed whereby entry to nursing homes would be determined by what came to be called 'aged care assessment teams' (initially known as geriatric assessment teams). By 1987 national guidelines were released, and the program expanded to include entry to all nursing homes. Each state developed its own assessment processes and databases, but eligibility was determined in all cases by the individual's score on the NH5, a nationally consistent set of dependency items. The process was progressively expanded to include hostels in the early 1990s.

These multi-disciplinary teams proved to be an effective restraint on demand for nursing home care. The long-established system of waiting lists, whereby people put their names down against a possible future need, often at several homes simultaneously, disappeared. The average dependency levels of residents in both nursing homes and hostels increased, indicative that improved targeting of available resources on those most in need had indeed occurred.

These changes to the assessment system were not operating in isolation, however. At the same time, the financial incentives referred to above were implemented to encourage service providers to admit higher dependency residents. The previous system of nursing home payment had been proved counter-productive in terms of targeting services on higher dependency residents, as the two levels of payment provided did not sufficiently recompense homes for the care costs of high dependency residents. The result had been a financial incentive for nursing home proprietors to admit lower dependency residents in preference to higher dependency ones.

The five levels of benefit associated with the new Resident Classification Instrument were developed to more adequately compensate service providers for the higher costs incurred in caring for more dependent residents. The financial incentives in the new system encouraged nursing homes to admit more highly dependent residents, thereby facilitating the access of those most in need to the most expensive component of the aged care service system.

Corresponding funding changes were implemented in the hostel sector to provide additional resources for the care of more dependent residents, and increase the financial viability of this sector. These increases were substantial, with, for example, the Personal Care Subsidy being increased from $58.70 per week in 1987 to $155.75 by 1991. From 1992 a three-level payment system was introduced to more closely match reimbursements to the care needs of more dependent residents. Again, the intention was to ensure that financial incentives, if any, operated to facilitate access among more highly dependent persons.

While the issue of financial incentives and disincentives was thus resolved within sectors, there remained an unresolved problem between sectors. The level of subsidy for high dependency hostel residents remained well below that paid for the lowest dependency nursing home residents, although there had been increasing evidence of overlap between the two populations in terms of dependency levels in recent years. In 1996 the federal subsidy for the highest level dependency residents in hostels was $242 per week, while that for the lowest level of dependency in nursing homes was $496 per week. A recent estimate by the federal Department of Human Services and Health (Duckett 1995) suggested that around one in five hostel residents had levels of dependency similar to those of nursing home residents in the moderate to low dependency care categories (RCI 3 to RCI 5). If this is the case, then the financial rewards for service providers, and the quality of care which can be provided, could be expected to make the hostel sector less attractive to service providers and service recipients alike.[12]

The question of the most appropriate distribution of resources among different sectors of the aged care service system may emerge as increasingly important over ensuing years. There are obvious incompatibilities in terms of the ways in which the three levels of care are funded, and in the presence or absence of means testing, asset testing and standards for user fees and contributions. The present systems of determining access to nursing homes and hostels differ (although both are determined by aged care assessment teams). There is no generally held schema for assessing clients for home-based care, with the exception of community aged care packages where eligibility is also determined by aged care assessment schemes. For the rest assessment for home care services is varied, and can involve multiple assessments where more than one agency is involved (for example, home help, home nursing and a respite care service may well perform separate assessments).

At the same time there is a growing overlap in the dependency levels of these client populations. To be sure it is more evident with lower dependency nursing home residents and higher dependency hostel residents, but the overlap with home-based clients will become clearer as the intensity of services provided in the community increases, together with its resource implications. While the issue of a generalised

[12] In the 1996–97 Budget, the federal government announced the intention of combining hostels and nursing homes into one uniform residential care sector. The details of how this is to be accomplished, or the time frames involved, remain unclear at the time of writing.

assessment procedure for community care services remains in its infancy, there is a need to recognise its importance in terms of equity between clients living at home and those in the residential care sector.

Equity of access

Perhaps, not surprisingly, given the trends already described, questions about equity of access have also received some attention under the Aged Care Reform Strategy. More broadly, the strategy was developed in the context of a federal Labor government with a strong commitment to social justice, and an overarching social justice strategy which ranged across all portfolios. Access among so-called special needs groups thus became an issue. As in any federal system, equity of access across state and territory boundaries was also contentious. In addition, there was the question of equity of funding among different providers of care.

The key special needs groups identified under the Aged Care Reform Strategy were persons from non-English-speaking backgrounds, indigenous Australians and those living in rural and remote communities. A number of policy changes were implemented to facilitate access among these groups. For persons from non-English-speaking backgrounds these included the development of ethnospecific services, as well as the development of culturally appropriate practices within mainstream services. A series of attempts was made to improve translation/interpreter provisions, including the availability of all aged care information brochures in a wide range of languages. Considerable attention was given to developing residential and home-based services that more appropriately met the needs of indigenous Australians, particularly those living in rural and remote communities, and retaining more traditional lifestyles. For rural and remote communities more generally the so-called 'multi-purpose centres' were developed to provide a range of state and federal government services from the one agency or outlet.

Geographic equity received a substantial boost under the reformed system. The previous system of submission-based planning had led to considerable variations in the supply of nursing home and hostel beds across state and territory boundaries, and also between rural and urban areas. The move to needs-based planning, combined with tighter control of new bed allocations, reduced, although it did not remove, those inequities. A system of aged care advisory committees was established in each state and territory to provide recommendations concerning the need for both new residential care places and home-based services.

In 1985 the level of residential provision ranged between 78 and 114 beds per thousand persons aged 70 and over in the different states and territories. By 1994 the variation had reduced substantially across all but one authority (the Northern Territory) with bed provision ratios ranging between 85 and 99.[13] The relative proportions of nursing homes and hostel places within that ratio also vary considerably from state to state, as does the supply of home-based care (Mathur 1996). Unfortunately, data on rural–urban variations are not presently available at the national level.

It has already been noted that the earlier two-tier funding arrangements for nursing homes were inefficient; they were, however, also inequitable. Within a particular benefit tier there were substantial differences in the levels of benefits being paid by the federal government, ostensibly for homes to provide the same level of care. The benefits varied by state and also according to whether the home was in the for-profit, charitable or state government sector.

In 1981, for example, a nursing home bed in Western Australia attracted an ordinary benefit payment from the federal government of $18.55 per day, while in Victoria proprietors received $31.65 (McLeay 1982: 68). With sector-based inequities, in 1984–85, average daily payments to the private-for-profit homes were around $32 per resident, while those to voluntary sector homes were $42 (*Nursing Homes and Hostels Review* 1986: 33).

Changes introduced in 1987 abolished the differential funding arrangements for the private-for-profit and voluntary sector nursing homes, replacing them with a single system of reimbursement. The phasing in of a standard level of payment for all states also commenced. The new reimbursement system had two basic components: the Standard Aggregated Module (SAM), which covered baseline costs (laundry, food, heating, accommodation etc.), and the Care Aggregated Module (CAM), which concerned the personal and nursing care requirements of residents. The latter benefit was differentially calculated on the basis of residents being classified into one of five dependency groups (as determined by the Resident Classification Instrument).

The RCI (Resident Classification Instrument) was subsequently subjected to minor changes in structure, and there was significant debate as to the appropriate financial remuneration associated with

---

[13] The Northern Territory moved from having one of the lowest levels of provision to having the highest (110) over this period, largely due to the development of special projects developed to meet the needs of the indigenous population. The Northern Territory has a higher concentration of Aboriginal and Torres Strait Islander peoples than any other Australian state or territory.

each level. The SAM and CAM funding systems have since been subject to review and minor change. An issue of ongoing debate concerns the level of funding required for adequate care of dementia patients. In order to implement the amalgamation of nursing homes and hostels proposed in the 1996–97 Budget, substantial revisions will need to be undertaken. Nonetheless, to date, the system in essence remains in place.

The funding systems for hostels and home-based care did not suffer from such state and territory and sector-based inequities, and there was not, therefore, the need for substantial reform evident in the nursing home sector. The modifications which did occur to the hostel payment system were described in the earlier discussion on targeting and financial incentives. The question of inter-sectoral equity, that is, the level of resources allocated and the services available to clients of the different components of the aged care system, remains largely unexamined at the present time.

Regulating quality of care and user rights

Prior to 1987 monitoring of the quality of care in nursing homes and hostels was based largely on input criteria, and administered by a variety of state and federal regulations. There had been a number of widely reported scandals in nursing homes involving poor quality care, and in particular the Giles Report (1985) pointed to the need for the federal government to become involved in the monitoring of nursing home standards. The Outcome Standards Monitoring Program was subsequently introduced into nursing homes in 1987, and extended to hostels in 1991. This program reviews the quality of care received by residents in terms of national standards, with an emphasis on the care outcomes for residents. It includes the potential to apply substantial sanctions (including withdrawal of Commonwealth benefits) where homes persistently fail to meet the required standards.

The standards themselves are detailed in Chapter 5; there are 31 nursing home standards and 25 hostel standards, all quite broadly defined. The standards monitoring teams are part of the federal Department, and receive nationally consistent training. Visits occur with 24 hours' notice. Whereas for a number of years homes and hostels were visited on an approximately two-year cycle, recent years have seen a shift to a risk management strategy, wherein only homes and hostels which register on one or more risk factors receive a standards monitoring visit.

Despite initial opposition by the nursing home industry the program was generally quite well accepted and there is some evidence to suggest that quality of care has improved. These findings are based on changes in the scores received by nursing homes and hostels over successive standards monitoring visits, and the results of a four-year national evaluation of the monitoring program in nursing homes. The outcome-based, client-centred focus of the standards monitoring procedures is innovative in an international context, and the procedures demonstrated high levels of reliability and validity in the national evaluation study.[14] However, with the change of federal government in 1996, and ongoing lobbying from some sectors of the residential care industry, a major redevelopment of the system is presently being undertaken by the federal Department of Health and Family Services.

Attempts are under way to develop regulatory strategies appropriate to home-based care services. A set of service standards was agreed to among the relevant state and federal authorities in the early 1990s; again, these are outcome oriented. To date, however, the problems of implementing such standards in a quality appraisal process have slowed progress, particularly in a context where the resources available for regulatory procedures are limited, and the number of agencies involved is substantial. In 1996 the Australian Institute of Health and Welfare (AIHW) was contracted to assist in the development of the Service Standards Instrument and a national pilot study undertaken.[15]

Another area of major activity was the development of a user rights strategy over the period from 1989 to 1991, involving both the residential and community care programs. These included a Charter of Residents' Rights and a proprietor and resident agreement for both nursing homes and hostels, whereby service providers are required to advise residents of their rights and to meet the specified obligations. These include both rights concerned with personal freedom and rights pertaining to the provision of services – for example, security of tenure.

There is some intersection and reinforcement between the user rights strategy and the outcome standards monitoring process which have speeded acceptance of the user rights focus. Residents' committees in nursing homes and hostels, for example, have flourished, encouraged by the Charter and the Agreement on the one hand, and are seen as a readily demonstrable way for proprietors to meet certain aspects of the regulatory standards on the other. A community visitors scheme was established in the residential sector, whereby isolated residents are provided with regular social contact on a volunteer basis;

[14] For details of the national evaluation see Braithwaite *et al.* (1990; 1993).
[15] For further details of the Service Standards Instrument and its development see Australian Institute of Health and Welfare (1997: Chapter 8).

with costs to the volunteers and administrative costs borne by the federal government.

A Statement of Rights and Responsibilities was also produced for clients of community services. For both home-based and residential care programs, clients have access to advocacy services (federally funded but independently auspiced agencies) and to complaints units (located within federal and state departments). Taken together, developments pertaining to the regulation of quality of care, and the recognition of the rights of clients of aged care services, have proceeded apace over the last decade, from a position where Australia could have been characterised as a laggard in the field to one where it has been at the forefront of some interesting developments in an international context.

Conclusion

The policy changes and developments described in this chapter summarise substantial and far-reaching reforms to the Australian aged care system. The process has involved not only the expansion and re-organisation of existing services, and changes to funding levels and strategies, but also the emergence of essentially new components such as intensive packages of home-based care, a regulatory system to improve quality of care in nursing homes and hostels, and user rights initiatives. The restructuring of services has been designed to maximise overall access to care by rationing the most resource-intensive services (nursing home beds) and targeting them to those most in need, with subsequent resource savings being directed towards the expansion of less intensive levels of care (hostel and home-based services).

Questions about the 'best' balance between residential and community care, and what constitutes an adequate supply of such services, will be increasingly brought into focus as the supply of nursing home beds continues to diminish. The need for cost containment has been and continues to be a driving force, as will demographically driven increases in the demand for services. While the Australian reforms have been broadly successful there are a number of aspects which are worthy of further scrutiny. In the following chapters some key elements of the reform are subjected to more intensive policy analysis, with a close eye kept on the implications of these changing patterns of provision for older people with disabilities and the carers who provide much of their support.

PART TWO

What's the Practice?

CHAPTER 3

Deinstitutionalisation and the Aged Care Reform Strategy

Introduction

Since 1985 Australia has been pursuing a course of a progressive deinstitutionalisation in the aged care field, under the policy directions set by the Aged Care Reform Strategy. The dimensions of that shift were broadly mapped in the preceding chapter, measured in terms of the supply of residential care beds and the relative proportion of overall aged care expenditure allocated to residential care. In this chapter a more detailed analysis of the changing balance of aged care services in Australia, and the consequences of those changes, is presented.

This shift away from residential care and towards home-based care has been a clearly documented part of the Aged Care Reform Strategy. It has not generally, however, been referred to under the rubric of deinstitutionalisation. That term has traditionally been used in the mental health and disability field to refer to the movement of particular individuals from an institutional context into the community. In Australia the classic case of deinstitutionalisation occurred in relation to the reduction of long-stay psychiatric beds, from 281 beds per 100 000 in the early 1960s to 40 beds per 100 000 in the early 1990s. Literally thousands of people were discharged from long-stay psychiatric institutions into the community over this period.

In aged care it would be more accurate to say that we are dealing with the deinstitutionalisation of a program structure, rather than the deinstitutionalisation of people. In aged care, processes of natural attrition allow the level of institutionalisation to be substantially reduced over a relatively short period without the discharge of actual individuals. Deinstitutionalisation in an aged care context is essentially an issue of non-admission rather than of discharge.

The changes of the last 10 years amount to considerably more than reducing the level of residential care; to view or construct the process in this way would be an inadequate rendering of the shifts which have occurred in the balance of care. While the overall level of residential care has indeed decreased from 99 to 92 beds per thousand persons aged 70 and over, there are a number of other elements in play:

- the ageing of the Australian aged population during this period, and the implications of that shift for changing levels of demand for residential care in a context of reduced supply;
- the changing balance within the residential care sector away from 'high intensity' nursing home beds and towards 'lower intensity' hostel places;
- the expansion of home-based care, not only in terms of the number and range of services but also in the intensity of provision which could appropriately be delivered at home;
- the emerging interface between home and residential care as a result of enhanced respite care provisions;
- the consequences of these shifts for the clients and potential clients of aged care services in Australia.

The reduction in residential care

The original policy direction which emerged as part of the Aged Care Reform Strategy was to maintain the level of residential care provision at 100 beds per thousand persons aged 70 and over, albeit with a shift away from nursing home care towards less intensive hostel provision. Subsequent years saw a marked and progressive reduction in that planned level of provision – by 1995 it was down to 90 beds per thousand. The actual level of provision also dropped during the period, from 99 beds per thousand in 1985, to 92 beds per thousand in 1995. The ratio of more intensive nursing home-type care to hostel care fell, in line with established policy directions.

The resources 'saved' by reducing the level of residential care were redirected to intensive forms of home-based care, referred to as community aged care packages. While still administered as part of the residential care system, and funded as such, community aged care packages are essentially part of the home-based care system of provision.

So far, however, this tells us little more than was covered in the preceding chapter.

How much of a reduction?

On the surface the reduction in residential care appears to be amply summarised by simply stating the reduction of seven beds per thousand persons aged 70 and over during the period from 1985 to 1994. However, this reduction in the supply of residential care was occurring in the context of rapid ageing of the aged population in Australia. Between 1985 and 1994, for example, the population aged 70 to 79 increased by 26 per cent, while that aged 80 and over increased by 46 per cent. The consequences were a substantially older aged population, and given the close relationship between age and handicap, one more likely to require some form of aged care services.[1] This distinctive shift in the profile of the aged population was thus undoubtedly associated with an increase in the proportion of highly dependent old people in the aged population.

If one assumes that the factors which determine existing use patterns are likely to impact on use in the future, then the demand for residential care was even more likely to rise as the age structure altered and dependency levels increased. To date, rates of institutionalisation have increased substantially with age in Australia, even among the highly dependent elderly. Whereas one in four highly dependent 70 to 79 year olds could be found in institutions in 1988, this proportion doubled among those aged 80 and over, so that one in every two highly dependent persons aged 80 and over was resident in institutional care (AIHW 1993: 220).

One explanation of such trends lies in the nature of the 'highly dependent' measure itself. Although the category is based on the most stringent available national categorisation of dependency, obviously it still contains individuals with a range of dependency levels. Very old people are more likely to be among the more dependent in the category, and hence more likely to require residential care. Another explanation lies in the likely availability of informal support; this too diminishes as old age advances, and spouses, siblings and children who are also ageing become less capable of intensive caring responsibilities, and more subject themselves to death and serious disability. In either case we know that institutionalisation rates are higher among the very old, and that this relationship holds even when the group under scrutiny is limited to the highly dependent aged.

---

[1] Whereas only 15 per cent of 70 to 79 year olds report a high level of dependency, 45 per cent of those aged 80 and over do so. High dependency here is defined as equivalent to the ABS category of 'profound and severe handicap'. This includes persons who require assistance with personal care activities such as moving around the house, eating, bathing, and dressing (ABS 1990).

There are good reasons for thinking that a planning measure for residential care based on the size of the population aged 70 and over will fail to take account of changing levels of need for residential care (and indeed for other forms of aged care) during this kind of population ageing.

If one assumes that the age- and sex-specific 'profound and severe handicap' rates (as defined by the Australian Bureau of Statistics) have remained constant, there must now be proportionately more highly dependent people in the aged population than there were in 1985, and that proportion must continue to increase into the next century.[2] When the planning ratios of 40 nursing home beds and 60 hostel beds per thousand persons aged 70 and over were developed (using 1983 data) 11 per cent of people aged 70 and over were 85 and over. By 2021 that proportion will be 16 per cent. These are quite different aged populations in terms of their likely level of need for aged care services, and planning ratios based on a 70 and over population denominator obviously obscure, rather than illuminate, that effect.

The argument is, of course, equally germane to the 65 and over population denominator more commonly used for international comparisons, and often used for comparisons over time in a range of national studies. The general effect is particularly marked, however, during periods when the internal structure of the aged population is changing rapidly, either because of a higher rate growth in the very old (leading to a likely underestimation of demand for care) or a high rate of growth among the young aged population (leading to a likely over-estimation of the need for care).

Of course, whether there is an over- or under-supply is a normative judgment, and one also affected by the point at which calibration or the relevant baseline was established. In other words, if the baseline is established during a period with a relatively high proportion of very old persons in the aged population, then the level of supply will presumably be ample if the proportion of young aged in the population increases. On the other hand, if the baseline is established at a time when the proportion of very old people is relatively low, then the actual availability of care will decrease substantially if the proportions of very old people in the aged population increase. Given the different rates and stages of growth in the aged population demonstrated in Chapter 1, such effects will obviously occur at different points of time in different countries, adding further complications to any trend analyses in the already difficult task of international comparison.

---

[2] Analyses of the ABS national survey data pertaining to disability and ageing gathered in 1981, 1988 and 1993 have demonstrated remarkable consistency in the age- and sex-specific 'profound and severe handicap' rates among the population aged 65 and over (AIHW: unpublished analyses).

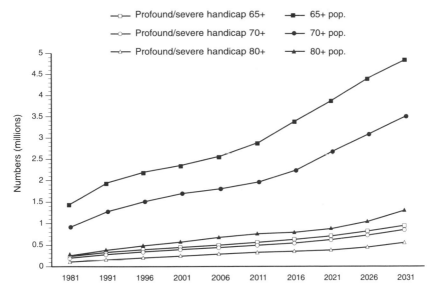

Figure 3.1 Patterns of growth 1981 to 2031
Source: Adapted from AIHW (1995).

Figure 3.1 illustrates past and projected patterns of population growth for six categories of older people. These include three age groups – the population aged 65 and over, that aged 70 and over, and that aged 80 and over – and three high dependency groups calculated on the basis of age- and sex-specific handicap rates – again for persons aged 65 and over, those aged 70 and over, and those aged 80 and over.[3] The changing patterns of growth are evident, as is the point that a level of supply linked to either the number of persons aged 65 and over or those aged 70 and over would diverge substantially over time from that linked to any one of the other denominators.

The remaining four groups (the population aged 80 and over, the highly dependent group aged 65 and over, the highly dependent group aged 70 and over, and the highly dependent group aged 80 and over) show similar rates of increase. Any of these would arguably provide a more accurate basis for comparisons over time or internationally; the highly dependent population aged 65 and over has, however, the advantage of being a more inclusive measure. Such a choice is still quite a conservative measure of change during periods of rapid growth in the very old population, however, given that use of residential care is much higher in the 80 and over age group even when dependency levels are taken into account. Nonetheless, there is

---

[3] The age- and sex-specific dependency rates were derived from the 1993 Survey of Disability, Ageing and Carers conducted by the Australian Bureau of Statistics.

Table 3.1   Changing provision of residential care (1985 to 1994)

	Residential places per 1000 persons 70+	Residential places per 1000, highly dependent persons 65+
1985	99	379
1994	92	361
Reduction 1985–1994	−7	−18

	Nursing home places per 1000 persons aged 70+	Nursing home places per 1000 highly dependent persons 65+
1985	67	255
1994	52	204
Reduction 1985–1994	−15	−51

quite a substantial difference achieved in mapping change using the two population denominators, as is demonstrated in Table 3.1.

If a denominator is used which takes into account the changing population structure, the reduction in residential care places is seen to be somewhat more substantial in relation to the number of persons in the likely target population. Thus, while the period has seen an overall reduction of residential care places per thousand persons aged 70 and over, the change in relation to the highly dependent population aged 65 and over is a reduction of 18 beds per thousand.

From nursing homes to hostels

While the total level of residential care places available was decreasing, a shift was also occurring in the proportion of residential care places allocated to nursing home and hostel levels of care. As the data presented in Table 3.1 illustrate, while overall residential care places declined by seven places per thousand over the period from 1985 to 1994, the decrease in the supply of nursing home beds during that period was substantially greater, being 15 beds per thousand persons aged 70 and over. Alternatively, in terms of the more targeted denominator included in the table this could be presented as a reduction of 51 nursing home beds per thousand highly dependent persons aged 65 and over.

The difference between these trends and those for residential care overall is obviously accounted for by an increase in the supply of hostel places (aimed at lower dependency persons requiring residential placement). The supply of hostel places increased over this period by eight places per thousand persons aged 70 and over, or 33 places per thousand highly dependent persons aged 65 and over.

The overall reduction in supply thus incorporated a substantial reduction in the provision of nursing home care (the high intensity end of the residential care sector) and a substantial (although not equivalent) increase in the less intensive level of hostel provision.

Changes in client profiles

The most obvious consequence of such changes has been a reduction in the proportion of the aged population accommodated in residential care, with a particular reduction in the proportion accommodated in nursing homes. This shift is evident in both age- and sex-specific institutionalisation rates, as well as the more general survey data indicating the proportion of highly dependent persons living in institutions.

These latter data show, for example, that between 1988 and 1993 the proportion of highly dependent persons aged 65–79 accommodated in institutions (nursing homes, hostels and hospitals) decreased from 21 per cent to 16 per cent, while for highly dependent persons aged 80 and over the proportion dropped from 50 per cent to 41 per cent (AIHW 1995: 191).

Analyses of age- and sex-specific institutionalisation rates for nursing homes reveal similar patterns. These data are only available at the national level from 1988, but even so quite substantial changes are evident. Overall, a 6 per cent drop occurred in the proportion of the population aged 60 and over accommodated in nursing homes. The reductions were much more pronounced among women than men, however, and slightly more pronounced among the older age groups. Thus while the proportion of men aged 60 to 69 living in nursing homes fell by 7 per cent, that for women fell by 14 per cent. Among women aged 80 and over the reduction was 18 per cent (Mathur 1996: 50–51).

For hostels the residency rates increased, although not sufficiently to accommodate the reductions in the nursing home sector (Mathur 1996: 52–53). Table 3.2 presents nursing home and hostel residency rates for Australia (the proportion of the age group in a nursing home or hostel) as at 30 June 1994.

Some, but by no means all, of the proportion of highly dependent persons previously accommodated in nursing homes would have been provided for by the expanded hostel sector. The corollary is, of course, an increase in the proportion of very old people living in the community (most marked among women), and more notably an increase in the proportion of highly dependent aged persons living in the community.

Not surprisingly these shifts have been associated with an increase in

Table 3.2   Nursing home and hostel residency rates, 30 June 1994

	Men	Women	Persons
% in nursing homes			
60–69	0.4%	0.3%	0.4%
70–79	1.6%	1.9%	1.8%
80+	7.0%	13.2%	11.1%
60+	1.6%	3.3%	2.5%
% in hostels			
60–69	0.2%	0.2%	0.2%
70–79	0.8%	1.4%	1.2%
80+	5.3%	10.0%	8.4%
60+	1.0%	2.5%	1.8%

Source: Adapted from Mathur (1996).

client dependency levels in both the nursing home and hostel sectors. Whereas in 1990 62 per cent of nursing home residents fell into the more dependent RCI categories (RCI 1–3), this proportion had increased to 72 per cent by 1994. For hostels, although national data are available for a more limited period, the proportion of residents in the high dependency 'Personal Care' categories increased from 54 per cent in 1992 to 66 per cent in 1994 (Mathur 1996). Such shifts are reasonably dramatic given the short time periods under scrutiny, and speak to quite substantial shifts in the levels of dependency in Australian nursing homes and hostels.

In addition, as noted in Chapter 2, increasing levels of dependency in both sectors have led to a situation where there is a significant overlap in the dependency levels of some clients of nursing homes and hostels – despite the quite dissimilar levels of care and resourcing supplied to the two sectors.

Future trends in residential care

While the trends reported above are of some interest in themselves, they also raise some important questions concerning the possible consequences of further intended decreases in the supply of both nursing home beds in particular and residential care places overall, particularly in the context of further ageing of the Australian population.

The pattern described above, with a higher rate of increase among the very old, is projected to continue into the next century. From 2001 to 2006 the number of people aged 80 and over will increase by 19 per cent, compared to a 6 per cent increase in those aged 70 and over. The trend is projected to reverse from 2011, with the numbers of younger aged increasing more rapidly than the older aged during the period to 2021, when the present pattern will recur.

In 1994, with colleagues at the Australian Institute of Health and Welfare, I undertook a series of projections based on then current (1993) patterns of service use, projected forward on the basis of age- and sex-specific nursing home and hostel utilisation rates. Some of the material from that work is presented below (Gibson and Liu 1995; AIHW 1995: 210–212).

Like all projections these analyses involved a number of assumptions. We knew that future patterns of residential care service use would in fact be largely determined by supply, particularly given the very high occupancy rates (in excess of 90 per cent) characteristic of both nursing homes and hostels in Australia in recent years (AIHW 1995: 213). Yet the projections given here are based on (then) current patterns of service use – patterns which would self-evidently have to decrease as the level of residential care being provided was reduced in line with government policy.

Our analyses were intended to provide an indication of the degree of difference between current patterns of use and those in the future as envisaged under the levels of provision set down by the Aged Care Reform Strategy. The patterns of residential care in 1993 provided a benchmark with which we were familiar – the levels of client dependency in the residential and community sectors, the viability of alternative home-based care arrangements, the adequacy of home-based care services – all were part of a working system of care, which, while not claimed as a perfect system, was certainly a reasonably well-functioning one. By 1993 persons admitted to nursing homes and hostels had for some years been assessed by multi-disciplinary teams to determine eligibility for entry; there was no suggestion in current policy analysis work that these people had been inappropriately placed in residential care.[4]

Some changes to the current system are incorporated into the model, otherwise the calculation would be of limited utility. While not officially documented, there is a general agreement in federal policy circles that nursing home care could well be appropriately limited to only those meeting the criteria for RCI categories 1 to 3 – the higher

---

[4] A small proportion of current residents would have been admitted prior to the implementation of the more stringent aged care assessment procedures. However, less than 10 per cent of these nursing home residents had a length of stay in excess of five years (AIHW 1993: 241).

dependency nursing home residents. Those in RCI categories 4 to 5, it is argued, could be appropriately cared for in hostels. At the same time there is some suggestion that the low dependency hostel clients (the so-called Hostel Care, as opposed to Personal Care, hostel residents) could be adequately accommodated elsewhere, probably in public or supported housing.

The projections presented here do no more than calculate the numbers associated with such changing scenarios, using 1993 utilisation rates. The projections are driven by demographic changes in the age and sex structure of the population, and the increased numbers of old people associated with population ageing. They do not include changes in occupancy rates and turnover, both of which could impact quite considerably on future patterns of use (although both have been stable in recent years). The data also assume that age- and sex-specific levels of dependency will remain relatively stable in the aged population; an assumption that would not be without its critics. However, in the absence of convincing evidence for either the 'pandemic of morbidity' or 'compression of morbidity' hypotheses (Robine, Mathers and Brouard, 1993), and given the relative stability of these rates in national surveys over the last decade and a half as reported earlier, such an assumption would appear to be a reasonable one.

Nursing home care

In 1993 there were 74 494 nursing home beds in Australia. Should the intended planning ratio be in place in 2011 there will be 78 600 beds, and by 2021, 106 900. To accommodate 1993 patterns of use, however, 119 300 beds in 2011 and 145 200 beds by 2021 would be required. On this projection, demand (at least on the basis of 1993 use rates) would exceed supply by a significant margin.

As already noted, however, the argument has been advanced that nursing home beds should in future be reserved for the more dependent nursing home residents (in current terms RCI categories 1 to 3). When service use patterns for only these residents were projected, the figures were somewhat more reassuring – 91 100 beds would be required by 2011 and 110 700 by 2021. Nonetheless a shortfall of nursing home care would still exist if we had intended to accommodate into the future our current categories of RCI 1 to 3 type residents. The projected shortfall would reach a peak of some 12 500 beds in 2011, declining to 3800 by 2021 when the growing numbers of (relatively healthy) 70- to 80-year-old baby boomers would ironically fuel an increased level of provision, as the official planning ratio is based on the numbers of people 70 and over.

Table 3.3 Projections of 1993 utilisation patterns and planned supply for nursing homes and hostels

	2001	2006	2011	2016	2021
Projection of nursing homes use based on 1993 RCI 1–3 residents only	70 600	80 700	91 100	100 200	110 700
Projection of hostel use based on 1993 hostel care and personal care plus nursing home RCI 4–5	87 000	99 500	112 400	123 400	136 300
Projection of hostel use based on 1993 hostel personal care only plus nursing home RCI 4–5	58 600	67 100	76 000	83 500	92 100
Planned supply for nursing homes	76 300	77 400	78 600	89 300	106 900
Planned supply for hostels	76 000	89 600	98 200	111 600	133 600
Planned supply for community aged care packages	17 000	18 100	19 600	22 300	26 700

Source: Adapted from AIHW 1995: 210.

Hostel care

Unlike nursing homes the level of provision of hostel places is set to increase under the present policy direction, from the 1993 level of 40 places per thousand persons aged 70 and over, to 50 places per thousand by 2011. The analyses presented here assume that this benchmark will be met. It should be noted, however, that while the federal government has control over nursing home bed approvals and can thus ensure that the reduction of nursing home beds to the planned level will be achieved, it cannot similarly ensure the expansion of the hostel sector. This is dependent on applications for new hostel places by the private-for-profit and private-not-for-profit sectors, which may or may not be forthcoming. In recent years, the expansion of the hostel sector has not met the levels envisaged by the federal government.

In 1993, 54 429 hostel places were available in Australia, and if the benchmark were to be reached by 2011, 98 200 places would be available. In 2021 the figure would be 133 600. Assuming that RCI level 4 and 5 nursing home residents would indeed be accommodated in hostel level care, as well as current residents, the projection suggests a likely requirement of 112 400 places by 2011, and 136 300 by 2021. Again, the projection suggests that the planned level of supply would not be capable of meeting that level of demand for this period, although the shortfall reduces substantially by 2021 as the increasing numbers of young aged begin to affect the size of the denominator (the number of people 70 and over) in the planning ratio. In 2011 the projected shortfall in hostel beds would be 14 200, reducing to 2700 by 2021.

If the lower level of 'Hostel Care' hostel residents are excluded from the projection the picture is a much more cheerful one. On this scenario, supply of hostel places exceeds demand for the entire period. The excess beds are more than sufficient to accommodate the shortfall noted above in the nursing home sector. On the other hand the level of care available in hostels, and in particular the more limited access to skilled nursing staff, may well not provide the quality of care required by many nursing home residents under such arrangements.

Moreover, there has been no account taken of the alternative arrangements which would or could be made for those hostel residents in the 'Hostel Care' category. While these persons may be appropriately cared for in the community, under private or public or sheltered housing arrangements with community-based support, such arrangements are not as yet forthcoming. Moreover, there is no empirical basis from which to assert that the Hostel Care category of hostel resident can best be accommodated in this way. While these are residents assumed to be without personal care needs, as they do not meet the eligibility criteria for a Personal Care benefit in the hostel, little is known about them, and national data provide no indication of their actual dependency levels.

Community aged care packages

Community aged care packages were established to provide more intensive home-based care to persons with levels of dependency akin to hostel residents eligible for the Personal Care subsidy. Arguably, they were designed to serve as a substitute for such care. Funding previously allocated to hostel places was reallocated to community aged care packages, with a planning target of 10 such packages per thousand persons aged 70 and over to be in place by around 2011. While the number of care packages has grown substantially the ratio of actual provision (two packages per thousand persons aged 70 and over in 1995) remains well below that specified by the planning ratio. At the planned level of provision (not the current levels) these care packages would meet the envisaged shortfall until 2006; by 2011 the shortfall would re-emerge and remain present through 2016, disappearing again by 2021.

There are dangers, however, in assuming that the community aged care packages are a viable substitute for hostel residents with personal care needs, or that they would necessarily be allocated to persons who would otherwise have sought residential care.

First, community aged care packages were developed to provide an alternative source of care for persons with dependency levels similar to Personal Care hostel residents. They are not intended to accommodate nursing home residents, and certainly not those of RCI 1 to 3, the envisaged residents of the nursing homes of the future. The shortfall in the nursing home sector is thus not appropriately taken up by community aged care packages.

Second, there is some evidence to suggest that care package clients are not, in fact, of a similar dependency profile to hostel residents receiving personal care benefits. Analyses of data from the first national survey on care package clients suggest that their dependency profiles are closer to those of community care clients than they are to those of hostel residents (Mathur *et al.* 1997).

Third, experience suggests that a significant proportion of care packages are likely to be accessed by people who would in any case have remained in the community and never entered residential care. While eligibility for nursing home or hostel care is determined by severity of disability, it is not, as we have seen, necessarily the case that those who remain in the community are less disabled. Most severely handicapped aged persons are cared for in the community; even among those aged 80 and over the level of institutionalisation is only 40 per cent. Meeting the eligibility requirements for admission to a hostel or nursing home in terms of severity of disability is a necessary, but not sufficient condition for entry to residential care. Other factors intervene, such as the availability of a range of formal and informal supports, and the willingness to 'make do' with inadequate assistance (or even no assistance) if that is the alternative to entering a residential care facility.

Intensive forms of home-based care will be accessed both by highly dependent people without informal carers, and those whose carers are carrying particularly onerous responsibilities. Assessment procedures will ensure that this is the case; the point being made is not that community aged care packages can be expected to slip down the level of need hierarchy to those who are less dependent or in less difficult circumstances. Rather, it is the case that there exists in the community a pool of highly dependent people who would be highly unlikely to enter residential care, but whose care requirements are such that they would be able to compete quite successfully on a 'need for service' basis with that subgroup of frail aged persons who would require relocation from residential care as the supply of such services diminishes in accordance with current policy directions. The ageing of the aged population means that in the home care sector, as in the residential care sector, the proportion of the very old and very dependent old is increasing and will continue to do so well into the next century.

The expansion of home-based care

Home-based services did expand quite dramatically over the period from 1985. This was partly to do with increased funding to existing home-based care services provided under the Home and Community Care program (HACC), partly due to the expansion of the range of services offered, and partly to do with the emergence of community options projects and community aged care packages, both essentially brokerage models aimed at persons who would not previously have been considered within the purview of home-based care services, having needs deemed to be more appropriately met in a residential care setting.

Unfortunately, the quality of national databases on home-based care in Australia does not allow accurate estimates of the changing quantity of home-based services at the client level. While the standard estimate of the number of clients served by HACC-funded services in any month stands at 215 000, it is only an estimate. Moreover, the same estimate has been given by the relevant federal department (currently the Department of Health and Family Services) over the period from 1991 to 1996. The exact number of clients is not known, and there is little by way of accurate information concerning the packages of services which they are receiving from the program.

These difficulties arise partly from the nature of the data collection on HACC clients, and partly from the nature of the HACC program itself. The collection is a sample survey, completed by each agency's staff with regard to approximately 10 per cent of its clients (the fraction does vary in some states, and for some agencies). The quality of the data is thus dependent on the quality of the agency's records, including its knowledge of what other services the client is receiving from agencies other than the one doing the reporting. This latter aspect tends to be poorly recorded.

The very structure of the HACC program, with a multitude of large and small agencies funded to provide a range of services (some

Table 3.4 Government expenditure for aged care services 1985–86 and 1993–94

	Current $m		Constant $m	
	1985–86	1993–94	1985–86	1993–94
Assessment	0.0	34.5	0.0	30.5
Home Care	192.2	627.0	233.8	553.4
Hostels	59.0	311.9	71.8	275.3
Nursing Homes	1010.1	1704.0	1228.8	1466.2
Total	1261.3	2677.4	1534.4	2363.1

Note: Constant prices calculated using the GFCE (Government Final Consumption Expenditure) deflator. Funding includes all Commonwealth funding of aged care services, plus state government funding of home-based care.
Source: Adapted from AIHW (1995: 205).

providing only one service, others virtually the full spectrum of home-based care), means that clients of the program may be receiving assistance from one, two, three or more agencies. The data generated by such agencies on their clients, therefore, do not refer to unique individuals, but include multiple references to one individual. There is no way of identifying these cases within the existing data set. Such difficulties simply do not occur in the residential care data, where facilities are centrally funded, the program centrally administered and the data centrally collected.

Other measures are available, however, which do allow some indication of the growth in home care services. Funding is commonly taken by economists and policy analysts as a standard measure over time and for cross-national comparisons, and such data are available. Similarly, reliable national data are available on the total hours of service delivered at the agency level (but not those received by individual clients) for a portion of the period under scrutiny here.

Expenditure patterns

Table 3.4 presents recurrent funding for aged care services over the period from 1985–86 to 1993–94 in both current and constant prices. In constant dollar terms, expenditure on HACC increased by 137 per cent, on hostels by 283 per cent and on nursing homes by 22 per cent. For aged care funding overall, expenditure increased by 54 per cent.

Of course, this quite considerable increase in expenditure was taking place in the context of a quite considerable increase in the at-risk

Table 3.5 Government expenditure per capita for aged care services 1985–86 to 1993–94

	Expenditure (constant $) per highly dependent person aged 65+		% increase 1985–86 to 1993–94
	1985–86	1993–94	
Assessment	0	82	na
Home care	826	1501	82%
Hostels	254	746	194%
Nursing homes	4339	4249	–2%
Total	5419	6400	18%

Note: Constant prices (1989–90 dollars) calculated using the GFCE (Government Final Consumption Expenditure) deflator. Funding includes all Commonwealth funding of aged care services, plus state government funding of home-based care.
Source: Adapted from AIHW (1995: 206).

population. Table 3.5 provides the same expenditure data, but calculated in terms of the number of highly dependent persons aged 65 and over. Expenditure has not only increased in absolute terms, it has also increased in relation to the target population. Overall, expenditure for aged care services increased by 18 per cent per highly dependent aged person. This growth occurred disproportionately in the earlier years of the period, with recent years seeing a marked slowing in annual growth rates. The exception to this pattern, however, was the decline in nursing home expenditure per highly dependent aged person (AIHW 1995: 206).

Taken together, these expenditure data demonstrate a number of important changes in the aged care system:

* Expenditure on aged care services not only increased in real terms, but also increased in relation to the number of highly dependent aged persons in the Australian community.
* Expenditure on home care not only increased in relation to the number of highly dependent aged persons in the community, but it also increased as a proportion of total aged care expenditure from 15 per cent to 23 per cent.
* Expenditure on nursing homes decreased from 80 per cent of total expenditure to 64 per cent, while that on hostels increased from 5 per cent to 12 per cent of total expenditure.
* Assessment, a critical component of the targeting strategy which underlies this reduction in the supply of residential aged care, remained at around 1 per cent of total expenditure.

Home-based services: Supply

Time series data on the supply of home-based services are limited; they are not available for all states or for all services, and only then for services funded under the HACC program (although these are the majority of such services). National averages have been calculated on a per frail aged person basis to allow some viable comparison of levels of provision at the two points in time for which reliable data were available (1989 and 1993–94).

For those services for which data were available, service provision appears to have increased in relation to the number of highly dependent aged persons in the community. This analysis uses hours or units of service per 1000 highly dependent persons aged 65 and over as the basis for comparison; the data refer to hours or units of service over a one-month period.

The number of delivered meals provided increased from 550 per 1000 highly dependent aged persons to 2870. The hours of centre-based day care provided increased from 550 to 1615 per thousand highly dependent aged persons, and those of in-home respite from 250 to 600 per thousand highly dependent aged persons (Mathur 1996).

For home help, the only other category for which time series data were available, the supply appears to have reduced from 2000 hours to 1640 per 1000 highly dependent aged persons. However, in 1993–94 a new data category of personal care was created and accounts for 420 hours per 1000 highly dependent aged persons (Mathur 1996). Some substantial part of this category would probably have formerly been categorised as home help; the remainder would have been home nursing.[5] It appears likely, therefore, that provision did not decrease over the period, although the nature of the service being provided may have shifted more towards personal care, and away from house cleaning and shopping activities. Table 3.6 provides the most recent national data on selected HACC services, again referring to services provided over a one-month period.

Overall, then, available evidence suggests that not only expenditure, but the hours of service supplied have increased. The HACC data listed above do not take account of the two community aged care packages now available per 1000 aged persons, which would further augment current levels of provision for home-based care. Of course, while the per capita base (the number of very dependent persons aged

---

[5] Unfortunately, data on home nursing are not available for the earlier period, making this comparison indicative rather than conclusive.

Table 3.6   Provision levels of HACC services 1993–94

	Hours per 1000 highly dependent people 65+	Hours per 1000 people 70+
Home help	1640	420
Personal care	420	110
Home nursing	790	200
Home respite	600	150
Centre day care	1620	410
Home meals (number)	2870	730

Source: Adapted from Mathur (1996).

65 and over) being used is a constant denominator in these comparisons, it must be remembered that the proportion of those highly dependent persons actually living in the community rather than in residential care increased quite markedly over the period. The extent to which the increase in provision has kept pace with the increase in need is one on which little concrete evidence is available, but obviously one of critical policy concern.

Anecdotally, HACC service providers claim an increasing difficulty in meeting levels of demand. They claim that their services are increasingly being directed towards more and more dependent persons, that the type of services which they are providing have moved from including both assistance with activities of daily living and instrumental activities of daily living to being concentrated on the former. This involves partially a process of natural attrition in less dependent clients, but also the actual termination of services to less dependent clients.

Some service providers also suggest that there is a tendency for a growing proportion of their resources to be directed towards the younger disabled; a population who are often both more severely handicapped and who have vocal advocates (parent carers, activists, lobby groups) to assert their particular needs. HACC services in Australia are available to both frail disabled older people and younger people with disabilities. If this is the case, frail older people may well not have been the recipients of the apparent growth in HACC services and HACC expenditure. Clear evidence to support these contentions remains unavailable.

Conclusion

While the expansion of home-based services in Australia dates from the mid-1980s and the emergence of the Aged Care Reform Strategy, the systems of service delivery in both residential and home-based care have continued to evolve since that time. One of the most significant developments has been a growing belief in and commitment to the maintenance of highly dependent frail older people in the community, with the support of home-based care services.

The earliest Commonwealth government initiatives in this direction were the community options projects, commenced in pilot form in 1987–88, but quite quickly implemented nationally. Although not without both difficulties and detractors the community options projects were seen to demonstrate that highly dependent persons could be maintained at home with the assistance of formal services. Community aged care packages were essentially the next generation of intensive home-based care services. While the projects run under these two auspices confirm findings from elsewhere that extremely dependent older people can indeed be maintained in their own homes, the extent to which such findings, often based on demonstration projects, can be broadly extended into the community remains unclear. The extent to which, and the instances and circumstances in which, they are the more appropriate alternative to residential care is also worthy of further scrutiny.

One of the recent corollaries of the increasing reliance on home-based care has been the growing acceptance of carers as legitimate clients for home-based care services. The role of informal support, while well recognised for over a decade, has come increasingly to centre stage in discussions of aged care policy and formal support programs. One visible result has been an increasingly vociferous demand for expanded respite care provisions.

The Australian system of respite provision is already well developed by international standards. Apart from day-care centres and home-based respite, residential respite care is also available in both nursing homes and hostels. The numbers of admissions have been growing substantially in recent years with a 146 per cent increase in respite admissions to nursing homes and a 43 per cent increase in admissions to hostels over the three-year period to 1994–95 (Gibson *et al.* 1996). This growth in residential respite care use demonstrates a growing interface between residential and home-based care, which was simply not characteristic of Australian aged care services in earlier decades. The system of aged care provision has indeed shifted dramatically away from residential care and in favour of home-based care. What has perhaps been less evident is the consequent shifts and changes in the nature of home-based and residential care services themselves – shifts which will continue to have implications in the way in which we think about aged care services well into the next century.

CHAPTER 4

The Feminisation of Ageing

Introduction

For those working in the fields of social gerontology or feminist studies, one of the recognised academic growth areas of the 1980s must surely have been the study of old women. As the previous feminist preoccupation with the reproductive phase of the life cycle gave way to a modest but emerging recognition of post-menopausal and ageing women, so too did at least some areas of social gerontology recognise the relevance of gender to the ageing process. This is not to suggest that old age became a central focus of feminist analysis, or that a feminist revolution took social gerontology by storm. Rather, a small group of researchers began to explore the co-incidence of age and gender – sparked in part (perhaps not surprisingly given the frequently observed link between biography and scholastic enterprise) by the movement of 'second wave' feminists into late middle and old age.[1]

Perhaps the most commonly offered explanation of the failure of feminists to engage with the problems of old age lies in the 'gerontophobic nature' of the wider society (Arber and Ginn 1991a). Such issues are perceived as unimportant and indeed unattractive in intellectual terms, as well as in those of society at large. A further explanation of the feminist neglect of ageing may well lie in its own intellectual origins. Feminism has always had a strong preoccupation with the division between public and private lives, between the reproductive and the productive spheres. This division, central to feminist theory and explanation, loses much of its potency in the later stages of the life cycle when women are no longer engaged in reproductive labour (at least as

[1] See, for example, the work by Greer (1991) and Friedan (1993).

70

it pertains to child-rearing) and men have withdrawn from the productive sphere. Conventional feminist categories of analysis are thus disturbed, perhaps explaining the perceived lack of relevance to the broader feminist project. The possible leverage that this disjuncture could provide to feminist theorists has sadly remained unexplored; these and other 'silences' form an important part of the more theoretical analyses of feminism and ageing put forward in Chapter 8.

The last decade has seen a considerable response to the absence of feminist analysis originally identified by authors such as Russell (1987), Reinharz (1986) and Allen (1988). There has been a growing awareness of the problems encountered by old women in an ageing society, ranging from the empirical to the polemical, and often much preoccupied with the double or triple jeopardy faced by women as they age. Curiously, there was less willingness to engage in analyses of social policy as they impacted on old women, despite the energy and force with which feminist social policy analysts were exploring other, quite closely related, areas.

Extensive feminist critiques of the sexism underlying much social policy – as developed by British feminists in the 1970s and continued there and elsewhere into the 1980s – stressed the consistent stereotyping of women as men's dependants and men as wage earners. Social provisions based on this assumed division of labour were thus seen to reinforce that dependency via a system which offered inadequate provision to, and discriminated against, women not in that position.[2]

This highly influential work serves both as a basis and a point of departure for the present analysis. While the tenor of those arguments was always broadly applicable to women in old age its application was limited, reflecting the previously noted tendency among feminist critics towards an engagement with the reproductive stage of the life cycle. Where it did occur attention was concentrated on two areas.

First, the underlying analytic focus on the sexist assumptions of female economic dependency led to a series of investigations illustrating the pension and superannuation inequities which emerge in the later stages of the life cycle (Land 1976, Rosenman 1982; 1986). Second, the preoccupation with women's public and private sphere responsibilities led to an extensive literature on the burdens of caring for the aged which confront women in the middle stages of their own life cycle (Finch and Groves 1983, Ungerson 1987 and Braithwaite 1990). It is perhaps ironic, as Arber and Ginn pointed out, that this

[2] Important examples of early path-breaking work include Bennett (1983), David and Land (1983), Land (1978; 1985), McIntosh (1978; 1979), Rose (1981), Scott (1984) and Wilson (1977).

kind of feminist analysis has contributed to 'a pathological view of elderly people' (Arber and Ginn 1991a), particularly where many of those older people are themselves women. These two lines of analysis, even in combination, fall far short of a systematic analysis of social provisions for older people.

The major thesis of this chapter is that in Australia, and indeed elsewhere, social provisions for the aged have failed to take account of the peculiar and particular problems confronting women in an ageing society. Recent years have seen a growing awareness of these issues, and the emergence of a range of empirical studies which canvass disparate elements of that debate. In this chapter, I attempt to systematise existing material and present a feminist analysis of social provisions for the aged.

The first section of the argument reviews available evidence on the extent of women's care of the aged. This is the area in which feminist analyses of aged care are already well known. Examples are drawn from a range of published research to document earlier arguments of this kind. The analysis is extended, however, by emphasising the role of old women themselves as providers of care, as well as recipients. The argument here is that the care of the aged bears a parasitic relationship to the unpaid and poorly paid labour of women in general, and that of older women in particular.[3]

The second and third stages of the argument present aspects of a feminist critique of social provisions for the aged less well developed in the existing literature. The second section examines the implications of existing patterns of expenditure and service delivery as distributed according to sex. In the third section, the mismatch between the particular needs and circumstances of women and the tenor of public provision is considered. In so far as available services and funding privilege the sex-specific needs and interests of men – the minority of older people – the argument is advanced that social policy for the aged is phallocentric.[4]

---

[3] 'Parasitism' has an honoured place in the history of feminist theory. Some first wave feminists – such as Gilman (1898), Schreiner (1911/1977) and Scott (1903) – understood 'sex parasitism' to refer to the analysis of modern woman as gradually reduced to being a 'creature of sex' getting her living not by productive labour but through a parasitic relationship with a man in return for sexual and domestic services which their socialist framework did not recognise as work. Conversely, and more recently, other feminists have identified men as parasitic upon women's work, sexuality and physical services. See, for example, Frye (1983); Leghorn and Parker (1981); and Woolf (1997).

[4] 'Phallocentrism' is used to characterise social policy formulations privileging and corresponding with the interests, experiences and preferences of men as a sexed group, advantaging them *vis-à-vis* women. 'Sexist' or sex discriminatory policies have generated campaigns for equality, and implicitly sameness – the unequal (female) party seeking extension of the same benefits or rights. Only some of the problems identified here with regard to social provisions for older women concern 'sexism',

Labours of love

Social policy provisions for frail and disabled older people are predicated on the expectation that women will provide the vast majority of care at no fiscal cost to the state and that much of the remainder will be subsidised by underpaid female labour. Like housework and child care, care of disabled older people is a labour of love borne for the most part by women at significant (short- and long-term) costs to themselves. These physical, emotional, psychological and financial costs borne by those caring for seriously disabled older people at home have been, to date, the major focus of feminist critiques of social policy pertaining to ageing. And while it is British feminists who developed these analyses (Finch and Groves 1983, Ungerson 1987), corroborative evidence has emerged with regard to such diverse systems of provision as Scandinavia (Woerness 1987), Australia (Braithwaite 1990, Rossiter 1984), the United States (Brody 1981, Brody and Schoonover 1986) and Canada (Gee and Kimball 1987). The dominant although not exclusive thrust of such analyses concerned adult non-aged women caring for elderly relatives, particularly elderly parents being cared for by daughters and daughters-in-law. The role of spouse carers has been less commonly articulated in connection with feminist analyses. While spouse carers figure in some of the empirical analyses, they have received less attention at a theoretical level. Yet spouses are the single largest category among carers of frail and disabled older people, and their apparent neglect in feminist work may be indicative of the 'geronto-phobic' explanation for the neglect of certain aspects of research on the aged discussed earlier.

The fact that both sexes have been shown to care for extremely dependent spouses may also have made spouse carers a less obvious subject for feminist analysis. Yet available evidence does point to a preponderance of wives over husbands in the caring role. Woerness (1987: 136), for example, reports three times as many women as men caring for a dependent spouse in Sweden. In Australia the findings are similar (Australian Council on the Ageing and Department of Community Services 1985; Kinnear and Graycar 1982). On the other hand, Arber and Gilbert (1989) and Arber and Ginn (1991b) suggest a more equal division of spouse care between the sexes in the United Kingdom, although the structure of the Office Population Census and Survey (OPCS) screening question, as noted by Arber and Ginn themselves, does render it particularly vulnerable to artifactually induced under-enumeration.

---

[4] (*cont.*) inequality and discrimination within social policies themselves. The pervasive 'man-centredness' of their conception and service delivery with its corollary of 'woman-blindness' is the more intractable problem. For a fuller discussion of phallocentrism see Grosz (1987).

There is undoubtedly an artifactual measurement problem at work confounding many of the findings and interpretations in this area. Care by female spouses is sufficiently part of the 'normal' female role to retain a certain level of 'invisibility', and hence is undoubtedly predisposed towards under-enumeration in many statistical collections. Wives 'do domestic duties' as part of their normal responsibilities. Studies such as the OPCS Informal Carers Survey reported by Arber and Ginn (1991b), for example, actually define 'caring' in their screening questions as not part of 'normal' family care or domestic provisioning work.

Even where the detailed description of domestic responsibilities was an integral part of the research design, gender blindness can emerge at the interpretive level, as exemplified by the not infrequent emphasis on the interdependence of married couples in old age. This is the comfortable notion that by judicious sharing of responsibilities the specific frailties of each partner may be 'cancelled out,' allowing quite disabled couples to remain in their own homes (Kendig 1983; 1986).

It is salutary to observe just what this 'interdependence' involves. Australian evidence on patterns of domestic responsibility in aged couple households with a highly dependent spouse can be used to illustrate this reciprocity. In households where the husbands were highly dependent their wives were primarily responsible for meal preparation (91 per cent of couples), housekeeping (82 per cent of couples) and doing shopping and errands (76 per cent of couples). In households where it was the wife who was highly dependent, the converse was not the case. Only 29 per cent of those husbands prepared the meals and 40 per cent were responsible for housekeeping, with a larger proportion (56 per cent) being responsible for shopping and errands. An imbalance in the services received is already evident, but in fact the asymmetry was even more marked. Half these highly dependent women were still preparing meals for their non-disabled spouse and one-third were responsible for the housework. The only ameliorating factor in these patterns is the greater responsibility of men for home maintenance tasks: 88 per cent of the male partners of disabled wives were primarily responsible for such tasks, and 48 per cent of those men, who while themselves disabled, were still undertaking home maintenance tasks. Nonetheless, the intermittent nature of such tasks, and their general lack of immediacy (a dripping tap can wait for several months in the way that meal preparation cannot), reduces the extent to which such responsibilities offset the contributions made by women.[5]

---

[5] Based on a re-analysis of data reported in Kendig (1983; 1986). Similar patterns, despite the measurement strategy used being more prone to the artifactual errors

Clearly, these women were not receiving an equivalent level of services from their male spouses to that provided where the circumstances were reversed, exposing marked inflexibility and non-reciprocity in the sexual division of labour. These disadvantages are further compounded by the fact that women on average outlive their spouses by approximately eight years.[6] Frail aged women are less likely than frail aged men to have a surviving spouse in the latter stages of the life cycle, and, as we have seen, even if women do have a spouse they are less likely to have him assume the domestic responsibilities than is a male in similar circumstances.

In Australia the analysis of nursing home resident statistics further demonstrates this propensity – while rates of institutionalisation (age standardised) are much higher for the never married than the married, the difference is much more dramatic for men than for women.[7] Marriage thus appears to provide greater protection from institutionalisation for men than it does for women; men are either less willing, or less capable, of maintaining a dependent spouse in the community.

While lifelong sexual divisions of labour underlie these patterns of responsibility, such continuity in no way undermines the central finding that it is older women rather than older men who maintain the independent household in old age. Moreover, that finding remains as salient for the non-disabled aged as it does for the disabled aged.[8] It is predominantly women's labour that maintains aged couples in their own homes, with consequent savings to the public sector. The use of concepts such as the interdependence of couples in old age, in combination with the devalued nature of women's private sphere responsibilities (exemplified by the relative invisibility of old women's 'normal' domestic responsibilities), obscures the non-reciprocity of women's situation in old age, and fails to recognise the extent to which social provision for the aged is parasitic upon the labour of old women.

Care of frail and disabled older people in the community is closely predicated on unpaid family labour, predominantly supplied by wives, daughters and daughters-in-law. The role played by formal

---

already described, were found in the Australian Council on the Aging and Department of Community Services (1985) report. Wright (1983) demonstrated a similar imbalance with sons caring for handicapped mothers in the United Kingdom.

[6] Expected years of widowhood vary by age cohort, but there is remarkably little cross-national variation in Western industrialised societies. So, for example, in Canada the cohort born between 1901 and 1910 averaged six years of widowhood, and that born between 1931 and 1940 will average 12 years (Gee and Kimball 1987: 83). In general, women continue to marry slightly older men, and life expectancy remains at around 71 years for men and 78 years for women (Rowland 1991: 48–53).

[7] Based on a re-analysis of data reported by Preston and O'Connell (1985: 53–59).

[8] See Kendig (1983) and also Bittman (1991) for an analysis of national time budget data. These patterns are consistent with cross-national evidence pointing to the persistence of traditional patterns of domestic responsibility in all age groups (Baxter 1991).

community-based services and institutional provision should be briefly considered in this context, as popular belief tends to overestimate the role of formal services relative to informal assistance. Not only do the vast majority of older people live in the community, so too do the vast majority of frail and disabled older people. Levels of institutionalisation among persons aged 65 and over are consistently around 5 to 6 per cent in a wide range of countries (see Chapter 1); quite clearly the majority of older people remain in the community (Woerness 1987, Rowland 1991).

Among those living in the community only a small minority use formal services. Even among the highly dependent older people in Australia only a minority used even one formal service, and less than 1 per cent received more than one form of assistance (Kendig 1983). In Scandinavia, Woerness reports on the basis of Norwegian Time Budget Survey data that informal care of the aged is eight times that provided by formal agencies. Despite differences in national social policies, informal care is consistently the predominant pattern in Australia, Britain, Canada, Scandinavia and the United States.[9]

The role of women in aged care is not, however, confined to their role in assisting family and friends. Women also dominate the provision of volunteer services. Not only are most volunteer workers women, but the predominance of females is even more marked in the service areas of volunteer work (those which relate to health education, family and personal well-being). Not surprisingly, in larger, hierarchical organisations women are located at the lower end of the organisational structure.[10]

The continuities between the position of women volunteers and that of paid women workers are evident. Women also predominate as paid labour in both the community and institutional sectors, indeed in many contexts the aged care labour force is virtually exclusively female. As is characteristic of many female dominated areas of the labour force, the work is for the most part classified as unskilled, is poorly paid, with little access to overtime payments and poor job security. Morale is often low, and rates of turnover high.

The issue of unpaid labour, however, emerges even here. One large-scale national study of Australian hostels revealed, despite the presence of the conditions described above, repeated instances of significant

---

[9] This point is consistently established in available literature. See, for example: Woerness (1987) on Scandinavia; Allen (1988) on the United Kingdom; Streib and Beck (1980) on the United States; and Gee and Kimball (1987: 86–88) on Canada and North America generally.

[10] See, for example, Baldock (1990), Hardwick and Graycar (1982), Paterson (1982) and Nemschoff (1981).

amounts of unpaid overtime being undertaken by these female workers. Staff remained behind to finish back rub rounds, or undertook small services for residents (shopping, errands) outside the institution (Peat, Marwick, Mitchell 1986). Such activities were seen as a 'normal' extension of the female caring role. While these data remain indicative, it seems likely that the provision of institutional care is subsidised not only by underpaid female labour, but by additional 'free' services volunteered by an already exploited labour force.

The labours of love offered by women caring for the aged in the community are ubiquitous and hence largely unacknowledged. These services would be, if acknowledged and appropriately costed, of momentous financial value.[11] The examples given here of the family care of frail and disabled older people, the domestic division of labour between aged couples, and the work of both voluntary and paid female workers show that social provisions for the aged rely heavily on women, and often ageing women, in their lifelong roles as unpaid domestic workers. This reliance constitutes the kind of sex parasitism identified by feminist theorist Marilyn Frye (1983) as characteristic of patriarchal societies. Parasitism might seem a strong word, especially if it could be shown that there are compensations for mostly longer living women – if services and policies then provided women with adequate assistance as they face widowhood, disability, institutionalisation, loss of income and other events associated with their own ageing. The evidence presented in subsequent sections of this article demonstrates, however, that this is not the case.

The pattern of public provision

As was noted earlier in this book the relative balance between home-based and residential care varies on a national basis. The United Kingdom traditionally had a comparatively high rate of provision of home-based care in relation to residential care, while the situation in Australia was the reverse. Yet the comparisons presented in Chapter 1 suggest that countries do not in a comparative sense emerge as high on one or the other, but rather tend if anything to be consistent in the level of generosity of their provisions in both the home-based and residential care sectors.

What can be consistently argued cross-nationally, however, is that an under-supply of either or both home-based or residential care

[11] Momentous may appear to overstate the case. But the value of women's unpaid labour has already been calculated, and the case proven, in other contexts (Waring 1988), while the total value of volunteer labour to society has recently begun to gain more general recognition (AIHW 1995: Chapter 2).

adversely impacts on women in particular, owing to their numerical predominance among both carers and the recipients of care.

Earlier feminist analyses of community care have correctly and succinctly pointed out that community care tends to mean family care, and that family care means care by women. It is not, however, the increasing emphasis on home-based care which is the problem, but rather the under-supply of either or both forms of public provision. Moves over the last decade to shift the balance of aged care away from institutions and towards the community do not necessarily adversely affect women or further exploit women. It is, after all, true that many and indeed most older people prefer to remain in their own homes rather than to enter an institution. Inadequate institutional care in terms of either quantity or quality will increase the burden on community-based carers owing to the absence of viable alternatives. Inadequate community-based services will force women into caring roles because of the absence of alternatives, or leave them in roles which they would willingly take on but without the support which they sorely need. Only an adequate supply of both residential and home-based care provides the range of options necessary to minimise the exploitation of informal caregivers.

Feminist critics of community care must, then, be careful to clearly delineate that it is the under-supply of formal services which is the major concern, rather than community-based care per se. That point having been made, there does remain a potentially dangerous ideological component which lurks within the community care rhetoric – the neo-conservative assumption that it is women's duty to assume such obligations.[12] If community care is formulated as a strategy to allow an inadequate supply and poor quality of residential care, then it exacerbates the sexual parasitism described earlier in this chapter. Yet to deny women (and men) who choose to care for a disabled person the right to do so (with adequate support) is to indulge in a privileging of public over private values consistent with an earlier androcentric stage of feminist analysis. Adequacy of provision in both arenas is the critical policy direction to be pursued.

Comments on and analyses of the potential impact of population ageing on the system of public provision, in terms of growing numbers and an expanding need for care, are almost ubiquitous. Yet the implications are rarely considered by feminist analysts of public policy. Levels of institutional care appear to remain relatively constant over time within national boundaries, with constancy in this instance

---

[12] See Aronson (1992) on the ideologies and assumptions which underlie women's decisions to care.

referring to a particular proportion of the population aged over 65 who are in residential care. But as has been argued in the previous chapter, a constant level of provision in those terms does not in fact mean a constant level of supply to older people in need of such care – the ageing of the aged population currently under way in countries such as Australia means that access to care is correspondingly reduced (see Chapter 3).

This need for increased levels of service provision to maintain parity is much less obvious in the community care sector, as the proportion of persons receiving assistance, and those who are not but may be in need of it, are much more difficult to identify. Moreover, there are much larger proportions of aged people involved, thus making the increases in absolute numbers far more dramatic. Compounding these trends are the higher rates of disability among the very old members of the aged population. The need for increasing levels of home-based services must be interpreted in the context of increasing demands on informal carers as well. Furthermore, as the gerontological transition proceeds there will be comparatively large cohorts entering old age, and comparatively small cohorts in the subsequent (supporting) generations. The demands on the children of frail older people will be significantly greater over the first three decades of the 21st century in countries such as Canada, the United States, New Zealand and Australia than they are in the 1990s (Rowland 1991: 187–207).

The gerontological transition will not only adversely affect women as providers of care. In combination with changing patterns of women's work force participation and perhaps changing ideologies surrounding women's caring obligations, it will also disproportionately affect women as recipients of care. It is women who are less likely to have a spouse carer, and therefore be more reliant on informal care from the next generation in the form of daughters and daughters-in-law who may well be less available, able or willing to undertake that role.

Apart from the broad issue of adequacy of supply and its adverse impact on and costs to women, there are a variety of ways in which the actual nature of public provision privileges male over female needs. The predominance of women among informal carers has been established, as has their cost-saving potential for the public purse.

A range of countries pay some form of attendant care allowance to the caregiver. In Australia the Domiciliary Nursing Care Benefit is set at less than one-fifth of the basic age pension entitlement, and less than one-tenth of the amount that would be expended by the federal government in providing institutional care. The payment is not means tested, however, and recipients may also qualify for a pension on old age or other grounds. Provisions in the United Kingdom are more generous, at around two-thirds of the invalidity benefit, or US$192 per month, although the benefit is strictly means tested. Michigan, one of the most generous of the United States programs, provides an average payment of US$250 per month, with no means testing of other income. Spouses, however, are disallowed.[13]

Payment levels in general are clearly low, and consistent with the low societal value attached to private sphere activities. It is largely women who bear the associated financial deprivations. It is also noteworthy that the United Kingdom benefit was extended to wives only after a legal challenge in the European Court of Justice on the grounds of equal treatment in 1986.

An interesting Australian corollary of this expectation that caring is part of women's natural role is demonstrated by the necessity to introduce in 1983 a 'spouse carers' pension – payable for men only. The situation came about because wives caring for husbands (aged or disabled) were automatically eligible for a pension because of their dependent (*sic*) status. Men caring for a disabled wife were not.[14]

On available evidence women are also disadvantaged with regard to community service provision. Old women, given a certain level of disability, seem to be less likely to receive community services than are old men. Hunt reported this finding for the United Kingdom as long ago as 1970, and more recently Allen (1988) has argued that this differential pattern of access continues. These patterns can also be found in Australian data – a re-analysis of large-scale survey data reported by the Australian Council on the Ageing and Department of Community Services (1985) confirms this finding. This is not to deny that the majority of service recipients are indeed old women. Rather the point is that men receive access to such services more easily, apparently because of their perceived (or perhaps actual) incapacity to care for themselves.

This bias does not just impact on care recipients, however. Women caring for the disabled aged at home are also less likely to receive public assistance, precisely because of normative expectations surrounding their capacity to cope. On rare occasions this perception is made explicit in policy documents, as was the case in the Australian state home care manual which specified that formal resources be directed

---

[13] See Keiher (1991) for a detailed comparison of these two benefits in the United Kingdom and the United States.

[14] This anomaly disappeared in 1985 with the introduction of a carer's pension payable to all persons caring for a significantly handicapped relative. This pension is available in addition to the Domiciliary Nursing Care Benefit which is an attendant care allowance paid only to those caring for a person assessed as requiring nursing home-level care.

towards those with least access to financial and personal resources – with personal resources defined as 'the person's family and friends' (Keens, Staden and Graycar 1983). On other occasions it is implicit. Aronson (1992), in describing patterns of caregiving in Canada, argues that public sector expectations of patterns of informal care provision are strongly sexually differentiated While consistent data are not broadly available, indicative evidence suggests that it is likely to be ubiquitous.

The use of institutional services shows a similar pattern. That is, although women are numerically predominant among persons over 65, and numerically predominant in residential care facilities, women at a given level of disability are less likely than men to use residential care. This broad trend has been remarked in the United Kingdom (Allen 1988). A more finely tuned analysis of Australian nursing home statistical data revealed that among never married, divorced and widowed residents there were significantly larger proportions of men than women who were independent with regard to activities of daily living.[15] The pattern did not hold, of course, for married men and women, where as it has been remarked earlier, the pattern is reversed due to the home-based care which women provide to disabled spouses.

Overall, then, once the effects of disability are controlled we find that government services, both residential and community based, are disproportionately directed towards old men – the minority of the aged population. Moreover, any inadequacy of provision in either the residential or home-based care sectors impacts most disadvantageously on women both as providers and recipients of care. An effective meaning to be drawn from this analysis is the assumption, indeed the enshrinement, of care by unpaid women within the family as a societal norm. This norm itself rests on the assumption (increasingly suspect) that women carers are supported in their turn by husbands or other (male) family breadwinners, leaving their labour available for unpaid caring responsibilities. The parallels with prescriptive norms surrounding the relative responsibilities of the public and private realm with regard to child care are obvious; in both cases the model is sexed and non-reciprocal – women provide care, men do not.[16]

The parasitism described here leads inexorably to the phallocentrism of the model of women as 'natural' servants and carers, men as 'natural' recipients of service and care. The implication of this phallocentric family care norm is to forestall the development of a plausible,

[15] Based on a re-analysis of data presented in Preston and O'Connell (1985: 84).
[16] In this section of the chapter, the focus of attention is on the assumptions underlying the system of public provision. This statement should not be taken as a denial of the substantial caring activities that some (almost invariably older) men do undertake.

equitable and adequately funded range of services catering for the diversity of situations, problems and preferences of aged men and women. Furthermore, the more politically powerful minority of the aged, men, have little objective interest in such a reorientation. Within prevailing circumstances their meals are still cooked, their clothes washed, the house cleaned, the shopping done, and their illnesses nursed by wives and/or female relatives, just as they were throughout earlier phases of the life course. 'The aged' are sexed, as fissured by sex-specific interests as at other phases in the life cycle. To identify the distinct unmet needs of older women is inevitably to challenge the allocation of resources and its basis in sexual politics and sexual economics.

Just as the character of the modern state has been argued to serve middle class interests (Goodin and Le Grand 1987), the structure of public provision for older people privileges the interests of men over those of women. We have seen that once levels of disability are taken into account, males consume a disproportionate share of both domiciliary and institutional services. Furthermore, certain elements of social policy for the aged still bear evidence to the assumption of traditional dependencies within the family. These assumptions, as others have observed in different contexts, serve to maintain and reinforce the subordinate position of women (Land 1978; 1985; McIntosh 1978; 1979). In the next section this argument is developed to explore the ways in which the type and structure of many existing provisions have been developed and maintained to more accurately align with the needs and preferences of older men than those of older women.

Sex-specific needs

What elements of women's lives impact differently from those of men on the resources and experiences which they bring to old age? In what ways might these give rise to sex-specific needs? The most obvious element is differential labour market participation, but community services, transport, recreation and social networks are also implicated. The limitations placed on women throughout their lives have particular ramifications in old age, when the cumulative impacts of disadvantage adversely affect women's capacities to secure solutions to everyday problems. A system of social provision geared for the actual needs of older women would act affirmatively in these areas in acknowledgment of lifelong inequities and culturally produced sexual differences.

Women's access to the labour market is in general terms both more fragmented over the life course and more likely to be concentrated in sectors and segments characterised by lower pay, less job security and less well-developed fringe benefits. One consequence of this is lower income in old age – whether via less access to private superannuation benefits, or, in countries where pensions are payable on an earnings-related basis, lower pensions, or through less accumulated capital and investment provisions. Women have less access to private superannuation and private income, are therefore consistently poorer than men in old age, and these adverse financial circumstances are further exacerbated by their greater longevity.[17]

Women are further disadvantaged by the structure of superannuation itself. Preservation arrangements, portability and employer vesting levels have in the past both discouraged women from joining superannuation schemes and reduced the level of benefits likely to be accrued for those who do. Moreover, entitlements based on husbands' superannuation arrangements are also problematic, particularly for widows and divorcees.[18]

It may be argued that sex-based inequalities in access to superannuation will disappear in the short to medium term; that the disparity is cohort specific. One detailed study of empirical trends conducted in Australia suggests that, on the contrary, the differential will persist for decades to come. Female labour force participation may have increased, but the nature of women's labour force participation is such that superannuation coverage remains low.[19]

In general terms it is clear that while retirement incomes remain dependent on long-term patterns of labour force participation, women's more attenuated patterns of attachment will continue to financially disadvantage them in old age. Attempts to improve women's coverage are commendable, yet they avoid addressing the wider structural issue wherein the dominant system of providing adequate income in old age is premised on the lifelong work force participation patterns of a minority of the aged population – men.

A second area in which women have sex-specific needs is that of community-based services. Traditionally, the emphasis in providing domiciliary services to the frail aged was on domiciliary nursing,

---

[17] See, for example, Rosenman (1986), Russell (1987) and Wiles (1987) who document the comparative disadvantage suffered by women in income terms, and its consequences for poverty in old age. Women, and particularly single women, are more likely to be solely reliant on public provision. Among the widowed, widows are almost three times as likely as widowers to suffer financial difficulty. See also the report of the Australian Human Rights Commission (1986) on superannuation.

[18] Rosenman (1986) points to the virtual absence of provision for divorced wives, and the reduced rates frequently available to widows.

[19] Dixon and Foster (1986: 348) quote Australian national statistics which demonstrate that working women in the 35–44 age category actually have lower superannuation coverage than those aged 55–59 (24 per cent compared to 35 per cent), and, of course, are also dramatically less well covered than equivalent aged males (61 per cent and 64 per cent respectively).

home-delivered meals and housekeeping services. Of these three services the latter two are, as we have seen, more likely to be accessed by males, once level of disability is taken into account. The point to be made here is that community provision has traditionally been inflected towards those services likely to be used or needed by males because of their socialisation, rather than those which females are likely to find, on the basis of their socialisation and experience, similarly difficult.

Australia provides a good example of a country in which the tenor of public provision was historically oriented towards services appropriate to males. So, for example, while the first federally funded domiciliary service available was delivered meals, in 1954, publicly funded household maintenance services were not generally introduced until the late 1980s, and are still not widely available. Yet survey data suggest that old women give up meal preparation only at marked levels of disability, and consistently encounter serious difficulties with minor household maintenance (Gibson and Rowland 1984; Coleman and Watson 1987).[20]

Minor household maintenance is an obvious example; an ongoing domestic activity essential to a reasonable standard of living, which few older women undertake for themselves, and where, at least in Australia, community service provision remains underdeveloped. One can go further and point to the lack of interest in this aspect of home-based care services among social scientists – published analyses of community services make remarkably few references to household maintenance. While the issue may be compounded in Australia where comparatively high levels of home ownership place a large number of older women in circumstances where they have such responsibilities, the point is generalisable to large segments of many other societies.

Another readily cited example which impacts more on women is the shortage of public assistance with shopping and errands. Particularly in the current generation of older women, car ownership and holding of a driver's licence are less common among women than men. Old women are also more likely to have mobility problems in terms of their functional health than are old men (Gibson 1983). Transport is thus another area which emerges as a particular problem for older women, and similarly as an area which has received much less attention in the development of community-based services for the aged. The relative under-development in many countries of institutional, community and home-based respite care services is yet another area which impacts disproportionately on women as the major carers of the disabled aged.

---

[20] Coleman and Watson (1987) describe an elderly woman who had no lighting in three rooms of her home because she couldn't change a light bulb.

Only in recent years have publicly funded respite services received serious attention and expansion in Australia (Gibson *et al.* 1996).

Recreational and leisure activities geared to the needs of older women have traditionally not been a priority for public provision. Women of these generations were discouraged from active lifelong involvement in sports and physical recreation; in old age these effects are particularly pernicious when many women are afflicted by disabling diseases for which certain forms of exercise are therapeutic – including arthritis, rheumatism and osteoporosis, but also more generally levels of cardio-vascular fitness. Age, sex and social stereotypes conspire to make municipal pools, aerobics classes, gymnasiums, tennis courts and bicycle tracks less than 'user friendly' to women in their fifties and sixties, let alone their seventies and eighties. Such difficulties are, of course, likely to be compounded by the effects of class and ethnicity among some subgroups of older women.

While old men may be similarly disadvantaged in some arenas, their lifelong patterns of participation and different social norms make them much more likely to be found on the golf links, at the bowling club, the tennis court or the swimming pool. As a consequence of the lack of specific facilities for aged women, and the cumulative lifelong impact of cultural norms concerning female participation in sport, old women more than old men are likely to experience their bodies as increasingly sedentary, unreliable, weak and fragile as they age. The consequent reduction in physical capacity, and associated withdrawal from activities outside their homes, has clear consequences for quality of life and the maintenance of social networks so important to the lifestyles and happiness of many older women.[21] The recent development of 'healthy ageing' programs is a welcome step in this direction; to maximise effectiveness, however, they must take into account the particular disadvantages accruing to this generation of older women.

The problems and difficulties described in this section are not unique to old women, but they encounter them disproportionately often and frequently with greater severity. It is clear that older women have in this sense sex-specific needs which have been inadequately addressed in the past, and remain less than adequately addressed by current systems of public provision. It is equally clear that many of these needs are consistent with unmet needs of women at other stages of the life cycle, and that the origin of those needs is a normative policy construction of women as dependent on and subservient to men. Such a policy construction is consistent with wider cultural meanings given

---

[21] For a description of the importance of social networks for expressive support in old age, and particularly for women, see Gibson and Mugford (1986).

to men, women and sexual relations as institutionalised within family life. And that construction has consistent adverse effects for the ways in which women experience old age in our society. In a context where appropriately tailored social provisions are lacking, the impact of much cumulative disadvantage over the life course is thus all too likely to coincide with the increasing levels of frailty and disability associated with in advanced old age.

CHAPTER 5

Regulating Quality of Care

Introduction

As has been outlined in preceding chapters, recent years saw quite substantial policy developments in the Australian aged care system. Under the broader rubric of a national social justice strategy, there was a systematic attempt to provide a more equitable, accessible and resource efficient system of service delivery for the frail and disabled aged. Some changes, such as those to the formulae determining nursing home funding, met with both debate and resistance. Others, such as those expanding the range and level of home-based care services, encountered widespread, although not entirely unequivocal, support. The subject matter of this chapter, the program implemented to regulate quality of care in Australian nursing homes (and later extended to hostels), belongs to a third group – those changes which went largely unremarked except by the members of the industry itself.

The regulatory system implemented in 1987 was designed from the outset to be heavily outcome oriented and resident focused. Prior to that time, arrangements for monitoring quality of care had involved both state and federal governments in a variety of roles, but all of them primarily concerned with assessing inputs to service provision. In the words of John Gillroy, the Executive Director of the then Australian Nursing Homes Association, while giving evidence to a Senate Select Committee on Private Hospitals and Nursing Homes, when inspectors visited nursing homes:

> They are not interested in patient care matters – they want to see whether there are cobwebs in the laundry (Giles Report 1985: 120).

The 1970s and 1980s were characterised by a growing concern at both the public and political levels as to the quality of care being provided in Australian nursing homes. The media drew attention to a series of scandals over this period, and consumer groups were vocal in various phone-ins and published reports. While there was evidence of concern about quality assurance practices in parliamentary reports as early as 1981 (Report of the Auditor-General 1981), the influential McLeay Report, released in 1982, did not recommend strengthening quality assurance practices in nursing homes and hostels. Indeed, the McLeay Report appeared to support the nursing home industry position which favoured self-regulation (1982: 76).

Four large consultancies concerning quality of care, staffing and the costs of care in nursing homes and hostels were commissioned by the federal government in 1985, evidence of continuing concern over quality assurance and cost containment issues. The mid-1980s also saw the release of two government reports which were to provide the political will, and the political muscle, to initiate significant changes to the existing system.

The Senate Select Committee on Private Hospitals and Nursing Homes (1985) gave strong bi-partisan parliamentary support to public anxieties about the quality of nursing home care. It took the unprecedented step of dramatising its concerns by including horrific photographs of pressure sores on the bodies of nursing home residents in the report tabled in federal Parliament. Chaired by Senator Patricia Giles, the committee recommended the development of new federal standards for nursing homes, to be implemented and monitored by a federally funded inspectorate.

In 1986 the Nursing Home and Hostels Review undertaken by the then Department of Community Services provided further support, recommending that a new system of federally based standards should be introduced. The new standards were to be focused on outcomes as they affected residents, rather than on inputs. Following extensive consultations with industry, consumer, professional and union groups, 31 outcome standards for Australian nursing homes were agreed and introduced in 1987. The standards constituted a key shift in regulatory focus, and one which was to put Australia at the international forefront of emerging developments in nursing home regulation by the early 1990s (Braithwaite *et al*. 1993).

An innovative regulatory system

The 31 standards which emerged from this process were grouped under seven broad objectives.[1] Yet they did not conform to the

---

[1] The standards were published in a report of the Commonwealth–State Working Party (1987) entitled *Living in a Nursing Home*.

traditional view of what nursing home standards, particularly regulatory standards, should look like. Even a brief perusal of the standards
(see Figure 5.1) reveals that they are concerned not only with quality of
care in the traditional sense, but with quality of life. It is also clear that
the standards are not linked to specific, easily measurable, objective
indicators of program performance. Statements such as 'Residents'
health will be maintained at the optimum level possible' do not automatically inspire confidence among evaluation researchers concerned
with identifying outcomes which can be readily translated into measurable indicators. These are not standards that at first glance appear to
conform to traditional views of outcome indicators as specific, objective
measures against which program performance can be assessed.

The content of the 31 standards is not, however, an adequate representation of the standards monitoring program. Arguably, the procedures involved in monitoring nursing home performance in terms
of the outcomes standards are as important a part of the outcome
orientation of the process as the content of the standards themselves.
To appreciate the outcome orientation of the Australian approach,
one must be familiar with the actual processes by which standards are
monitored in the field.

The monitoring process

The procedure commences with 24 hours' notice to the nursing home
of the impending visit. The initial visit is generally conducted by at least
two standards monitors over one or two days. The standards monitors
observe the facility, its staff and residents, and conduct interviews with
(capable) residents and a number of key staff. The visit also includes
more casual encounters with a range of other residents, visitors and
staff, and reviews of some patient care documentation. The process is
resident centred and outcome oriented in that the central issue is a
concern with the (observed or potential) outcomes for residents, and
information supplied by the residents and their relatives is an important component.

Thus, for example, appraisal of the extent to which the nursing
home meets the dignity and privacy standards is assessed according to
whether or not residents are observed to be treated with respect for
their privacy and dignity, and to the comments which they or their relatives make in this regard. The teams have certain factors which they
look for with regard to particular standards (e.g. showering male and
female patients in full view of each other) but these do not form part of
a detailed check list or inventory which is systematically worked
through for each home. The process emphasises flexibility, and is

Figure 5.1 Objectives and outcome standards for Australian nursing homes

Objective 1 Health care: Residents' health will be maintained at the optimum level possible.
  1.1 Residents are enabled to receive appropriate medical care by a medical practitioner of their choice when needed.
  1.2 Residents are enabled and encouraged to make informed choices about their individual care plans.
  1.3 All residents are as free from pain as possible.
  1.4 All residents are adequately nourished and adequately hydrated.
  1.5 Residents are enabled to maintain continence.
  1.6 Residents are enabled to maintain, and if possible improve, their mobility and dexterity.
  1.7 Residents have clean healthy skin consistent with their age and general health.
  1.8 Residents are enabled to maintain oral and dental health.
  1.9 Sensory losses are identified and corrected so that residents are able to communicate effectively.

Objective 2 Social independence: Residents will be enabled to achieve a maximum degree of independence as members of society.
  2.1 Residents are enabled and encouraged to have visitors of their choice and to maintain personal contacts.
  2.2 Residents are enabled and encouraged to maintain control of their financial affairs.
  2.3 Residents have maximum freedom of movement within and from the nursing home, restricted only for safety reasons.
  2.4 Provision is made for residents with different religious, personal and cultural customs.
  2.5 Residents are enabled and encouraged to maintain their responsibilities and obligations as citizens.

Objective 3 Freedom of choice: Each resident's right to exercise freedom of choice will be recognised and respected whenever this does not infringe on the rights of other people.
  3.1 The nursing home has policies which have been developed in consultation with residents and which:
      – enable residents to make decisions and exercise choices regarding their daily activities
      – provide an appropriate balance between residents' rights and effective management of the nursing home
      – are interpreted flexibly, taking into account individual resident needs.
  3.2 Residents and their representatives are enabled to comment or complain about conditions in the nursing home.

Objective 4 Home-like environment: The design, furnishings and routines of the nursing home will resemble the individual's home as far as reasonably possible.
  4.1 Management of the nursing home is attempting to create and maintain a home-like environment.
  4.2 The nursing home has policies which enable residents to feel secure in their accommodation.

Objective 5 Privacy and dignity: The dignity and privacy of nursing home residents will be respected.
  5.1 The dignity of residents is respected by nursing home staff.
  5.2 Private property is not taken, lent or given to other people without the owner's permission.
  5.3 Residents are enabled to undertake personal activities, including bathing, toileting and dressing in private.

5.4 The nursing home is free from undue noise.

5.5 Information about residents is treated confidentially.

5.6 Nursing home practices support the resident's right to die with dignity.

Objective 6 Variety of experience: Residents will be encouraged and enabled to participate in a wide variety of experiences appropriate to their needs and interests.

6.1 Residents are enabled to participate in a wide range of activities appropriate to their interests and capacities.

Objective 7 Safety: The nursing home environment and practices will ensure the safety of residents, visitors and staff.

7.1 The resident's right to participate in activities which may involve a degree of risk is respected.

7.2 Nursing home design, equipment and practices contribute to a safe environment for residents, staff and visitors.

7.3 Residents, visitors and staff are protected from infection and infestation.

7.4 Residents and staff are protected from the hazards of fire and natural disasters.

7.5 The security of buildings, contents and people within the nursing home is safeguarded.

7.6 Physical and other forms of restraint are used correctly and appropriately.

oriented towards specifying the desired effect of the caring process on the resident (i.e. privacy and dignity be maintained), rather than toward specifying the processes by which that end is to be obtained (separate showers for male and female residents).

Within 48 hours of the initial visit the team generally returns for a compliance discussion at which the director of nursing is given the interim findings on all 31 standards. The nursing home can dispute findings at this stage, and teams may change their ratings as a result. The action plans which the nursing home might implement to come into compliance with the standards are discussed. The nursing home should receive its report within 10 days of the initial visit, and is then given up to four weeks from receipt to submit their action plans. Where homes are found to be seriously in breach of the standards sanctions include the withdrawal of Commonwealth funding for any new residents and the withdrawal of all Commonwealth funding from the nursing home.

The Australian shift towards an outcome orientation is consistent with movements in the American regulatory philosophy of the last decade. But the American approach has been one of maintaining a balanced regulatory model which emphasises inputs – both structure and process – as well as outcomes.[2] The American system mandates the

---

[2] In a review of the British system of nursing home regulation, Day *et al.* (1996), while arguing for an increase in attention to outcomes, express a similar view in favour of input and process standards as well as outcomes.

inputs required to achieve specified outcomes. And the requirements at both the input and outcome levels are often very specific, as, for example, in the case of pre-specified acceptable error rates in medication rounds.

The Australian federal system is explicitly outcome oriented, and is based on the assumption that attempts to mandate particular inputs seriously compromise the nature of an outcome-based regulatory system. Under this model, outcomes for residents are what count, structures and processes are important only in that they deliver desired outcomes, and these outcomes are themselves defined largely in subjective terms – the perceptions of the residents themselves, relatives and team members. This is the theory of the Australian regulatory system. How does it perform in practice?

In the remainder of this section, a range of analyses and publications undertaken under the auspices of the Nursing Home Regulation in Action Project relevant to the implementation process in nursing homes are reviewed. In subsequent sections, recent developments in the standards monitoring procedures in both nursing homes and hostels are analysed, and changes in the quality of care provided in nursing homes and hostels since the implementation of the new system considered.

The Nursing Home Regulation in Action Project

The present chapter, in reviewing and evaluating the implementation of this new approach to the regulation of residential care, draws heavily on some of the findings from a large-scale evaluation of the outcome standards monitoring program in nursing homes conducted from 1987 to 1992. The Nursing Home Regulation in Action Project was a large-scale, cross-national study of the implementation and subsequent development of the standards monitoring program in Australian nursing homes.[3]

The project was conceived from the outset as a formative evaluation – one which fed back to the key players in the program the results and

---

[3] For further reading see Braithwaite *et al.* (1990; 1991; 1993) and Braithwaite and Braithwaite (1995). The Nursing Home Regulation in Action Project was based at the Australian National University, with the core research team comprising John Braithwaite, Valerie Braithwaite, Toni Makkai and myself (although I was then based at the University of Queensland). It was one of the most detailed appraisals of a regulatory program ever undertaken, attracted funding not only from the Department of Community Services in Australia, but also from the American Bar Foundation, the Australian National University and the University of Queensland. The primary data collection period was from 1987 to 1992.

findings of the evaluation as they emerged, rather than waiting to the end of the five-year period to reveal what had been wrong with the program all along. One consequence of such an evaluative style (at least if implemented successfully) is a program which evolves and improves in response to the ongoing evaluation findings. A formative evaluation can only be successful with the co-operation of the key stakeholders in the program – in this instance most particularly the industry and the responsible federal department. The support of these stakeholders was essential to that process, and the results of the evaluation suggest that the standards monitoring program, and more broadly the Australian nursing home industry, has benefited from their own willingness to engage actively in the evaluation process.

That commitment to a formative evaluation model is, in my view, perhaps the most important factor in defining the methodological approach taken in this research project. Yet other, more conventionally described aspects of project methodology are also worthy of note.

The study combined both quantitative and qualitative research techniques. In the quantitative component, directors of nursing in 410 nursing homes in four states were interviewed. At the same time, semi-structured interviews were conducted with the proprietors and interested staff in each of these homes. The interviews occurred after the first standards monitoring visit, and contained material on the nursing home, the director of nursing, her experience of and reactions to the standards monitoring visit, her appraisal of the standards on several dimensions, together with information on her attitudes and reported behaviour on a range of issues relating to nursing home care. For 406 of those homes the standards monitoring team also completed a questionnaire on the standards monitoring process in that home. For each home final compliance scores on the standards were recorded.

The study design was longitudinal. By the time the quantitative fieldwork was concluded, 224 of the 410 directors of nursing in the first wave had experienced their second standards monitoring visit. A mailed questionnaire was completed by 165 of those directors of nursing, and again compliance scores were obtained for those homes where the standards monitoring procedure had been completed.

The nursing homes included in the study were initially selected via a random sampling method. Owing to delays in the completion rate achieved by the standards monitors, it was necessary to augment the sample size with a supplementary sample. A range of checks showed the homes to be representative of Australian nursing homes, and that the supplementary sample did not differ from the original random selected sample.

The quantitative component of the study also included a demographic analysis of the characteristics of residents in the nursing homes using the federal government database, a questionnaire sent to each person who had worked as a standards monitor, and a reliability study of 50 standards monitoring visits where an independent monitor employed by the research group rated each of the homes while it was undergoing its standards monitoring visit.

The qualitative component of the study included comparative fieldwork in the United States and England, involving the observation of 44 inspection visits in 22 American states, and visits to 50 British nursing homes with inspectors, 30 of them for the purpose of conducting inspections. The American fieldwork also involved interviews with most of the key regulatory players nationally and in the 24 states visited, totalling more than 300 people. In Britain, interviews were conducted with nursing home inspections staff, nursing home staff, and residents in 13 local authorities, as well as key people in the national government, industry associations and advocacy groups.

The Australian qualitative fieldwork included 58 observations of standards monitors at work in Australian nursing homes. Research staff also attended industry association executive meetings, industry liaison committee meetings, various conferences and workshops, training courses for standards monitors, standards review days, and a range of other events. Key players were interviewed over the six years of fieldwork, some more than 10 times. These included office holders in industry associations in all states, union officials, leading activists in advocacy groups, and key bureaucrats in federal and state government departments.

The final report, 'Raising the Standard', was completed in draft form in mid-1992, sent out for comment to all key players, modified and finalised late in 1992. It was not publicly released until August 1993, but at that time was launched and applauded by the responsible Minister (and then Deputy Prime Minister), Mr Brian Howe. The report was generally positive in its concluding evaluation of the standards monitoring process in Australia, although not uncritically so. The opening paragraph notes:

> [T]he Australian standards monitoring program has some deficiencies in comparison to the regulatory systems that have been observed in the United States, England, Japan and Canada, but in its fundamentals it is a better designed process than that operating in any of these countries. In the opinion of the consultants, over the long haul it is the Australian regulatory process that stands a better chance ... of securing substantial improvements in the quality of nursing home life and better value for the taxpayer's dollar (Braithwaite *et al.* 1993: xi).

Evaluating the standards

The success of the Australian outcome standards monitoring program could be appraised on a number of dimensions. The focus of discussion adopted here is with the performance of the standards as reliable outcome measures for determining quality of care in Australian nursing homes. Three discrete questions are considered:

- Are the standards really concerned with outcomes, rather than with processes or structures, and are they assessable as such?
- Is the subjectivity of the standards a cause for concern, particularly in terms of the validity of the process?
- Does the subjective and non-specific nature of the outcome standards compromise reliability?

Are the Australian standards really outcome standards?

The concern about whether or not particular measures constitute outcome or process indicators is not uncommon in the evaluation literature. The relative advantages of process and outcome measures, a debate which dominated much of the evaluation literature in the mid to late 1970s, are rarely now at issue; we have recognised, albeit not before time, that both are useful and relevant. Yet the distinction itself, so useful when initially conceptualised by Donabedian (1966), frequently impedes rather than facilitates the formulation of much evaluation research. One problem continually resurfaces: there is a failure to recognise that the distinction between process and outcome is relational rather than absolute – a point to which I shall return in more detail in Chapter 8. A corollary of this failure, more central to present purposes, is the not infrequent tendency to uncritically equate process evaluation with subjective appraisals, and outcome evaluation with 'hard' objective measures.

A large part of the confusion concerning what constitutes 'real' outcome measures emerged from the extremely varied nature of the fields in which evaluators work. For evaluators with clearly agreed outcome measures to hand – education test scores, recidivism rates, neo-natal death rates, post-operative infection rates – the question of the distinction between process and outcome was a non-issue. For those evaluators working with programs aimed at 'improving community health' or 'reducing the effects of domestic violence' the issues were not simply salient, they were omnipresent. In the case of domestic violence, for example, was program outcome to be measured in terms of the number of women who consult the service, the number of women removed from untenable domestic situations, a reduction in the reported admission rates to local hospitals, or a reduction in the level of domestic violence being perpetrated in the community? The point being made here can be put quite succinctly – depending on one's perspective, a particular measure can be either a process or an outcome measure – one man's process is another woman's outcome.

The implications for the aforementioned tendency to equate outcome with objective measures, and process with subjective ones are obvious. If the distinction between outcome and process is agreed to be relational rather than absolute, then the formulation of outcome measures as somehow more inherently objective is in error on logical grounds alone. Moreover, it can be readily demonstrated that outcome measures can be either subjective (client satisfaction) or objective (postoperative infection rates), and process measures similarly (clients were treated with dignity or the number of clients seen).

If these components of the process/outcome distinction are recognised, the terms, and Donabedian's conceptualisation (1966), remain extremely useful to the evaluator. It is the confusion which has developed around the distinction which is the problem, rather than the distinction itself. To what extent, then, can the Australian standards be said to function as outcome standards?

I have already commented that outcomes are often conceived as more objective, defined indicators of program performance. This is certainly the case in the American literature on health outcomes. From this perspective, many of the Australian standards would not be classified as outcome standards at all. Take as an example standard 4.1 (*Management of the nursing home is attempting to create and maintain a home-like environment*). In American gerontologists' terms, and indeed in classic evaluation terms such as that proposed by Donabedian, this would constitute a structural standard. But qualitative fieldwork suggests that whether or not a standard is outcome oriented is much less to do with the wording of the standard than with the process and definition by which it is determined whether or not the standard is met. And the procedures by which the Australian standards are monitored do indeed focus, in most instances, on the outcomes for residents, rather than on program inputs or program processes.

The relevant outcome, and the concern which must be and is probed in the Australian context, is whether residents perceive themselves to live in a home-like or an institutional atmosphere. What team members primarily do on the standard described above is to observe and question residents about their perceptions of their private space and the communal areas. They are not concerned with counting how many pictures hang on the walls, but rather with whether residents have pictures on their walls if they want them there, and equally, whether they do not have pictures on their walls if that is the kind of environment they want. The likelihood of empty conformity (such as the Chicago nursing home which featured as part of its decor pages ripped out of magazines fixed to the wall with Blu-Tack) with input require-ments is avoided. The ultimate reference remains, as it should be, the satisfaction and perceptions of the residents.

Of course, an inappropriate process can see the standards defined in input terms. For example, several directors of nursing and proprietors in South Australia complained about teams asking for changes in the arrangement of chairs in lounge rooms, from around the periphery of the room to clustered 'conversational' groupings. Residents who did not like the change then asked for the chairs to be changed back; the conversational groupings were not the ones they defined as comfort-able and home-like within their present environment. (Interestingly, but tangentially, an American study suggests that residents frequently do prefer the arrangement of chairs around the perimeter (Duffy *et al.* 1986).)

The issue here is not which is the 'best arrangement', but rather that the focus should have been with what the residents preferred. It is thus the process by which teams find the standards to be met or not met, rather than the content of the standards, which defines the outcome orientation.

The standards, when appraised in this way, did indeed function as outcome standards, focused on the perceptions and experiences of the residents. There was, however, a caveat to these generally positive find-ings. The fieldwork undertaken for the Nursing Home Regulation in Action Project suggested that three of the 31 standards were not as well served by a process which relies on observed outcomes for residents (Braithwaite *et al.* 1993: 13–18).

All three of these standards were ones where inputs could be clearly related to outcomes, and where the outcomes in question were both low incidence and high risk. This is well exemplified by standard 7.4 (*Residents and staff are protected from the hazards of fire and natural disasters*). There is little dispute that buildings with high fire safety standards are less likely to inflict loss of life in case of fires. Moreover, getting burnt to death in a fire is clearly a very undesirable outcome. This is not an area where one would wish to discard the evidence on poor inputs, while waiting to see evidence of impacts on residents.

The two other standards met those same criteria. These were stan-dards 7.2 (*Nursing home design, equipment and practices contribute to a safe environment for residents, staff and visitors*) and 7.3 (*Residents, visitors and staff are protected from infection and infestation*). The results of the evaluation suggested that these standards were indeed most properly investigated in relation to inputs and processes, as well as in relation to outcomes.

The remaining 28 standards were appropriately and successfully assessed in terms of their outcomes for residents. Even if the definition of these standards as outcome oriented is accepted, however, their broadly defined nature inevitably raises questions about their objectivity, particularly for those more familiar with the narrowly defined objective indicators employed in the American regulatory process.

Are the standards too subjective?

The Australian system is essentially concerned with establishing through dialogue the kinds of outcomes which are subjectively important to residents. Whether a standard is found to be met or not met rests not with a range of pre-specified 'objectively' determined criteria, but with the team members' judgment concerning the outcome for residents of quite broadly defined standards such as 5.1 (*The dignity of residents is respected by nursing home staff*). Yet these kinds of criteria are typically those that have been seen as difficult to operationalise in terms of specific outcome indicators in the relevant literature. How do such criteria work in the field?

Reliability, the extent to which such ratings can be replicated, is obviously a critical issue, and is dealt with separately below. But what of other correlates and concerns over this level of subjectivity? Three emerge as of particular relevance.

First, some critics have argued that the resident-centred nature of the process presupposes a certain level of capacity (physical and mental) among nursing home residents. In particular, it is argued that an approach which depends on residents to define outcomes cannot work effectively in homes with high levels of very sick or disabled residents. Analyses undertaken as part of the Nursing Home Regulation in Action Project show that this is not, in fact, the case. The reliability of ratings remains high in such homes. Moreover, while it may be more difficult and time consuming in such contexts to ascertain resident preferences, experienced standards monitors were observed doing so effectively even in homes with very disabled residents (Braithwaite *et al.* 1993: Appendix B).

Second, there is the likelihood that different residents in different homes will have different perceptions of what constitutes the best outcomes for them. In fact, this individuality lies at the centre of a subjective appraisal, and should more accurately be regarded as an advantage rather than as a disadvantage of the approach. Such variations reflect the reality of individual experience in nursing homes – we do not remove any of this variation by mandating an objectively determined indicator which, by definition, many of the residents if consulted would not agree with. The resident focused, subjectively determined nature of the Australian process gives standards monitors, residents and nursing home staff the opportunity to work out the optimal outcomes for the residents in that home at that time, which may well vary from resident to resident and from home to home. Subjectivity in this sense is a strength rather than a weakness of the process.

Third, there is the more general issue of the adequacy of resident perceptions as a basis for appraising outcomes. There may indeed be circumstances whereby a radical resident-centred approach requires some qualification. The most obvious example is the case which was often cited by the nursing home industry – the problem of complaints raised by demented residents which may bear little resemblance to actual events. The point is a valid one; but the experienced standards monitor will gather relevant information from a range of sources, and not be reliant on a single source. Moreover, the very examples of such problems cited by the industry tend to be those which emerge at compliance discussions: the meeting with relevant nursing home staff which follows one or two days after the inspection visit, and at which the findings and observations of the standards monitoring team members are discussed with nursing home staff. It is at this point that misunderstandings of this kind can be clarified by staff, and that clarification is a further contribution to the validity of the standards monitors' findings.

The more serious problem concerning the adequacy of using resident perceptions as the basis for appraising outcomes is less often mentioned. This is the problem of institutionalisation, whereby resident expectations have been so adversely affected, and their experiences so dehumanising, that they do not share the views of members of their community of orientation as to what constitutes appropriate care or treatment.

In one observed instance, female and male residents were showered together in full view of each other. The problem for the standards monitoring team was that residents had come to accept this and did not complain of it, although this would not be regarded by most people as consistent with the privacy and dignity standards. Arguably, this would not have been the view of the residents prior to their perceptions being shaped by a very inflexible regime. There may indeed be a case for arguing here that the privacy and dignity standard is not met because it breaches certain basic rights and practices in the community from which these residents came. In the strict interpretation of a resident-centred approach, however, it may be possible to argue that the standard is not breached. (It is of interest in passing that other standards, such as providing residents with freedom of choice, would clearly have been breached by this practice.)

Fourth, it is useful to take into account the views of the directors of nursing, the persons charged with responsibility for implementing the standards in their homes, and whose quality of care is appraised against the standards. If the standards are indeed too subjective to be an appropriate basis against which to measure performance, we might expect the directors of nursing charged with implementing the standards to object to them, if not in terms of their desirability, certainly in terms of their practicality and clarity.

In the quantitative data gathered during interviews with 410 directors of nursing, the vast majority responded favourably not only to the desirability but also to the clarity and practicality of the standards. At least 95 per cent of the directors of nursing thought each of the individual standards was desirable. At the time of their first standards monitoring visit, more than 96 per cent of directors of nursing reported that the standards were clear for 27 of the 31 standards. The perceived clarity had increased even further by the end of the second wave of standards monitoring visits. Two-thirds of the directors of nursing indicated that their understanding of the program had improved further since their first visit. At least three-quarters of directors of nursing had no doubts about the practicality of the standards, and for most of the standards, more than 90 per cent of directors of nursing regarded them as practical (Braithwaite *et al.* 1993: 36–38).

The heading in this section of the present chapter asked the question 'Are the standards too subjective?'. The results of the evaluation yield a reasonably clear negative response. Yet it must be recognised before concluding that had the question been whether or not the standards are subjective, the answer would equally clearly have been in the affirmative. The argument being put is that the standards are indeed subjective, that in their present form they functioned well as indicators of outcomes for residents, and that their subjectivity impeded neither their practicality, their reliability nor their validity.

Is reliability compromised by this approach?

If outcome standards are appraised in this way there remains a concern that emphasising outcomes which are subjectively important to residents will lead inevitably to a lack of reliability. There is a common perception, sometimes explicit, sometimes implicit, that 'harder' objective measures are a more replicable and hence reliable basis for program evaluation than 'softer' subjective ones. If indeed the standards cannot be reliably implemented, then they do not meet the most basic criteria for assessing quality of care. Concerns about reliability stem partly from this emphasis on residents' subjective appraisals, but also partly from the broadly defined nature of the standards themselves.

The research design for the Nursing Home Regulation in Action Project specifically addressed the issue of reliability. In 50 Victorian and New South Wales nursing homes, two independent sets of ratings on the 31 outcome standards were completed. The findings from these studies have been subjected to detailed quantitative analysis which is reported elsewhere (Braithwaite *et al.* 1991; Braithwaite and Braithwaite 1995). In broad terms, however, a high level of agreement was recorded for all standards, with 21 of the standards being agreed in at least 90 per cent of cases. The lowest agreement rating was 78 per cent (standard 1.5). Agreement in this study required exactly the same rating to be made on the three-point scale. The evidence accumulated in those analyses lent no support to the argument that the subjective elements of the process compromised either the reliability or the validity of the outcome standards.

Issues of ongoing concern

This system of nursing home regulation is based on a set of outcome standards which are broadly specified and defined in terms of the subjectively perceived impact on nursing home residents. The program has been successfully implemented, with support from both regulators and the industry, and impressive results in terms of reliability and validity. The outcome orientation of the standards is found to rest on the process by which standards are appraised, rather than with the content of those standards. Moreover, the subjectivity and lack of specificity characteristic of the process have not adversely affected its implementation.

What emerges very clearly from this account, however, is a regulatory program which is highly process dependent. In other words, when the processes in which the teams engage are appropriate ones, where the focus is firmly on outcomes for residents, where the relationship between standards monitors and nursing home staff is one of mutual respect, and where compliance discussions and the subsequent development of action plans occur against a general backdrop of a concern to provide the best quality of care for residents, all will be well. The fieldwork undertaken for the Nursing Home Regulation in Action Project showed that these conditions were indeed generally met – hence the generally positive evaluation findings on the regulatory program.

There were, however, issues of ongoing concern at the time of completing the final project report in 1992. These included the issue of visits without notice, the timeliness of the inspection process, and the willingness and capacity to invoke sanctions in cases where homes were clearly providing inadequate care. Each of these three aspects is dealt with below. There is also the continuing possibility that notwithstanding the reported success of the regulatory program, there will be a move away from the process to one of self-regulation and accreditation. Proposals to make such a change appear and reappear intermittently, supported by various sectors of the nursing home industry. Now, with the election of a Liberal Party government in the 1996 election, the proposed changes also have the support of the federal Minister for Health and Human Services.

Visits without notice

In 1989, when the interim report of the Nursing Home Regulation in Action Project was completed (Braithwaite *et al.* 1990), nursing homes received a three-month advance warning of an impending visit, and a one-week notification of the actual date of the standards monitoring visit. At the same time the final report of the Ronalds consultancy on Residents' Rights in Nursing Homes and Hostels (1989) had recommended against advance notice for visits, and a number of directors of nursing and proprietors in the nursing home industry had expressed similar views.

The arguments in favour of visits without notice were clear. Advance notice gives nursing homes providing poor quality care time to 'tart up' their homes, to bring in additional staff, temporarily modify care practices (place buzzers in reach of residents, for example), improve the quality and quantity of food offered at meal times, and generally improve the look and cleanliness of the home. Directors of nursing and proprietors who feel that their homes could meet the standards on any day of the year may justifiably resent other homes which have been temporarily upgraded in order to obtain the same ratings – ratings which are, after all, publicly available.

In 1989, when the interim consultancy report recommended in favour of retaining visits with notice, there were seen to be advantages which offset the disadvantages described above. It was important, for example, in the early stages of the regulatory program to develop better relationships between the teams and industry, and to facilitate the educational and consultative components of the standards monitoring program. In some states there was a history of quite adversarial input-oriented inspections to put to rest – for example, the practice of unannounced 'night raids' at 3.00 or 4.00 a.m. to ascertain whether or not there was a sufficient supply of clean linen in the linen cupboards (this being the time when supplies could be expected to be most depleted).

By 1992 the final report of the project recommended that all advance notice of visits should cease. Abuses of the system of advanced warning increased over the years, and became sufficiently widespread to partially undermine the legitimacy of the standards monitoring process. Public and industry confidence are critical elements of a successful regulatory program, and these were being adversely affected.

The issue remains one of some contention, but in 1993 the period of advance notification was reduced from one week to 24 hours. In 1994 the three months' warning of 'intent to visit' was also dropped. The 24-hour notice remains in place, although not for homes declared as being of 'high risk'. While the factors determining exactly what constitutes a 'high risk' home have not been definitively identified, relevant issues include the frequency and nature of complaints about care made to complaints units or advocacy services, previous poor performance against the standards, and a change in either the proprietor or the senior staff of the home. For follow-up visits, which target homes that have not performed adequately against the standards, visits without notice have been standard practice for some time.

Timeliness

Timeliness is dependent on both the efficiency of the regulatory process and the resources available to the regulatory program. In the first five years of the program, productivity increased substantially. Early on, the rate of completion of inspections would have placed homes in some states on a three- to four-year inspection cycle, perhaps worse. At the end of that period the proposed two-year inspection cycle had either been achieved or close to achieved in all states.

In 1994 the Keys Committee (established by the federal government to appraise and implement the recommendations of three major consultancies into aspects of the nursing home industry in Australia) supported proposals that a two- to three-year inspection cycle was not adequate, and advocated a so-called 'risk management' strategy.[4] Under these arrangements, homes which had a record of good performance against the standards could expect a visit only once every three

---

[4] The Keys Committee, formally titled the Nursing Home Consultancy Committee, was convened by the Minister for Housing, Local Government and Community Services in 1994, with a brief to consider the recommendations of the consultancy on Resident Classification Instrument Documentation (Macri 1993), the Review of the Structure of Nursing Home Funding Arrangements (Gregory 1993; 1994) and the evaluation of nursing home regulation (Braithwaite *et al.* 1993). Members of the consultative committee included representatives of the not-for-profit and for-profit sectors of the nursing home industry, relevant unions, professional associations and consumer groups.

to four years, with available resources being concentrated on more frequent visits to homes with poorer records, or where various other
events or reports suggested a shorter inspection cycle was required.
The alternative strategy of allocating increased resources to the regulatory program, to retain at least a two-year cycle for all homes, was
rejected by the committee.

Sanctions

Any regulatory program relies on a set of sanctions which will be
brought into force if the relevant actors fail to come into compliance
with the relevant standards. The nursing home regulatory system is no
exception, and in fact the provisions conform very well to the regulatory pyramid proposed by Ayres and Braithwaite (1992: Chapter 2) as
the most efficient and effective form of regulatory control. The regulatory pyramid implies a system where most breaches of standards are
dealt with at the broad base of the triangle, through negotiation and
persuasion.

The outcomes standards monitoring program has performed well in
this regard, almost from the time of its inception. The problems which
did occur were to do with the minority of homes which could not be
dealt with in the context of a regulatory culture based largely on praise,
consultation and encouragement. The difficulties concerned the ease
and willingness with which regulators could move up the regulatory
pyramid, to escalate to more severe sanction stages when homes had
proved themselves unable or unwilling to meet the required standards
of care. It proved possible for homes to bluff, bluster and generally
bully their way through prolonged negotiations, which led to a perceived weakness of the regulatory system at these levels. This is not to
suggest that enforcement procedures did not occur, but rather that
there were undesirable delays and a number of failures to invoke
sanctions when they were well deserved.

Several attempts were made after 1993 to streamline the sanctions
procedures, with more rapid movement up the sanctions pyramid
being balanced by earlier access to the Standards Monitoring Review
Panel. The Panel reviews complaints and disclaimers brought by nursing home proprietors against the findings of the standards monitoring
process. It is, however, noteworthy that the very clear recommendations made by the national evaluation team in 1993 to render sanctions
automatic in certain circumstances (for example, those where homes
are rated as requiring 'urgent action' on a majority of the 31 standards)
have not been implemented, even in a modified form. The only

response to the recommendations in the Keys Committee report is to affirm in general terms that there is a need to ensure that sanctions are invoked where appropriate, and are seen to be so invoked. The federal government response, which generally conformed to a format providing an issue by issue response to each of the Keys Committee recommendations, contained no mention of this issue at all.

Nonetheless, some enforcement procedures have occurred. Between January 1990 and December 1994, 102 notices of intent to declare that homes failed to reach standards were issued. Once notices of intent are issued the homes have 30 days to respond; in 59 cases the declarations were made and in 31 of those cases financial sanctions were imposed. While exact numbers are not available over that period standards monitoring teams would have carried out in the vicinity of 2800 inspections.

As an interesting afterword the most recent media scandals concerning poor quality of care in Australian nursing homes (in Victoria in 1995 and Canberra in 1996) incorporate a heavy use of material derived from the standards monitoring reports on those homes. Indeed, in two cases, the trigger for the stories was the (now routine) public release of the standards monitoring reports. While problems may remain in imposing official sanctions, the requirement to publish standards monitoring reports appears to have ensured one further avenue of public accountability.

Implementing the outcome standards approach in hostels

While the outcome standards monitoring program in nursing homes underwent rigorous evaluation and progressive modification from its inception in 1987, plans were in place to extend the program to aged persons hostels. By 1991 the standards had been revised and modified for implementation in aged persons' hostels, emerging as 25 standards grouped under six broad objectives.

The standards as they were implemented for hostels were very similar to those already in place in nursing homes; this was most obvious at the level of the six broad objectives, where the similarities to the nursing homes standards are marked. The hostel standards, however, include significantly more detail, and are noticeably more wordy than those in place for nursing homes. In some cases, such as those standards pertaining to the resident/proprietor agreement, they appear to move away from the outcome-oriented resident focused approach of the nursing home standards on which they were based. The standards for hostels are listed in Figure 5.2.

Figure 5.2 Objectives and outcome standards for Australian hostels

Objective 1 Freedom of choice and exercising rights: Each resident is to have active control of his or her life.

   1.1 Before moving into the hostel, each resident must be given the opportunity to learn about the lifestyle of residents of the hostel.

   1.2 Before moving into the hostel, each resident, or a representative of the resident, must be given full opportunity to discuss with a responsible hostel staff member the resident's rights and responsibilities.

   1.3 Hostel management must ensure that:

     (a) each resident has, or is offered, a Formal Agreement with the operator of the hostel that: (i) treats the parties as equals; and (ii) sets out clearly the rights and obligations of each party; and (iii) includes equitable termination provisions; and

     (b) each resident, either directly or through a representative, is: (i) informed of, and assisted to understand, the resident's rights; and (ii) whenever necessary – able to talk to a responsible hostel staff member about any agreement between the resident and the hostel operator; and (iii) at liberty to seek the services of an interpreter, a translator or a legal practitioner for independent assistance.

   1.4 Hostel management and staff must be available for discussion about a resident's freedom of choice sufficiently to enable each resident, or representative of the resident:

     (a) to make informed decisions and choices about the resident's daily activities; and

     (b) to participate in decision-making processes that affect the resident's life-style.

   1.5 To ensure that the rights and responsibilities of each resident, as a member of Australian society and as a resident of the hostel, are observed:

     (a) a balance must be obtained between the rights and responsibilities of each resident individually and the rights and responsibilities of residents as a group;

     (b) to the extent practicable, each resident must be assisted to exercise his or her rights and to fulfil his or her responsibilities;

     (c) each resident, either directly or through a representative, must be able to draw attention to, or comment on, unsatisfactory conditions in the hostel;

     (d) prompt action must be taken to identify the cause of any dissatisfaction and, if possible, to resolve the problem.

   1.6 Each incoming resident, either directly or through a representative, must be assisted to understand the fees and other charges of the hostel and be given a written explanation of the services that are provided for those fees and charges.

   1.7 Each resident must be given:

     (a) at least once a year, a written schedule and explanation of the costs and fees and other charges of the hostel; and

     (b) a reasonable period of time before the change is to occur – a written schedule and explanations of any changes in the fees and other charges.

Objective 2 Care needs: The care needs of each resident to be identified and met.

   2.1 The care needs of each incoming resident must be identified.

   2.2 Each incoming resident must be given support in adjusting to hostel living.

   2.3 The care needs of each resident must be continually monitored, general care services being provided as necessary and each resident having access to professional health care as necessary.

Figure 5.2 (cont'd)

2.4 The manner in which the resident's care and personal needs are fulfilled must comply with the following principles:
  (a) the independence and dignity of the resident are to be upheld;
  (b) awareness of, and behaviour compatible with, the cultural and linguistic background of the resident are to be demonstrated;
  (c) the needs of the resident and the manner in which they are met are to be identified by communication and negotiation with the resident, either directly or through a representative;
  (d) regular review of services provided to the resident is to be undertaken with the resident, either directly or through a representative;
  (e) the resident is to be encouraged and assisted to make informed choices about the options available to him or her for his or her care in the hostel.
2.5 That the individual care needs of people with dementia, recurrent confusion and cognitive impairment are identified, and that these residents participate in a program that enhances their quality of life and care.

Objective 3 Dignity and privacy: The dignity and privacy of each resident is to be respected.
3.1 Each resident must be treated with respect for his or her dignity.
3.2 Each resident must have personal space in which to display and securely store personal effects.
3.3 Personal effects of a resident must not be used by other persons without the consent of the resident.
3.4 Each resident must be free to carry out activities of a personal nature in private or, if necessary, with the discreet assistance of hostel staff.
3.5 Information about residents must be treated in confidence.

Objective 4 Social independence: Each resident should exercise maximum social independence.
4.1 Each resident must be able to receive guests of his or her choice in private and in other suitable areas of the hostel.
4.2 To provide continuity with each resident's lifestyle before becoming a resident, he or she must be allowed opportunity:
  (a) to engage, to the extent practicable, in spiritual, cultural and leisure activities that are significant to him or her; and
  (b) to participate in local community life; and
  (c) to keep informed of current events and to vote in community elections.
4.3 Each resident must be assisted to the degree required to remain independent in the conduct of his or her financial dealings.
4.4 An appropriate balance must be maintained between the independence and the safety of each resident.

Objective 5 Variety of experience: Residents must have the opportunity to participate in a variety of activities and experiences of interest to them.
5.1 Each resident must have the opportunity to give expression to, and to engage in activities relevant to, his or her various interests and cultural or linguistic background.
5.2 Each resident's right to participate in activities that may involve some personal risk must be respected.

Objective 6 Home-like environment: A hostel is to provide a home-like environment for the comfort, safety and well-being of residents.
6.1 Each resident must be provided with a comfortable and home-like environment.
6.2 The hostel must afford each resident a clean and safe environment.

Impact on quality of care: Nursing homes and hostels

The outcome standards monitoring program for hostels and nursing homes is regulatory in function – that is, it is concerned with maintaining and improving the quality of care being delivered via a process of site visits in combination with education and consultative strategies. The data generated by this regulatory process can, however, also be used to explore the extent to which homes and hostels have improved (or failed to improve) their performance in terms of the national standards.

There are caveats to be considered in interpreting data derived from a regulatory process in this way. The standards monitoring process in nursing homes was progressively modified during its implementation, with consequent potential for differences in the ways in which homes were scored over time. Over the first few years of the program there was also qualitative evidence to suggest that the standards monitors became more stringent in their ratings, as industry understanding of what was required improved. At the same time, national training programs were undertaken to increase comparability in ratings against the standards across state and regional boundaries. Against these problems, however, can be placed the research evidence reported earlier concerning the high levels of validity and reliability associated with the nursing home standards.

For hostels the caveats have less force. The hostel standards monitoring program benefited from the already completed learning curve of those involved in implementing the process in nursing homes. On the other hand, the more recent implementation date means that the data available cover a shorter time period, dating only from 1991–92.

Nursing homes

On the basis of these data, the overall standards of quality of care in Australian nursing homes have improved since the implementation of the national outcome standards. In 1989–90, the average total compliance score at the team's initial visit was 52.5, out of a possible total of 62. For the next three years the national average stabilised at 51. In 1993, the average score had increased to 53, and in 1994 it increased again to 55 (AIHW 1995: 228). Ratings against each of the 31 standards are given in Table 5.1.

In terms of performance against the individual standards, while there was general improvement on all standards over the period, for some the change was quite marked. There were a number of standards for which the proportion of homes receiving a met rating increased by 20 per cent or more. These included three standards (1.1, 1.5, 1.6)

Table 5.1 Percentage of nursing homes meeting the
outcome standards, Australia 1989–90 to 1993–94

Standard	1989–90	1993–94
1.1	55.1	81.2
1.2	69.6	81.0
1.3	88.9	93.8
1.4	67.1	86.7
1.5	50.9	76.7
1.6	66.7	91.2
1.7	88.9	94.0
1.8	76.1	95.9
1.9	78.0	94.8
2.1	73.8	95.5
2.2	75.5	86.6
2.3	86.6	93.3
2.4	86.0	96.7
2.5	93.1	99.3
3.1	73.4	79.5
3.2	70.2	89.3
4.1	54.5	79.8
4.2	58.7	82.9
5.1	62.9	70.9
5.2	70.0	88.4
5.3	49.7	70.2
5.4	80.9	92.6
5.5	77.4	91.0
5.6	84.3	93.3
6.1	57.9	82.6
7.1	80.5	91.6
7.2	39.0	48.6
7.3	56.8	70.2
7.4	44.9	70.9
7.5	79.7	89.3
7.6	60.8	75.7
No. of visits	477	580

Source: HSH 1995 unpublished data (AIHW 1995).

pertaining to objective 1, all of which are concerned with maintaining
the residents' health at an optimum level. One standard pertaining to
social independence (2.1) and one pertaining to social participation
(6.1) also showed substantial improvement in nursing home ratings, as
did both standards relating to a home-like environment (4.1 and 4.2).
There was also a marked increase in the proportion of homes meeting
the fire safety standard (7.4).

In 1989–90, three standards (5.3, 7.2, 7.4) were met by less than half
the nursing homes; in 1993–94 only one (7.2) remained in this

category. Standard 7.2 concerns nursing home design, equipment and practices and their contribution to a safe environment for residents, staff and visitors. On all others, the minimum proportion of homes meeting individual standards in 1993–94 was 70 per cent.

Hostels

In 1991–92 the first year in which the hostel outcome standards were in place the general performance was reasonable. Of the 25 standards, 14 were met by at least three-quarters of the hostels, and a further 9 by at least half. Two standards were not, however, being met by the majority of hostels. One of these was standard 1.3, which concerns the Formal Agreement on residents' rights (including termination provisions) between residents and the hostel. This was met by only 42 per cent of hostels. The second standard was 6.2, which concerns the provision of a clean and safe environment. This was met by only 33 per cent of hostels.

By 1993–94, 22 of the 25 standards were met by at least three-quarters of the hostels visited, and all standards were met by the majority of homes. The three standards which were giving hostels most difficulty at that time were standard 1.3 (the Formal Agreement and associated provisions concerning residents' rights, met by only 53 per cent of hostels), standard 1.6 (concerning the provision of written and verbal explanations of the hostels' policies concerning fees and charges, met by 71 per cent of hostels) and standard 6.2 (concerning the provision of a clean and safe environment met by only 52 per cent of hostels). The full set of compliance scores against each of the standards is presented in Table 5.2

Overall, the evidence of the compliance scores generated by the standards monitoring program in both nursing homes and hostels suggests that standards of care have indeed improved in the Australian residential care sector, and that this improvement is continuing. There remains, however, room for further improvement. In 1993–94, 14 of the 25 hostels standards, and 13 of the 31 nursing home standards, were met by at least 90 per cent of homes.

Regulating home-based care

This chapter has concentrated on regulation and quality of care in the residential care sector. In 1991 guidelines for seven National Service Standards were agreed and published for the Home and Community Care program (HACC 1991). These are further broken down into 27 'consumer outcomes', but function as guidelines, and, unlike the

Table 5.2 Percentage of hostels meeting the outcome standards, Australia 1991–92 to 1993–94

Standard	1991–92	1993–94
1.1	91.7	97.3
1.2	85.8	93.6
1.3	42.2	52.8
1.4	67.1	81.9
1.5	66.5	78.9
1.6	60.6	71.0
1.7	52.9	81.3
2.1	76.6	94.0
2.2	94.2	97.5
2.3	78.3	87.1
2.4	52.6	75.3
2.5	74.5	77.0
3.1	82.2	94.0
3.2	80.0	94.7
3.3	93.8	98.2
3.4	67.4	79.9
3.5	78.2	93.3
4.1	87.1	97.8
4.2	91.1	98.2
4.3	87.4	95.1
4.4	88.9	92.2
5.1	68.6	79.5
5.2	89.8	96.6
6.1	79.1	90.2
6.2	32.6	52.3
No. of visits	477	580

Source: HSH 1995 unpublished data (AIHW 1995).

nursing home and hostel standards, do not as yet include a monitoring function. The need to develop a quality assurance or regulatory system for home-based care has generally been agreed, but attempts to date have not been successful. Given the range and degree of fragmentation of home-based care services in Australia, and the involvement of several levels of government, as well as the private-for-profit and not-for-profit sectors, in the funding and provision of such services, the difficulties in agreeing on and implementing such a system are indeed formidable. The problems are an amalgam of political, conceptual and methodological difficulties which will not be easily resolved.

Present developments are focused on a self-appraisal system, supported by varying levels of external review. In cases of complaint or other risk factors, the process would move largely into the external review arena. The arguments advanced in favour of some elements of self-appraisal are largely to do with the resource implications of an externally monitored system. The growing use of contracting out in the community services sector, however, makes the need for some form of reliable outcome-based quality appraisal even more pressing. The Australian Institute of Health and Welfare is currently engaged in a testing and development phase intended to produce an instrument suitable for use in a national pilot.

Conclusion

This chapter began with a report on the successful implementation of a regulatory system for nursing homes based on standards which are outcome oriented, resident focused, non-specific and subjectively determined. The findings speak positively to the capacity of a recent Australian innovation to contribute to the maintenance of an adequate standard of care in both nursing homes and hostels. There remain, however, some issues of ongoing concern, particularly with regard to the adequate resourcing of the regulatory program, and the availability and use of formal sanctions within the regulatory structure.

National data generated by the outcome standards monitoring process suggest that there has been general improvement in the quality of care provided in Australian nursing homes and hostels in recent years. The outcome standards monitoring process has been in place in Australian nursing homes since 1987, and in hostels since 1991. For home-based care, although national service standards have been agreed, a national quality assurance or regulatory program has yet to be developed.

CHAPTER 6

Implementing User Rights Strategies

Introduction

User rights emerged as a visible component of the Australian government's aged care policy in 1988, with the commissioning of the Ronalds consultancy on residents' rights in nursing homes and hostels. Subsequent years saw the extension of user rights strategies to the Home and Community Care program, which provides home-based care not only to frail and disabled older people but also to younger people with disabilities. In 1993 the arena of concern expanded again to include the rights of older people more generally, not only those who were recipients of aged care services.[1]

Australia can be characterised as a country where such issues have been held as of concern only in relatively recent times, but one where the available evidence and examples from countries such as the United States were rapidly assembled into a relatively comprehensive user rights strategy. The implementation of these policies, and where possible the appraisal of their impact, forms the subject matter of the present chapter.

While the commissioning of the Ronalds consultancy achieved considerable visibility for the issues surrounding residents' rights in nursing homes and hostels, a recurrent concern with residents' rights had

---

[1] *The Working Party on the Protection of Frail Older People in the Community (1994)* was established to explore the risk of abuse in the community, where abuse was taken to include physical, psychological, emotional, material and financial abuse, and neglect. The focus of this chapter is, however, on the implementation of user rights strategies with regard to aged care services. The more general preoccupations concerning elder abuse addressed by the Working Group, as well as the legal structures established or expanded under various forms of guardianship legislation during this period, are beyond the scope of the present discussion.

manifested itself over the preceding decade. In the late 1970s and early 1980s nursing homes had begun to attract public and media attention with a series of horror stories concerning mistreatment or neglect among nursing home residents. In 1981 in Perth and 1982 in Sydney, concerned community groups held phone-ins concerning the abuse of older people in residential settings. The Sydney phone-in received over 500 calls in 24 hours, mostly concerned with conditions in nursing homes and hostels, and led to the release of the uncompromisingly titled report *Prisoners of Neglect: A Study of Abuse of Elderly People*.

Around the same time, *Choice*, the flagship publication of the Australian consumer movement, conducted a reader survey into residential conditions which confirmed the concerns being voiced by community groups of one kind and another. By 1986 the Aged Care Coalition had published similar findings in *If Only I'd Known: A Study of the Experiences of Elderly Residents in Boarding Homes, Hostels and Self Care Units*.

These actions by community groups were not without their parallels in the parliamentary system. Government committees and inquiries canvassed such issues throughout the 1980s (including the McLeay Report in 1982, the Giles Report in 1985, the Joint Review of Hostel Care Subsidy Arrangements in 1985 and the Nursing Homes and Hostels Review in 1986). From both the community groups and the parliamentary reports there emerged similar concerns about the rights of residents and the quality of care, concerns which led to rapid policy developments in the late 1980s with regard to residents' rights, as well as those pertaining to nursing home and hostel regulation discussed in the preceding chapter.

Nor was there a dearth of support in the bureaucracy for such reforms. As early as 1987 the Commonwealth Government's Office for the Aged had produced a discussion document, *Toward a Comprehensive User Rights Mechanism*, which opened with the following statement:

> The first thing that can be said about user rights and complaint mechanisms is that they are a concept whose time has come. The issue isn't whether or not we implement them, but how and when.

Although concern can be traced back over much of the 1980s it was the commissioning of the Ronalds Reports (1988; 1989) which gave residents' rights greater public visibility and which established for the first time a specific and explicit policy agenda. Through a series of interviews with residents and proprietors and rounds of public meetings, Ronalds built a picture of a residential care system which generated a loss of both independence and personal privacy, and was characterised by undue regimentation, a lack of security of tenure, and a generalised sense of fear, anxiety and the absence of personal control.

The final report on *Residents' Rights in Nursing Homes and Hostels* (Ronalds 1989) proposed a series of strategies – some already partially in existence, others not – to promote residents' rights. The four principles underlying the more specific recommendations were:

- that residents have the right to be treated as individuals;
- that consumer participation and involvement in decision-making requires adequate information;
- that participation and consultation are central to a sense of personal control; and
- that residents' rights are not reduced by an inability to personally exercise those rights.

The report contained 43 recommendations, some of several constituent parts, not all of which can usefully be summarised here. Nonetheless, six priority areas were identified, which convey the major thrust of the findings (1989: 97–98):

- the implementation of a Charter of Residents' Rights and Responsibilities;
- the development and implementation of a legally binding contractual agreement between residents and proprietors, to be signed as soon as possible to the date of entry, which provided plain English information on a range of topics including basic services, financial arrangements, tenure, and internal complaints procedures;
- the establishment and resourcing of mechanisms to enable resident participation and involvement;
- development and strengthening of the departmental complaints handling mechanisms;
- improved access to information on the nature of aged care services, their availability, and the rights and choices of older people for both residents and their relatives, as well as education of the general community in this regard; and
- the establishment of independent advocacy services and a Community Visitors Scheme to facilitate advocacy services.

Implementing user rights strategies

The years from 1988 thus saw a qualitative shift in the way in which user rights (and more specifically residents' rights) came to be understood, a broadening of the more traditional view of protecting 'powerless' consumers to one which incorporated a concept of aged consumers as active participants in that process, and a more aggressive policy commitment to implementing these changes. Yet while a range of programs and service modifications were implemented, progress on a number of fronts remained uneven.

Residential care

Legislation supporting two of the key proposals of the Ronalds Report, the Charter of Residents' Rights and Responsibilities and the Resident/ Proprietor Agreement, was passed in December 1989. The actual Charter was approved by Parliament in December 1990, and has been in force in Commonwealth-funded nursing homes and hostels since April 1991. The Charter lists a series of rights pertaining to personal independence, choice, privacy, quality of care, access to medical and related services, personal property, personal finances and so forth.

The Charter is underpinned in a legal context by the Resident/ Proprietor Agreement. A common form of the Agreement received parliamentary approval in December 1990, and implementation in nursing homes commenced in December 1991. Proprietors were invited to offer the Agreement to all residents from that date, and were initially to report on progress on a biannual basis; the first report being due on 31 July 1992. The Agreement guaranteed a number of rights listed in the Charter, and was intended to provide both a legal basis and a source of information for residents, prospective residents, and their friends and family.

Departmental complaints units were established in all states and territories by 1992. These units considered complaints concerning home-based as well as residential care services, but only those facilities which were in receipt of government funding. Private boarding houses, for example, were thus outside the scope of these arrangements, although this sector is known to accommodate persons with a range of physical and intellectual disabilities and health problems.

Federal funds were also provided to establish independent advocacy services; by 1991 these were active in all states and territories. The first National Conference for Residential Aged Care Advocacy Services was held in 1991, and provided a context in which advocacy staff could exchange experiences and information in what was a relatively new field of endeavour for some. The advocacy services were intended to function as an advocate of the resident, unlike the ombudsman schemes in the United States that are essentially concerned with fair arbitration and reconciliation of disputes. While federally funded, the advocacy services were established under the auspices of non-government agencies or community groups, in an attempt to ensure their independent status.

The Community Visitors Scheme proposed by the Ronalds Report was implemented in pilot form in 1990, but in an altered form which explicitly excluded the advocacy role envisaged in that report. The Scheme was subsequently implemented on a national basis, and functions as a 'friendly visitor' service for older people in residential care facilities. While the presence of a community visitor may potentially help to reduce the powerlessness experienced by isolated frail and disabled older people in such settings, the scheme does not provide the grassroots support to advocacy services which was originally envisaged. The potential for outreach to various homes, hostels and even home-based care services was thus lost.

The same period saw the establishment of Aged Consumer Forums in each state, and an equivalent body at the national level, intended to represent the views of aged persons in policy discussions and negotiations. Moreover, the state-based advisory councils which review the regional allocation of aged care services (both residential and home-based) now include consumer representatives.

These rights-based strategies thus included initiatives at both the strategic planning and the operational or service delivery levels. Consumer participation and representation were sought on national and state planning committees, and via the creation of representative committees where none had existed. User rights were supported at the service delivery level by the implementation of the various complaints and advocacy services. Taken in their entirety these changes constituted a significant shift in their own right. Almost simultaneously, however, a discrete development had occurred in the form of the outcome-based regulatory program for nursing homes and hostels – discussed in the previous chapter – which incorporated a strong user rights component.

The broader implications and experiences of the standards monitoring program as it impacted on quality of care in the residential sector have already been discussed. Nonetheless, of the 31 standards for nursing homes and the 25 for hostels the majority are consistent with, and in many cases could be considered an integral part of, a residents' rights strategy. In a more specific sense, certain standards can be identified which relate directly to residents' rights. These are discussed in more detail later in this chapter.

Clearly, recent years have seen the implementation of a number of user rights initiatives in the residential care field. While some, such as the complaints units and certain of the advocacy services, progressively extended their field of influence to include home-based care, others, such as the aged care advisory councils, were established to deal with home-based as well as residential care services. The Aged Consumer Forums and the various Offices of the Aged within most state governments have a more general brief, including any and all aspects of interest and relevance to older persons, not simply older persons as service users. Developments specifically related to home-based care also occurred, although these have generally lagged behind those in the residential care area.

Home-based care

In 1990 a Statement of Rights and Responsibilities for HACC was released, aimed at facilitating an environment where service providers were aware of the rights of service users, and wherein service users felt comfortable about exercising those rights.[2] The Statement was released in a context where consumers already had representation on the program planning advisory committees in each state, and where advocacy services and complaints units were either established or under development. The two key complementary developments specified in the preamble to the Statement are the National Service Standards for HACC and the provision of national training material for service providers, both emphasising the importance of consumer rights in the service relationship.

The HACC National Service Standards were the subject of extensive consultation among federal, state and territory governments, service providers and consumers from 1989, and were released in 1991 (HACC, 1991).[3] Like the outcome standards developed for nursing homes and hostels, these guidelines were intended to form the basis for assessing quality of care with a view to ensuring an adequate level of performance by service providers. As noted in the preceding chapter, however, the HACC National Service Standards have yet to form the basis of a regulatory program, or any form of program accountability concerned with achievement against the service standards. For the time being there are no national data on performance in this regard available for the HACC program, and thus no basis on which to appraise progress.

---

[2] A full text version of the Statement may be found in Appendix 3 of the *Report of the Working Party on the Protection of Frail Older People in the Community (1994)*.

[3] A listing of the HACC Service Standards is found in *Getting It Right: Guidelines for the Home and Community Care Program National Service Standards*, AGPS, Canberra.

Like the outcome standards for hostels and nursing homes, however, there are some of particular relevance to user rights, and indeed virtually all were at least tangentially related. Of the seven broad objectives (comprised of 27 'consumer outcomes'), three focus explicitly on user rights issues:

- Objective 2 To ensure that each consumer is informed about his or her rights and responsibilities and the services available, and consulted about any changes required.
- Objective 6 To ensure that each consumer has access to fair and equitable procedures for dealing with complaints and disputes.
- Objective 7 To ensure that each consumer has access to an advocate of his or her choice.

Assessing the consequences

Up to this point I have provided evidence of both activity and intent with regard to facilitating user rights within the Australian aged care system. The full impact of such developments will not be manifested in the short term, and in some ways it is probably premature to assess achievements. Nonetheless, there are some aspects which can be considered in the short to medium term, and on which data are presently available. Others, in particular those in the home care sector, must await either the implementation of a national monitoring scheme, or some large-scale sustained research inquiries directed towards those specific ends.

At the strategic planning level the simple inclusion of consumers on the key planning bodies may be taken as a measure of success. The aged care advisory councils in each state and territory advise the relevant Minister concerning regional resource allocation, funding priorities and program planning, and the formal inclusion of consumers on such bodies is an important achievement. In a more general sense the Aged Consumer Forums in each state and at the national level, together with the various pensioner lobby groups and others such as the National Carers' Association (established with federal funding), function as both an information exchange and training ground for the participants, and a source of consumer opinion for all levels of government.

In addition there is some evidence that consumers and carers are increasingly being given the opportunity to act on steering committees or boards responsible for various services. Community options projects, for example, particularly those sponsored by community groups, frequently include consumer representatives on their steering committees and advisory boards. There is also a growing recognition among service providers of the resource implications of asking consumers and carers to act in this regard (they generally get paid neither for their time nor for the costs involved in attending such meetings). The simple fact that such issues are being discussed is further evidence of the increasing tendency to seek some form of user input at the local or grassroots level.

For most consumers, however, the real test of a user rights strategy occurs at the provider–user interface – in other words, the everyday experiences of prospective and continuing clients. What evidence is available to suggest that user rights mechanisms have actually changed the nature and manner in which aged care services are delivered in this country?

The most detailed data available apply to residential care, and were gathered as part of the Nursing Home Regulation in Action Project described in the previous chapter. Commencing in 1987, and concluding in 1993, the project covered the key period during which user rights strategies were being introduced in the residential care sector.

A brief description of the research design has already been given. The components of particular relevance here, however, were the first and second wave interviews with directors of nursing (the chief executives of the nursing homes). These interviews ranged over a number of topics, including the attitudes of the directors of nursing to the principles underlying the outcomes standards (including user rights) and their experience of and reaction to the standards monitoring process itself.[4]

Directors of nursing are the senior management officers in Australian nursing homes. Broad policy and financial trajectories may be set by proprietors or management committees, but it is the directors of nursing who are primarily responsible for the quality of life and quality of care experienced by nursing home residents in individual homes. Their level of commitment to residents' rights is, therefore, a central element in developing resident participation and freedom of choice in Australian nursing homes.

---

[4] In the first wave 410 interviews were completed. They took place between 1988 and 1990, in nursing homes in and surrounding four large capital cities – Adelaide, Brisbane, Melbourne and Sydney. In the second wave of quantitative data collection, directors of nursing were sent a mailed questionnaire following their second standards monitoring visit some two years later. Homes which had closed, those where a new director of nursing had been appointed in the intervening period, and those which did not receive a second visit within the allotted time span, were excluded. Of a total of 224 questionnaires mailed out in the second wave 165 were returned within the allocated time period. Additional information on project methodology was presented in Chapter 5. A more detailed account is available elsewhere (Braithwaite *et al.* 1990; 1993).

After the first standards monitoring visit, directors of nursing were asked to appraise all standards in terms of their desirability and practicality. The standards, as noted in the previous chapter, enjoyed very high degrees of support from the outset. For 28 of the 31 standards at least 97 per cent of directors of nursing had no doubts about their desirability. With regard to practicality, support was somewhat less unanimous but nonetheless widespread. Twenty-five of the 31 standards were viewed as practical by at least 90 per cent of directors of nursing.

The vast majority of respondents supported all standards, and virtually all respondents supported the vast majority of standards in terms of both practicality and desirability. Where concerns about standards did arise, however, they did so in relation to standards specifically concerned with residents' rights.

The three standards which attracted some concern with regard to desirability were standards 1.2, 2.2 and 7.1, albeit among a small minority of respondents (4–5 per cent). These are the standards to do with residents making informed choices concerning care plans (1.2), maintaining control of financial affairs (2.2) and participating in activities which may involve a degree of risk (7.1). For practicality, the four standards about which most doubts were raised were again standards 1.2, 2.2 and 7.1 (by 20 per cent, 24 per cent and 14 per cent of directors of nursing respectively), plus one additional standard (3.1) requiring that nursing home policies be developed in consultation with residents (22 per cent of directors of nursing doubted the practicality of this standard).

The qualitative evidence gathered during the interviews reveals that the underlying concerns were indeed to do with a lack of commitment and understanding to the principles underlying user rights. Directors of nursing expressed concern that confused residents were not capable of such involvement (Standards 1.2, 2.2 and 7.1), and indeed that residents did not want that responsibility, particularly in relation to standard 1.2. Care plans were held to be a professional responsibility ('We as professional nurses should make the decision'; 'I think we should be the spokesperson for residents'.). This theme of professional responsibility was frequently mentioned in relation to standard 7.1 concerning risk-taking behaviour, particularly where the consequences were likely to involve physical injury.

This latter standard provides perhaps the best example of the potential conflict between residents' rights and the duty of care – between individual rights and professional responsibility. If a resident insists on climbing furniture to reach a high cupboard in her room, it is the director of nursing who must explain the subsequent broken hip if she falls; and it is thus perhaps not surprising that residents are not 'enabled' to engage in such activities. On the other hand, while a frail older woman living in the community who decides to 'jump the fence' to visit a neighbour may be ill advised to do so, she is unlikely to be prevented from engaging in this activity by visiting domiciliary care workers, and they would certainly not feel professionally responsible for her activities.

The situation is often further complicated by the attitudes and behaviour of relatives in a residential care context. One director of nursing recounted the case of a resident who had a minor balance problem, which resulted in very occasional falls. To date these had been without serious consequence. In her professional view, physically restraining the resident was unnecessary, and would have led to reduced muscle tone and impaired mobility, not to mention an unpleasant experience for the resident concerned. Yet her son and daughter-in-law were arguing strongly that she should be so restrained – for her own protection. As this director of nursing wryly observed: 'People don't like to see their elderly parents with broken limbs'.

The implementation of a user rights philosophy, then, not only can lead to conflict with notions of professional responsibility within the particular service, it can also conflict with dominant norms in the wider community, not to mention those held by the specific service recipient and his or her concerned family members.

In the second wave of data collection, directors of nursing were asked to reflect on a number of items concerning how their approach had changed over the intervening period since the first interview (about two years). Taking a broad definition of residents' rights, particular interest attaches to their responses to the item 'I am more resident oriented and less task oriented than I was in 1987'. Forty per cent of respondents agreed with this statement, 40 per cent neither agreed nor disagreed and the remaining 20 per cent disagreed. Presumably a proportion of the respondents who disagreed did so because they felt that their commitment to a resident focus was already high at the beginning of the program.

Of course, 'resident focus' is a sufficiently broad term to be consistent with even very traditional models of patient care. Responses to four more specific items, however, also suggest the emergence of a more positive approach. Directors of nursing were asked whether their commitment to each of a series of items had gone up or down in the period from 1987. About two-thirds of respondents reported that their commitment to emphasising residents' rights had gone up, and well over half said that their commitment to involving both residents and their relatives in decision-making had increased. The fourth item, allowing

Table 6.1 Percentage of nursing homes receiving a 'met' rating on various rights-based standards 1989–90 and 1993–94

Nursing home standard	1989–90	1993–94
1.2 (informed choices about individual care plans)	70%	81%
2.2 (maintaining control of financial affairs)	76%	87%
2.3 (maximum freedom of movement within and from the nursing home)	87%	93%
2.5 (maintaining responsibilities and obligations as citizens)	93%	99%
3.1 (policies developed in consultation with residents)	73%	80%
3.2 (ability to comment and complain about conditions in nursing homes)	70%	89%
4.1 (security of accommodation)	59%	83%
7.1 (right to participate in activities involving a degree of risk)	81%	92%

Source: Adapted from AIHW (1995: 384).

residents to take risks, reflects a more controversial aspect of residents' rights, and not surprisingly received somewhat less support. Nonetheless, 43 per cent of directors of nursing reported an increased commitment in this regard. No more than 2 per cent of respondents indicated a reduction in commitment to any of these items.

Taken together these data suggest a significant improvement in the acceptance of a residents' rights philosophy in the nursing home context over this period which saw a number of key developments concerning individual rights. Unfortunately, similar data are not available for other service areas. However, the nursing home standards and hostels standards described in the previous chapter, on which data are gathered routinely to determine compliance at a national level, provide a further source of information.

For both nursing homes and hostels, performance against all the specifically rights-oriented standards had improved over the period for which national data are available. Performance on individual standards is set out in Tables 6.1 and 6.2. While a detailed appraisal of performance against individual standards is left to the reader, it is of some note that a minority of nursing homes (10 per cent) and hostels (21 per cent) continued not to meet the standards concerning the availability of a complaints procedure.

Some other more specific indicators of progress in the user rights field are also available concerning residential care. In the period from

Table 6.2   Percentage of hostels receiving a 'met' rating on various rights-based standards 1991–92 and 1993–94

Hostel standard	1991–92	1993–94
1.4 (residents are enabled to make informed choices and decisions about daily activities and to participate in decision-making)	67%	82%
1.5 (residents to exercise their rights and responsibilities, and to draw attention to unsatisfactory conditions)	67%	79%
2.4 (care and personal needs to be identified by communication and negotiation, the resident is encouraged to make informed choices)	53%	75%
4.2 (the opportunity to engage in spiritual, cultural and leisure activities, to participate in local community life, and to vote in elections)	91%	98%
4.3 (assisted to remain independent in the conduct of financial dealings)	87%	95%
5.2 (right to participate in activities that may involve some personal risk)	90%	97%

Source: Adapted from AIHW (1995: 385).

1986 to 1991 there was a dramatic increase in the proportion of homes with residents' committees. In New South Wales, Queensland and South Australia, residents' committees became the rule, rather than the exception, and in Victoria they came into being in the majority of homes. One reason for this rapid growth was undoubtedly the belief in the nursing home industry that having a functioning residents' committee would contribute quite substantially to being rated in compliance with standard 3.2, concerning appropriate avenues for comment and complaint. A growth in the number of committees does not, however, of itself ensure the existence of a viable avenue for resident participation. Indeed, a more cynical view may well be that they mask the absence of such avenues in any real sense.

More detailed data collected on resident committees suggest that they do indeed have a limited function in this regard. Two-thirds of committees met on a monthly basis, with only 1 per cent meeting more often. The remainder met less frequently. Over half the committee meetings were attended by 12 or fewer residents. The most commonly discussed topics were food (84 per cent of committees), activities (51 per cent) and outings (52 per cent). Issues of nursing home policy, or something pertaining to the structure of the nursing home or its equipment, had been raised by one-third of committees. The specific and sensitive issue of complaints against staff had been raised by only 14 per cent of committees, and comments pertaining to departmental policies on nursing homes by 10 per cent.

Taken together with the qualitative fieldwork these findings suggest that it would be a mistake to place too much weight on the growth in numbers of residents' committees as an indication of significant increases in effective resident participation. In general, of those residents' meetings attended in the course of project fieldwork, most did not act as important vehicles for resident participation in formulating nursing home policies and influencing practices. Many functioned more as a conduit for information from management to residents than as an avenue of influence from residents to management. Many were preoccupied with the 'bread and butter' issues of food, activities and outings, rather than with more grandiose aspects of consumer empowerment. Nonetheless, the importance of the actual issues discussed to nursing home residents themselves should not be dismissed lightly.

Another aspect of consumer empowerment on which data are available concerns the signing of the resident/proprietor agreement in hostels. This agreement is actually specifically mentioned in one of the hostel outcome standards (this is not the case for the nursing home standards). On the most recent data (1993–94), only 53 per cent of hostels surveyed met this particular standard. Moreover, it was one of three standards on which performance was clearly well below all others. (One of the other two being concerned with the related issue of providing information concerning fees and charges.)

Towards evaluation and explanation

These data reveal some progress towards increasing the level of resident participation in nursing homes and hostels, but also some limitations. Commitment among directors of nursing towards the philosophy of residents' rights, for example, was undoubtedly high. The proportion of homes and hostels which met the relevant standards had increased over the period since their implementation, suggesting that the quantity and quality of resident participation in key decision-making processes may have improved. Moreover, even in nursing homes and hostels that met the required ratings on both occasions, there may well have been development in the level and range of resident involvement and consultation.

Certainly, the data collected in the Nursing Home Regulation in Action Project suggested that many directors of nursing felt this to be the case in their nursing homes. On the other hand, despite the verging on universal support for the majority of standards reported in that study, those standards which raised most doubts related directly to residents' rights.

The dramatic increase in the number of residents' committees is somewhat offset by the limited roles played by those committees. Moreover, observations of committees in the United States suggest that this is not a purely Australian phenomenon. Indeed, one particular event which occurred in the American fieldwork cautions us against placing too much faith in the mere existence of residents' committees. On this occasion the door to the meeting room was physically barred by a staff member to prevent a particular resident from attending the committee meeting, and eventually, after several attempts at entry, locked – and this with an 'overseas observer' present.

As we have seen, the procedures adopted in the standards monitoring visit are themselves demonstrably resident focused, and strongly oriented towards outcomes for residents (Chapter 5). While direct equivalent data on hostels are not at hand, the very nature of the standards monitoring program, as it has been implemented in both hostels and nursing homes, suggests that that would be the case.[5] Yet there was very little involvement of residents from that point on in the process. Very few compliance discussions (in which the performance of the home against the standards is discussed) involve residents, or their representatives. Residents were not regularly participating in the development of the action plans constructed to deal with areas of non-compliance with the standards.

While this may not be held to be appropriate if the issue in question is, for example, the comparative benefits of sterilising procedures, it may indeed be appropriate with regard to such standards as creating a home-like environment, preferred menu choices or the range of activities offered by the home. In approximately half the nursing homes studied in the Nursing Home Regulation in Action Project, residents and their relatives had not been informed about the outcome of the first standards monitoring visit in any way. And in only 11 per cent had the report actually been made available via the residents' committee in a systematic way.

Thus, although residents were made the focus of the standards monitoring procedure they did not and have not become an integral part of it. They are certainly not active participants. And while the rhetoric of residents' rights did indeed become manifest in many nursing homes, the reality is more one of relatively modest achievement.

With regard to home-based care, there is little that can be said at the

---

[5] See Chapter 5 for further details of this process.

national level. Apart from the presence of consumers and carers on various committees and some agency boards there is little evidence available to document progress on user rights. Even at the committee level there tends to be 'a user or carer representative' in a board or committee dominated by service providers or government (and non-government) bureaucrats.

In the community options service delivery system, which takes as a key element of service delivery the involvement of the consumer in service planning, evidence of an emerging user rights philosophy is not readily available. The national evaluation document does not report progress in this particular area, an oversight which is perhaps more telling than the data which might have been collected.

In a detailed evaluation of one such service undertaken over the period from 1990 to 1992, attention was specifically directed to this issue (Gibson *et al.* 1992). The constraints imposed by the frailty, lack of knowledge and the previous experiences of the clients themselves emerged as a significant issue. While the majority of the 37 clients interviewed in this study said that their wishes had been taken into account, the picture which emerged was more one where clients had been able to indicate agreement or disagreement with the proffered services: 'They put suggestions forward and asked me if I wanted it'.

Another theme was a concern among clients of not to be too 'pushy' or demanding: 'I was just so thrilled to think I was getting help that I didn't want to be pushy. I told [the Project Co-ordinator] what was involved in caring for [husband], and listened to her suggestions about what help I might need.'

These project staff clearly did take the philosophy of involving clients quite seriously, despite the difficulties and limitations which they encountered in doing so. Yet they were working within a context of other more traditional service providers. During one observational period, the community service broker had to attempt to deal with a frail older woman caring for a seriously disabled spouse who had been 'scolded' by a domiciliary nurse when she realised that the woman was using two periods of day care per week, one provided by another domiciliary nursing service (both, incidentally, private-not-for-profit services). Despite ultimate resolution (as a result of complex inter-service negotiations) and a personal apology by the delinquent service provider, the carer withdrew her husband from the program, despite her need for the support. In a climate such as this, at least on the basis of anecdotal evidence, we have quite a long way to go.

Another 'silence' from which we may tell much about progress on user rights is the failure to incorporate such issues into the national aged care assessment system. The assessment system was introduced to promote equity of access to scarce resources, in this case the aged residential care system. The aged care assessment teams determine eligibility for admission to nursing homes and hostels throughout the country. Yet there is no appeals procedure, no involvement of consumers, and no attempt to consider the implications of user rights issues at any level. The aged care assessment teams are not subject to any form of standards monitoring, other than the informal pressure which may emerge from their professional peers in a community or local context.

Conclusion

In many ways, these findings are not surprising. The user rights movement in Australia is relatively young; the onset of the various user rights strategies is quite recent. Evaluation of these processes is of value not in a summative sense of defining success or failure, but in a formative mode to identify weaknesses and strengths which can be incorporated into ongoing program developments. A move to further develop the user rights program will require even greater commitment from service providers, increased awareness among and perhaps active education of consumers, expanded resources, and some further attention to the integration between rights and regulatory strategies across the various arenas in which aged care services are designed and delivered.

While there has been undoubted progress in the residents' rights area in Australia in recent years, the structural constraints operating in this area remain formidable. There is, however, also room for optimism. As the impacts of the standards monitoring procedures, current policy initiatives to upgrade and develop in-service training, the prospective emergence of monitoring procedures for home-based care, and growing community acceptance of the rights of aged persons converge and interact over the next few years some further development of user rights may yet emerge.

PART THREE

Reconceptualising Problems, Reorienting Solutions

CHAPTER 7

The 'Problem of Old Women' Redefined

Introduction

In the first and second sections of this book, I have engaged with, analysed and evaluated Australian aged care policies – sometimes favourably, sometimes not. In all cases, however, those analyses have been undertaken within the frameworks imposed by the policies themselves. The focus has been on policies and programs in terms of the constructions which *they* place on social problems, and in terms of *their* self-defined goals and tasks. The perspectives adopted have been consistent with dominant discourses, with accepted wisdoms as to what constitutes a public issue or a personal trouble. In the remaining chapters of this book, however, the ways in which those problems have been constructed, and policy solutions inflected by those constructions, become themselves subject matter for broader theoretical reflections. What aspects – be they personal troubles, public issues or somewhere in between – are eclipsed by the very nature of our social policies? And how might our particular understandings (or misunderstandings) of the resources and difficulties confronting older individuals distort or modify our perceptions of the nature of the problem and limit or pre-determine what constitutes an appropriate solution? It is to the first of these constructions – the 'problem of old women' – that I now turn.

As described in Chapter 4, ageing, at least among a subset of gerontological researchers, has come to be regarded as a gendered issue. From somewhat neglected origins the particular circumstances confronting old women soon emerged in a veritable deluge of material concerning the difficulties associated with being old and female. The social problems approach neglected by earlier analysts was invoked with a vengeance, and in pieces ranging in style from the empirical to the polemical the disadvantages which accrue to older women were extensively documented and analysed.

In this chapter, I certainly do not wish to take issue with the relevance of gender to the study of ageing, nor to disagree with the particular disadvantages likely to be encountered by old women outlined earlier in this book. This is not a recanting of the views put forward in the earlier chapter, but rather an attempt to examine the 'problem of old women' from a different perspective, and from that perspective to reconsider the relevance of our policy directions and solutions. It is the extent to which unremitting negativity has come to characterise the study of old women, and its reflection and reinforcement of pervasive images of old women in society at large, which constitutes the central focus of this chapter.

It is my contention that the particular lens through which old women have come to be viewed is one which selectively includes only certain elements of the experience of being old and female. The 'problem of old women' referred to in the opening paragraph of this chapter has thus a dual significance. The problems likely to be encountered by particular old women in particular social and historical contexts have become so central to scholarly discourse that there is a danger of viewing old women only in terms of those problems. From there it is a dangerously short step to constructing old women as a problem for society. The problems that society poses for old women may thus disappear as the problems that old women pose for society take hold.

By focusing on issues of disadvantage, feminist analyses of old age have tended to unintentionally obscure not only the heterogeneity of old women, but perhaps more importantly the aspects of being old and female which are a source of both celebration and strength. While there is no doubt that women face a number of adverse physical, emotional, mental, social and economic eventualities in their old age, such eventualities do not adequately represent the totality of their experiences.

The construction of disadvantage

Documentation of the disadvantages confronting older women proceeded apace during the 1980s, across a wide variety of difficulties and problems. Some took as a starting point heterosexual relationships. The combination of men tending to marry younger women and the greater longevity of women lead to a greater incidence of widowhood among women. The same factors, combined with the perceived lesser sexual attractiveness of older women, lead to a lower likelihood of remarriage for old women. The absence of a spouse in old age is associated with a range of potentially negative domestic, psychological, social, and financial consequences. Spouses often act as a significant source of assistance in the case of serious illness or disability, provide social and emotional support, sexual fulfilment, physical contact, and financial security, as well as someone with whom to share caring and domestic labour.[1] Moreover, the loss of perceived sexual attractiveness and reproductive function experienced by old women has been related to poor self-esteem, and the way in which they are devalued by society at large (Allen 1988, Arber and Ginn 1991b, Gee and Kimball 1987, Sontag 1975, and Russell 1987).[2]

Other analysts focused more on the adequacy of public provisions. In Chapter 4, I argued that much social provision for the aged may be characterised as both phallocentric and parasitic upon the labour of old women. Writing from a political economy perspective, a number of authors emphasised the disadvantaged position of old women with regard to income and housing (Estes, Gerarg and Clarke 1984, Coleman and Watson 1987, Hess 1985, Minkler and Stone 1985, Peace 1986, Rodeheaver 1987, Rosenman 1986, and Woerness 1987). Attention was also focused on measures of disability and health status, use of medical and hospital services, and rates of institutionalisation (Arber and Ginn 1991b, Gee and Kimball 1987, Hess 1980). There is now a considerable body of literature to document the fact that the problem of ageing is really a problem of and for old women; we have come a long way from de Beauvoir's (1972) confident assertion that the problem of old age was really the problem of old men.

Nor should the personal and socio-economic disadvantages suffered by old women have come as much of a surprise; it is after all the same finding which would be revealed by any comparative analysis of young or middle-aged men and women. Women's poorer health, lower income, less adequate housing and so forth do not suddenly appear in old age; they are continuous with and contingent upon a lifetime of cumulative disadvantage.

Any analysis of the position of old women (particularly policy-oriented analysis) must take this into account. A review of the evidence in the fields of health, income, housing, living arrangements, social provisions and personal relationships makes compelling reading – the

---

[1] Although as was demonstrated in Chapter 4, these advantages accrue more frequently to male, rather than female, spouses.

[2] Within the constraints imposed by a single chapter it has frequently been necessary to focus on what is common among older women rather than on their specificities and differences. It is important to recognise at the outset, however, that old women are a heterogeneous population – by virtue of race, class and sexuality, and not least of all, the cumulative consequences of a lifetime of diverse experiences and opportunities.

disadvantaged position of older women emerges as beyond dispute. Yet such analyses by their very nature fail to take account of the advantages which may accrue to old women by virtue of the same lifelong patterns of gender-specific behaviour. In attempting to redress the balance and identify the peculiar difficulties faced by women in old age, good earlier insights may well have been pushed beyond the limits of maximum utility. The relatively recent preoccupation with the particular disadvantages associated with being old and female which dominates current debate threatens that all evidence will be viewed through the one interpretive lens – the unfortunate life circumstances of older women.

Despite its emergence from a feminist perspective, this preoccupation with the 'problem of old women' is, in some curious sense, predicated on both a male and a midlife perspective. While the importance of the adversities described above should not be minimised, there are a number of positive elements pertinent to women's experience of old age which either remain unaddressed or, if considered, are elided, reconstructed or misconstrued in the dominant discourses in both social gerontology and social policy. By reconstruction, I refer to the ways in which aspects of women's lives which could be seen as advantages appear more as disadvantages. This is illustrated below in relation to women's longevity, their social networks and their coping skills. Other elements are simply not there, or at best dealt with in a peripheral way. These are the areas of silence in our understanding of the circumstances of old women – their greater experience of and investment in the private sphere, their involvement in the informal economy, and their more frequent experience in moving between formal and informal sectors, public and private spheres, over the life course. Finally, there are the misconstructions, or the areas where the evidence fails to support our taken for granted truths about gender differences in old age.

The reconstructions

Women's greater longevity has been acknowledged for some decades but curiously, as Friedan (1993) observed, was not subjected to sustained critical scrutiny until quite recently. And perhaps more curiously, while attention has focused on the explanation of the observed difference, there has been a continuing tendency not to incorporate the advantages of greater longevity for women into analyses of their position.

Gee and Kimball (1987: 40), in an analysis of older women's health, demonstrate this preoccupation with the 'problem of old women' in a lengthy discussion of the competing explanations offered for older women's higher rates of morbidity, psychotropic drug use, prescription drug use (more generally), medical services and so on. Their conclusion is of particular interest:

> ... as we have seen, the theoretical concern in studies focussing on sex differentials in morbidity has been on why women are more likely than men to be sick with minor, less life-threatening illnesses. An equally important, perhaps more important, question is why are women less likely to contract major illnesses and diseases?

To rephrase that question we might have asked why is it that men are more likely to contract major diseases and die from them? The point at issue is not the wording of the comparison, but rather with the fact that women appear so firmly entrenched in their category of 'other' that even here where the questions for men are of life-threatening significance, and where the authors are attempting to shift the focus of inquiry to a more positive note (at least for women's health), the theoretical emphasis is on women's difference from the (male) norm pertaining to major morbidity, rather than on explaining male divergences from the female.

More generally, however, the focus in comparative analyses of male and female health has remained on women's disadvantaged state. The advantages (less major disease, as pointed out by Gee and Kimball above) are rarely discussed in this literature. A more extreme, indeed verging on the bizarre, example of this preoccupation with the negative is the tendency to construct women's greater longevity as a disadvantage, and the consequent 'surplus of women' as a social problem:

> Women live longer than men, they are usually poorer than men, and because their husbands die earlier, they are more likely to live alone and, in extreme old age, to be institutionalised (Gee and Kimball 1987: 40).

or

> Women are given the dubious privilege of living longer than men, after years of financial and psychological dependency – ill-prepared to survive on their own, much less to use their added years with enjoyment and fulfilment (Lewis and Butler, 1984: 203).

The 'dubious privilege' referred to by Lewis and Butler is used to underline their argument concerning women's social and economic disadvantage. While as a rhetorical device it undoubtedly illustrates the adverse financial and other circumstances confronting older women, the suggestion that life itself becomes a burden and a 'dubious privilege' is perhaps to take the argument too far, and certainly illustrates the lack of balance characteristic of this literature. It is also this 'problem' for which Gee and Kimball (1987) go on to propose a solution in terms of improving men's health as a key policy direction. While the logic of such a conclusion is inescapable, it is curious indeed that it should be proposed as a solution to the 'problem' of women's greater longevity (and the associated disadvantages) rather than as a solution to the problem of men's shorter lifespan.

Such arguments may appear to be cheap shots. These authors were, after all, concerned with something else, the social construction of disadvantage in old age as it impacts on old women. But it is the dominance of a paradigm which can construct greater longevity, even in passing, as a social problem that is at issue here. While women in any birth cohort are indeed considerably more likely to experience high levels of disability and low levels of income than are men, they are also more likely to be alive. Few older women are likely to view their own longevity in quite the terms which characterise this literature. We may safely assume that the majority of the human race, given a choice of the male or female average lifespan, would choose the latter, despite the greater likelihood of objectively poorer life circumstances during that period. Indeed, the literature on morale in old age is redolent with examples of relatively high subjective perceptions of well-being in relatively poor (from the standpoint of the social scientist) objective circumstances (Herzog and Rodgers 1981, Rudinger and Thomae 1990).

It is worth considering that this problem of lack of fit between objective and subjective indicators of well-being in old age may be at least influenced by the midlife perspective of most researchers. Calasanti and Zajicek (1993), among others, have argued that when women are analysed within a conceptual model derived from men's experiences, the result is that anomalies are explained as sex differences, and research which purports to be gender neutral actually reinforces gender hierarchies. If the argument is applied to age, rather than gender, it is possible to begin to consider that research on old age, when conducted from one dominant (midlife) perspective, may well not be 'age neutral' in its consequences and conclusions. The perceived disparity between objective circumstances and subjective well-being may be a disparity from the perspective of the researchers – it is not necessarily a disparity, however, from the perspective of the researched.

Another area where the positive aspects of being female in old age tend to disappear from academic view is that of social networks and social support. Much is made of the greater propensity of old women to experience widowhood, which is readily associated with a range of financial, social, psychological and sexual difficulties. Comparatively little is made, however, of the closer instrumental and affective ties which women experience with family and friends.[3]

Certainly there is ample empirical evidence that these stronger networks do exist. Gibson and Mugford (1986) reported on the higher levels of emotional and social support experienced by old women, and Peace (1986) and Demetrakopoulos (1983) on the greater social contacts and friendship bonds of elderly women. Rossi (1986: 168) argued more broadly that it is women who maintain the communal and social bonds; men without spouses are thus particularly at risk of isolation from the social collectivity. Yet despite this knowledge it is widowhood and the associated social isolation which dominate more general analyses of older women's position in society.

As a consequence it is widowhood and not network strength that is used as an independent variable in the analysis of service use, institutionalisation, patterns of volunteering, health status, paid work patterns and so on. Where the focus is on one element of the private sphere, such as friendship, women's advantageous or at least their more liberally endowed position is generally recognised. It is when the focus of analysis broadens – and particularly in multivariate models predicting a range of outcomes in old age – that the picture tends to revert, with variables such as widowhood assuming a more central role and others, for example, the strength of female friendships, disappearing from view in explaining various aspects of the personal and public life of older people.[4]

And yet these elements of women's lives have important consequences for their old age. Women have frequently had a lifetime of experience in maintaining and establishing social bonds within families, friendship networks, neighbourhoods, voluntary associations, school associations and so forth, certainly more so in general than men. It is women who move in and out of the work force with their family responsibilities, women who are more likely to change towns because their husbands have moved jobs, women who have to establish the new friendship groups at the children's new school and so on. They are thus simply better equipped to maintain and redevelop their social networks

[3] In the context of a society and a gerontological literature which tends to assume heterosexual couples as a basic unit, it is worthwhile noting that such arguments could be applied even more strongly for lesbian and/or never married women.

[4] This is not to suggest that attempts, such as the recent paper by Nelson (1993), are not made to explore the impact of social support more generally on other variables. Part of the explanation may also lie in measurement difficulty, good network measures are not as easily acquired as a single indicator on marital status. It should be noted, however, that such technical difficulties have not prevented the emergence of a massive and increasingly complex empirical literature on the correlates of, for example, social class.

when confronted with the vicissitudes frequently attendant on old age. Death of spouses, family and friends is undisputedly a more frequent experience as one ages, the erosion of established networks an unavoidable corollary. The very interruptedness of the traditional female life course tends to provide a context in which the re-establishment or replacement of network members is not a new experience.

The importance of social networks, and particularly emotional and social support, has been demonstrated in connection with quality of life issues, the capacity to cope with stressful life events, and with regard to health and longevity (Antonucci 1990, House and Kahn 1985). Better social network support has been positively associated in the literature with coping capacity in the face of stressful life events (George 1989 and Krause 1987). There is some direct evidence that women generally have better coping capacities than men; this is certainly a quality that becomes more rather than less critical with the onset of old age. Thus, for example, men are much more likely than women to become sick or indeed die in the period following widowhood.[5] Women are indeed more likely to experience widowhood than men, but as Rossi comments 'it is perhaps fortunate that it is elderly women rather than men who tend to outlive their spouses' (1986: 160).

Women's greater longevity, stronger social networks and personal coping capacities are recognised in existing literature. Yet these strengths tend to appear only in relation to their problems – the loss of a spouse, their greater caring responsibilities and so on. The capacity of older women to deal successfully with these changing life circumstances is subject to a peculiar eclipsing – it is the changing life circumstances and their problematic nature which remain paramount.

The silences

Other potential areas of advantage remain largely uninvestigated in relation to women in old age. Women, particularly the current generation of old women, have by and large spent much of their time in the so-called private sphere. It appears to have gone largely unremarked that women's life-course experiences may well advantage them in old age – a life phase which essentially involves exclusion from the world of paid work. Given the low labour force participation rates of women in late midlife and old age, the structure and organisation of their lives are most likely to be premised on private sphere activities. It is thus virtually certain that for most women the transition from mid- to late-life

---

[5] This finding seems to be generally supported in the literature, although some age-related differences appear. For a recent review paper see Mendes de Leon *et al.* (1993).

will contain significantly more continuities in terms of interests, activities, social participation and so forth than it does for men.

Recently, studies of retirement have begun to explore some of these issues. Young and Schuller (1991), for example, although predominantly concerned with men in retirement, consider the positive implications of women's greater involvement in a variety of paid and unpaid, formal and informal activities. Interestingly this broadening of focus in the retirement literature appears to coincide with the acceleration of early retirement among men in their fifties and early sixties (Jacobs, Kohli and Rein 1991: 63–66). Retirement is now a much less clear-cut event; it may, for example, be an alternative to unemployment, or signal the beginning of a second career. As older men's labour market attachment becomes more tenuous and varied, it becomes more like that experienced by women over their life course. The changing nature of male retirement therefore coincides with an increasing willingness to consider the construction and definition of retirement within the ageing literature (Adelmann, Antonucci and Jackson 1993, Rosenman 1995).

Another area of silence is old women's involvement in the domestic (informal) and unofficial (black) economies. Recent years have seen a growing recognition of the size and relevance of the domestic and unofficial economic sectors, particularly among analysts in the social policy and labour force fields (Baxter and Gibson 1990, Offe and Heinze 1992, Waring 1988). There is, moreover, some evidence that the extent of unofficial economic activities is linked to economic downturns and to the availability of leisure hours (Rose 1985). If Rose is correct, it seems not unrealistic to argue that as both are likely to be present in the lives of many old women (and indeed a number of old men), they may well be heavily involved in a range of non-market activities. The current generation of aged people grew to maturity through the most severe economic downturn of the century, and may well be predisposed towards a system of exchanging goods and services.

While such activities may well be of relevance to both sexes, there are some indications to suggest that they may be particularly so for women. Women are likely to be poorer than men, and less able to maintain themselves comfortably within the official economic sector. Given that the majority of old women would have had less experience of paid work than old men, this is an area where women may have had more opportunity to be involved over their life course. Moreover, the processes of barter and exchange characteristic of the unofficial economy may well be facilitated by the larger and more active networks characteristic of old women. Some support is indeed offered for such a hypothesis by Herzog *et al.* (1989) in their account of the continuing differences in both the amount and nature of productive work which men and women undertake in old age. Further support comes from Danigelis and McIntosh's (1993) finding that among whites, women spend more time in unpaid activity in the home, more time in unpaid activity outside the home, and more time in productive activity overall. Such statements remain largely in the realm of conjecture at the present time; yet these and other as yet unspecified areas of investigation may tell us a great deal about the lives of older women which remains hidden at the present time.

The inaccuracies

It is my contention that we do not know as much about the lives of old women, and the ways in which their lives differ from old men, as is often believed. Our knowledge is partial, and we have failed to recognise some of the more obvious anomalies and inadequacies. It is possible to illustrate this using both qualitative and quantitative material.

Let me start with the general academic construction of the 'problem of old women'. This preoccupation with women's comparative disadvantage in old age is not necessarily shared by old women themselves. While much reported qualitative research has been redolent with difficulties experienced by old women (Russell 1987, Coleman and Watson 1987), the comments of old women when explicitly asked about the relative positions of men and women in old age are instructive. In a qualitative study which I undertook in the mid-1980s, responses to this question generally favoured women over men, with the main thrust of their comments concerning the advantages of continuities in the experiences and life skills accrued by women.[6] This view is exemplified by two excerpts from these interviews, one from a 67-year-old married woman and the other from a 76-year-old unmarried woman:

> Well, I think women, like in every other sphere of life can cope better than men . . . Men, especially married men who've had women to care for them for many years, are inclined to lean on their wives and have things done for them. And if there's anything wrong with them men are always bad patients. I think women can cope with things better because they're more strong-willed than men (Mrs H).

> I went to a Retirement course. They advocated that women learn the 'business side' of things, and that men . . . men should learn to look after themselves (Miss H).

---

[6] These data were collected in a study undertaken jointly with Judith Allen and Frances Boyle. Forty qualitative interviews were conducted, covering a broad range of issues. The interviews took place in a major Australian city, Brisbane, over the period from 1985 to 1986.

Blieszner's (1993) recent work offers some quantitative evidence in support of this argument. While she does not directly address the more general absence of attention to various positive aspects of women's experiences of old age, she does provide a useful illustration of the argument. Her article takes as a starting point the lack of attention focused on the capacity to manage everyday living in previous work on adaptation to widowhood; she finds that women are indeed more likely than men to manage in this regard. Other qualitative studies, concerned with particular women's competence and capacity to survive, can also be found (Day 1991). This perspective has yet, however, to acquire the status of a dominant paradigm.

The second example offered here involving the misconstruction of available evidence is more quantitatively grounded, and focuses on a brief critical appraisal of one of the more common explanations of women's greater likelihood of institutionalisation.[7] The received wisdom is that it is women's (and particularly wives') care which keeps men out of nursing homes in old age. Women, in comparison, are less likely to have husbands due to their greater propensity to widowhood, and hence more likely – in the absence of a caring spouse – to be institutionalised. But there are difficulties with that interpretation.

Rates of institutionalisation are in fact almost identical for men and women until age 70, and quite similar (albeit higher for women) until age 80. It is only over age 80 that the really significant divergences occur. Yet women are markedly more likely to be widowed than men throughout all of these age ranges. While rates of widowhood do increase with advancing age they do not increase as quickly as do those for institutionalisation. Widowhood, therefore, is at best only a very partial explanation of the observed sex differences.

Perhaps it is women's better networks which compensate for the absence of a spouse – but why then are women so much more likely than men to be admitted to institutions from the age of 80 onward? Admittedly, this informal network is more likely to be eroded in very old age, but so too are over-80-year-old men more likely to be widowed, and to have more attenuated networks than their younger counterparts.

Or perhaps the explanation lies in some difference in the ways in which illness and disability affect women and men which emerges once they are over 80. Perhaps at this point severity of disability increasingly dominates other factors such as the availability of informal care in old age. If severe levels of disability become the dominant determinant to the virtual exclusion of all else, why do severely disabled very old

---

[7] For more detailed statistical data concerning the differential rates of disability and institutionalisation experienced by men and women in old age as discussed in this chapter see AIHW (1993: ch 5 and 1995: ch 5).

women have twice the institutionalisation rates of severely disabled very old men?

The point being made is that we really do not know the answers to these questions. The 'comfortable wisdom' can be shown to have some very uncomfortable inadequacies.

Towards an explanation

The recent preoccupation with the 'problem of old women', then, can legitimately be said to have rendered invisible some more positive aspects of ageing for old women. I have argued that this has occurred through a variety of processes, including the reconstruction of positive qualities such as women's greater longevity, the academic silence that surrounds certain favourable aspects of old women's lives, and by the failure to identify inaccuracies or at least conflicting pieces of evidence underlying what have become conventional wisdoms.

Such arguments are gaining increasing legitimacy with regard to race, class and gender. In particular, recent feminist analyses of race have explored the inclusion and exclusion of certain groups from formal scholarship, and the distortions and incomplete information which result (Andersen and Collins 1992). Yet the notion that age is just such a powerful agent in processes of inclusion and exclusion has been oddly missing; it seems that just as traditional malestream scholars have difficulty in considering, let alone accepting, the notion that their system of knowledge excludes female perspectives, so too have feminist scholars who easily apply such insights to divisions of race and class resisted the claim that age can function as a selective filter on the social world.

The preoccupation of this chapter has been with the predominant way in which older women have been constructed and viewed from a social problems perspective, and with the lack of balance which emerges as such a process gains pace in feminist and gerontological literature. By reflecting genuine problems and difficulties in the absence of equally genuine capacities and strengths, we run the risk of re-inventing and reinforcing a self-concept and a societal concept of old women as a dependent group with little to offer society and much to demand. It does not take a large intellectual leap to consider some of the consequences of such a creation, particularly with the plight of 'welfare mothers' in the United States as an example.

The argument would remain incomplete, however, without some attempt at a more detailed explanation of the emergence of the 'problem of old women'. The 'problem' is a multifaceted one; what is offered by way of explanation is thus not one but four explanations, each in its own way true, each more compelling in convergence than in isolation.

The first, most obvious and most quickly dealt with explanation is that there is more than an element of truth in the construction – old women really do have a number of problems.

The second, and perhaps most powerful explanation, may be found in intellectual history. The study of old women emerged at the co-incidence of social gerontology and women's studies, both of which have a traditional concern with social problems and the social construc-tion of disadvantage. It is hardly surprising that those social scientists interested in both social gerontology and feminism would be preoccu-pied with questions of inequality and social disadvantage as they impact on old women. Their intellectual history predisposed a focus on what was wrong with older women – how they were socially disadvan-taged and what could be done to correct that disadvantage.

Women's studies more generally quickly moved beyond a stage whereby women's position is understood in relation to men; the so-called androgynous phase referred to by Eisenstein (1984). Yet while the 1970s and 1980s in 'mainstream' women's studies were charac-terised by a growing interest in women-centred issues such as house-work, motherhood, incest and so forth, there was no equivalent shift in work on gender and ageing. In the 1990s debates rage at a theoretical level concerning the politics of difference versus the politics of equality, but the field of gender and ageing remains relatively untouched.

It has been argued that the sociological preoccupation with paid pro-ductive work (which dates from the founding fathers of the discipline) led to a theoretical incapacity to successfully interrogate questions of both gender and age as these were groups outside the paid work force (Arber and Ginn 1991a, Roberts 1981, Stacey and Thorne 1985). So too it can be argued that similar difficulties emerged in relation to the feminist preoccupation with women's reproductive and sexual func-tions. Old women, culturally divorced from paid productive labour, reproductive labour or sexual services, could not be easily incorpo-rated into any feminist framework – be it Marxist, socialist or radical in orientation. It is thus perhaps not surprising that our understanding and analysis of old women should 'stall' at the more traditional level of a preoccupation with social problems and the social construction of inequality.

We are only now seeing some coherent moves beyond this position. Calasanti and her colleagues (Calasanti 1993a, 1993b, Calasanti and Zajicek 1993), for example, have begun to develop a feminist perspec-tive on old age which incorporates differences associated with the intertwinings of class, race and gender into the conceptual analysis itself. Yet even in these more sophisticated accounts, a resistance to age as a similar source of bias is evident. In the same special journal issue on socialist feminist approaches to ageing in which this work by

Calasanti and her colleagues was published, Hendricks argues that to apply a feminist perspective to the study of ageing means that all findings 'must be closely scrutinised for any possible "centredness" – whether this be "male bias, class bias, or racial/ethnic bias"' (1993).[8] While this list is not held by its author to be complete, the failure to include age as a source of potential 'centredness' is quite striking in a piece on the relativity of gender in ageing research.

A third explanation emerges from methodological limitations inherent in much of the quantitative work underpinning the gerontological literature. A decade ago Hess observed that 'most gerontologists were slow to realise that this young–old distinction was in most respects a gender difference' (1985: 320). I would argue that the confusion of age- and sex-based distinctions continues to adversely affect analytic work in this area. The high correlations among age, sex, disability and marital status alone confound many bi-variate analyses, and there is a scarcity of theoretically informed (particularly informed by feminist theory) multivariate analysis in this literature. Where multivariate work has been undertaken, sex is frequently taken into account as 'just another variable'. Thus, when the effects of variables such as lower income, greater disability, better social support, widowhood and extreme old age are taken into account we find reports that sex does not account for any additional variance (Edwards and Klemmack 1973, Leonard 1981). Yet it is exactly these differences – some socially constructed, some biologically – which constitute the meaning of the categories male and female. The fact that the experience of being old and female is one characterised by lower income, greater disability, better social support, higher social participation, greater continuities, widowhood and extreme old age, or in other words some coherent sense of what it means to be old and female as distinct from old and male, somehow fades into invisibility in such multivariate analyses.

Finally, and in a sense underlying much of what has gone before, we may look for explanations in the standpoint from which much gerontological and feminist research has been undertaken. In some odd way, social gerontology and the policy analysis work associated with it, even that undertaken from a feminist perspective, has failed to fully escape from a male, midlife standpoint.

Social gerontologists cannot sensibly be accused of gerontophobia – the charge that Arber and Ginn (1991a) laid against sociology in pointing to its failure as a discipline to engage with the later stages of the life cycle, and which others have laid against feminism for similar failures (Allen 1988, Russell 1987, Reinharz 1986). Nor are those feminists who

[8] An issue of the *Journal of Aging Studies* (1993, vol. 7, no. 2) is devoted to this topic.

choose to work on questions of old age reasonable targets for that criticism. Social gerontologists are, however, subject to dominant paradigms and high- and low-status areas of interest within their discipline, just as are political scientists (political theory versus local government) or economists (econometricians versus health economists). In social gerontology, as in sociology, work on public sphere issues (retirement, income security etc.) retains more prestige than that on the private sphere (friendship networks, the informal economy). Ironically, perhaps, some would classify social gerontology in its entirety as something of an intellectual ghetto for these very same reasons.

The arguments made in this chapter may be seen to vary in the intensity with which they can be applied to particular sub-fields within gerontology. Women's superior network strength is generally well recognised; the advantages which that might confer in transitions such as retirement are only just beginning to be recognised. While social gerontologists have successfully stepped outside certain disciplinary traditions in terms of their substantive preoccupation with a group who are by and large excluded from the public sphere, they have yet remained in some senses implicitly embedded in those intellectual histories.

Conclusion

In 1987 Dorothy Smith wrote of the 'peculiar eclipsing' of women in academic discourse. In some curious way there has been a peculiar eclipsing of old women as old women in much of the work undertaken to date. It is the argument of this chapter that the study of old women has been defined by a preoccupation with male and midlife problems and perspectives. A moment's reflection will reveal that it is certainly the case that we tend to refer to gender differences most often in terms of women's difference – women live longer, are higher users of prescription drugs, have higher rates of institutional care and so on. We do not generally refer to men living shorter lives, being lower users of prescription drugs, or having lower rates of institutional care.

This of itself is not important. The comparisons are valid in either direction. It becomes an issue in my view when the orientation of the research – the problems posed, the research strategies employed, and the solutions proposed – reflect that presumption of men as the dominant group. Compare, as another example, the amount of research done on the discontinuities associated with moving out of the paid work force in old age (a predominantly male experience) with that on the continuities which women experience by virtue of not leaving the paid work force.

If we wish to account for women's greater longevity we may need to examine, for example, the things that women do and that men do not do, in addition to the more traditional approach of focusing on things that women do not do (or do less of) in comparison to men – such as working in dangerous physical environments, smoking and drinking.[9]

I have in mind a number of things which we already know about old women, as well as some which we as yet do not know. These are characteristics such as readily providing and receiving social and emotional support, and engaging in a more complex and often diffuse range of activities and responsibilities throughout the life cycle. There is also the frequent cultivation of interests and activities which 'fit' with the competing demands of other activities and responsibilities, and are thus more amenable to the processes of selection and compensation which have been recognised in contemporary psychological literature as critical elements in successful ageing (Baltes and Baltes 1990).

Disabled feminists have recently initiated an autocritique of the feminist literature on caring, pointing to its preoccupation with the needs and perspectives of carers, to the virtual exclusion of those being cared for (Graham 1993, Morris 1993a). It is possible to argue, in a similar vein, that there is a need to recognise the ageism and to some lesser extent the androcentrism which continues to inflect our understanding of the problems, and the solutions, relevant to the study of gender and ageing.

We have come, in a sense, full circle to a more general version of points raised throughout this chapter. There is a need to focus not only on how women differ from men, but what is unique about them. On not only what their problems and disadvantages are, but on what they do well, and on what they can, and do, contribute.

---

[9] While the frequency of smoking and drinking among women has been increasing in recent years, these patterns are not generally applicable to the current and previous generations of older women whose lifestyles and experiences form the basis of the currently observed differentials in longevity between men and women.

CHAPTER 8

The Gordian Knot: Defining Outcomes in Aged Care

Introduction

We have now seen some 30 years of preoccupation with outcome measurement among policy analysts and social planners. From the rise of the social indicators movement in the 1960s, through the emerging preoccupation with program evaluation in the 1970s, and on to the performance indicators of the 1980s, the need to identify the outcomes of policy interventions has been ubiquitous. In 1966 Avedis Donabedian divided the measurement of quality of care into the three domains of structure, process and outcome, and in a remarkably short period of time it emerged that outcome was the greatest of the three.

In the 1970s and 1980s there was a growing demand for health and welfare services in a context of increasing concern over escalating public expenditure. Within this general framework the need to establish program effectiveness and efficiency rapidly became the accepted wisdom. The social indicators movement was one of the earliest manifestations of the trend towards improving the capacity to demonstrate the effectiveness of public programs.

In March 1966 the President of the United States directed the Secretary of Health, Education and Welfare 'to search for ways to improve the Nation's ability to chart its social progress'. In 1969 the resulting Panel on Social Indicators, co-chaired by Daniel Bell and Alice M. Rivlin, produced a report on the social condition of the nation, the introduction of which makes an eloquent statement of the need for 'social', as well as economic indicators, in a context where this eminent panel of social scientists clearly felt that economic efficiency should not be the only measure of public sector performance (1969: iii, xii–xiii).

In recognition of the difficulty of the task in which they had

147

engaged, the panel elected not to describe the result of their three-year project as a 'Social Report on the Nation', but rather as a step towards the development of one. The letter of transmittal accompanying the report suggests that a first true 'Social Report' might, if appropriate resources were made available, be produced in a further two years. In hindsight the difficulties which we continue to encounter in obtaining good measures of program performance make that estimate appear somewhat optimistic.[1]

In the 1970s program evaluation came of age, and a huge industry and literature developed. The aims and intentions were clear – in the words of one of the leading exponents, Harry P. Hatry (1980: 159), the task was 'to attempt to determine what the effects (impacts) of the program have been over a specific period of time'. The problems were also clear – in Hatry's words again – 'program effects are often unclear, are often ill-defined, and can be quite messy to measure'. Again, the measurement of outcomes was recognised as important; and as literally thousands of subsequent evaluations were to show, difficult.

In the 1990s the concerns with growing demand and fiscal constraint – and the preoccupation with effectiveness and efficiency – which drove these developments in earlier decades, remain relevant, but these are now compounded by new trends. In many developed countries the way in which governments fund and supply services has undergone significant change – a change generally referred to as the shift from the provider to the regulatory state (Day *et al.* 1996, Power 1994).[2] With the emergence of quasi-markets and 'contracting out' as standard strategies in service provision, the accountability of service providers has come under increased scrutiny (Day and Klein 1987). Almost by definition, accountability requires that providers demonstrate that the service has been provided, and provided with due attention to considerations of quality and effectiveness. An even greater emphasis on outcome measurement was inevitable.

In federal and some state government departments, outcome or performance indicators are definitely the statistical fashion statement

---

[1] For useful accounts of the social indicators movement at this time, and the difficulties attendant on measuring program performance, see Gross (1966) and Rivlin (1971).

[2] The move from provision to regulation has occurred in different ways and to different degrees, but some form of privatisation of health and welfare services is recognisable in a number of countries. In Britain it has taken the form of quasi-markets (Le Grand and Bartlett 1993), while in the United States and in Australia the process is more accurately described as one of 'contracting out' (Smith and Lipsky 1993, Fine 1995). Whatever the structure and terminology, as services formerly provided by government are increasingly provided by the private-for-profit or not-for-profit sectors, systems of regulation and accountability gain considerably in importance.

of the 1990s.[3] In 1995 the (then) Industry Commission instituted an annual cycle of performance monitoring for the community service sector, a project which made considerable demands on the various agencies responsible for relevant state and national data collections. The Commission encountered a number of difficulties in attempting to meet its charter – the 'state of the art' in available collections was frequently not sufficient to support the required objectives.[4]

There is, however, no hint of emerging disenchantment with the process. Under the Liberal federal government elected in 1996, a National Commission of Audit was established (incorporating and expanding the Industry Commission functions described above). One of the first tasks set for the Commission by Cabinet was a review of the federal government's financial position, with extremely broad terms of reference. The executive summary of the subsequent report adopted as one of its 'common sense principles' the desirability of 'setting up accountability and performance monitoring frameworks against desired outcomes' (1996: vii–ix).

Outcome indicators have achieved the status of a taken for granted good in contemporary social science and policy circles; these days their superiority over process, structure or input measures goes largely unchallenged. While the many advocates of outcome measures would admit that there can be difficulties in both defining and measuring progress against outcome indicators, their desirability remains uncontested.[5] Hoyes *et al.* (1992: 2) start from the premise that 'Performance measurement in social care is bedevilled with theoretical, methodological and practical problems.' Yet while the subject matter of their book analyses the feasibility of measuring such impacts – including a discussion of problems and solutions, successes and failures – the desirability of the end-game remains unchallenged.

Similarly, while the search for 'good' outcome indicators in aged care more generally has arguably met with limited success, the possibility that outcome measures may simply not be particularly appropriate or

---

[3] For recent examples of this preoccupation, see the Victorian government's document *A Guide to Output-based Funding* (H&CS 1994), or the annual Program Performance Statements produced by the (now) Department of Health and Family Services.

[4] There were some concerns expressed about the quality of some of the indicators published in the first report of this project (Industry Commission 1995, Steering Committee for the Review of Commonwealth/State Service Provision 1995, *Report on Government Service Provision*). The difficulties of acquiring and interpreting such data from available databases are, of course, immense. Indeed, the difficulties were such that it did not prove possible to amass sufficient material for a section on aged care services in that first volume. It is, however, intended for inclusion in the next volume.

[5] See, for example, the collection edited by Smith (1996) entitled *Measuring Outcomes in the Public Sector*.

desirable in aged care services has rarely been raised. Researchers and policy analysts continue with the quest for reliable and objective outcome indicators. While the energy and creativity of the process are to be commended, this chapter subjects the task itself to critical scrutiny. In short, it is past time to consider, in popular parlance, whether or not the game is worth the candle.

The problems

In defining outcomes for aged care, one of the key problems derives directly from the nature of the client population and the kinds of services which they require. Caring for frail or disabled older people involves a pastiche of medical, paramedical, pharmaceutical, psychological, social, housekeeping, personal care and accommodation services. The clientele are characterised by multiple morbidities, comprising a complex amalgam of chronic, episodic and acute conditions. Disease trajectories are highly individual and unpredictable, frequently variable on a daily basis, and often degenerative. Mental, psychological and physical problems may interact to produce highly variable manifestations which are not infrequently dependent on the caring environment itself.[6]

Identifying outcome indicators in such a field is not an easy task. Elements of measures developed and employed unproblematically in acute care services are not readily transferable. Rates of recovery or cure, for example, have limited relevance in a chronic care context – they certainly cannot be used as a performance indicator in, for example, nursing home care.

Discharge or length of stay is a common component in various indicators derived for appraising acute health care systems, and in some instances is employed as an indicator in its own right. A reduction in average length of stay in the acute care system implies successful treatment completed in a briefer time period, and hence at less expense and with improved efficiency. It may be necessary or desirable for particular purposes to build in additional indicators – for example, ensuring that recovery occurred or that procedures were completed within the specified length of stay – but in the acute care area this is frequently not a particularly difficult problem. If, for example, post-operative hospitalisation periods are reduced, with no adverse consequences in terms of readmission or death, then an improvement in efficiency has arguably been achieved, and length of stay, in combination with the specified controls, is the appropriate indicator.

---

[6] See, for example, the work of Baltes (1988) and Baltes and Silverberg (1994) discussed in Chapter 10.

Discharge or length of stay have quite different meanings, however, in a chronic care system. What does it mean in the context of a nursing home, as opposed to an acute care hospital, if length of stay is reduced? One response would be to note that there is necessarily a concurrent increase in turnover, and that the number of older persons making use of the service has thus increased. More people served, the same number of beds and the same cost could lead us to a claim of improved efficiency. Another response, less attuned to the use of the concept within an acute care framework, would be to ask just what a reduced length of stay implies? Are residents dying earlier, for example, and what does that say about quality of care? Are they being discharged to fend for themselves under difficult and inappropriate circumstances? Or alternatively, has admission been delayed, so that the period over which care is required is reduced? If admissions are delayed more and more, due to constraints on supply, will a point be reached at which nursing homes are essentially providing palliative care? When this happens, have we perhaps ceased to have a chronic care facility?

At a more conceptual level it becomes clear that the outcomes of aged care services are something of a vexed issue. If it is not cure that we are seeking, what is the alternative? The ultimate outcome for clients in an aged care service system is clearly death. Is it a shortening or a lengthening of the time period until that event which is desired? And how can it be determined whether lengthening or shortening has occurred – that is, how can we go about determining a particular individual's life expectancy? The very nature of the clientele makes such a prediction difficult at the individual level, and impossible for aggregate populations. While we can generate with reasonable utility norms for individuals with specific conditions (say, advanced renal failure), the co-morbidities characteristic of, for example, nursing home residents make such a prediction impossible. There is little comfort for those in search of objective generalisable outcome indicators there.

Nor do the problems associated with outcome measurement remain at the conceptual level. There are political difficulties, in that indicators of good or bad outcomes are not matters for idle academic debate. In contemporary health and welfare systems these are measures of accountability, determining whether appropriate value is gained for the taxpayers' dollar. For the nursing home proprietor who derives most of his or her income from government sources, the capacity to meet the required outcomes at a standard which guarantees continued funding is a matter of some personal interest, and the process by which such indicators are determined is subject to fierce political lobbying and contestation by the relevant industry bodies.

Small wonder if agreement on appropriate indicators becomes something of a vexed issue. To these conceptual and political

problems, however, one must add the practical problems of measurement and monitoring in the real world. While vast strides in technol-
ogy mean that ever-increasing levels of sophistication are possible
in database construction and maintenance, the practicalities of such
systems remains a moot point.

In aged care systems the decentralised and complex nature of the
service system means that the number of players is immense, and the
degree of variability in size, function and available resources considerable. To this must be added the range of data systems already in place,
and the investment in and commitment to those systems which has
developed over time. Even if the conceptual problems were to be overcome, and the political tensions resolved, purely pragmatic difficulties
associated with routine measurement of client outcomes in a diverse
system would remain an issue requiring considerable resources to
resolve.

Problems of politics and pragmatics in data development are hardly
unique to the aged care field. If the conceptual difficulties could be
overcome, then sufficient commitment and resources invested over a
period of time could potentially take care of the rest. But can the lack of
conceptual clarity surrounding the nature of outcomes in aged care
services be overcome in ways which meet the implicit and explicit reasons for wanting outcome measures in the first instance? It is to this
question that the remainder of this chapter is addressed.

Is 'real' outcome measurement possible?

A preoccupation with outcome measurement assumes that 'real' outcome measures do exist. Yet in the case of aged care we have seen that
some difficulties arise in specifying what the agreed outcome is, at least
at a broad conceptual level. Moreover, the distinction between process
and outcome measures is one which has bedevilled the field of program evaluation for decades. Inputs are generally more readily dis-
tinguished, although some components, such as quality of staff, can
appear in several categories of the input/process/outcome type
schemas. Researchers and analysts have, however, attempted to cir-
cumvent these difficulties. One set of strategies can best be summarised
under the rubric of opposing 'care outcomes' to 'cure outcomes', and
a second, more common approach involves reliance on measures of
output where specification of outcomes proves too difficult.

Outcome versus process

The distinction between process and outcome measures of program
performance stems from the 1960s, the trilogy of structure, process

and outcome measures being identified in a seminal article by Avedis Donabedian concerning the appraisal of quality of care in acute medical facilities. Since that time it has become commonplace, and indeed there can be no doubt that the distinction has proved to be a useful one. It is, however, important to appreciate that the distinction is an artificial construct, and one which is heavily context specific.

The point is most easily illustrated with regard to the superficially simple example of national immunisation programs. The process is readily identified as the procedures put in place to administer the vaccine, the outcome as the number of people vaccinated.[7] Alternatively, one may view the number of people vaccinated per day or per month as a process measure, with the outcome measure being the proportion of the target population vaccinated – say, for example, a 95 per cent immunisation rate among teenage girls against rubella. From another perspective, that 95 per cent immunisation rate may become the process measure, and the incidence rate of the disease in the general population over the subsequent years the outcome. And so on.

Clearly, what constitutes a process or an outcome measure in this example is context specific – it depends essentially on the limits which one wishes to draw around the object or program under scrutiny. In the case of nursing care provided to a bed-bound patient, one might argue that appropriate outcome measures would be the presence or absence of pressure sores and some maintenance of muscle tone. Alternatively, a case could be made that these are process measures, while the outcome measures are patient comfort and quality of life. From another perspective (that is, a facility rather than individual level of analysis), a high proportion of bed-bound residents in a residential facility may be regarded as an indicator of poor quality care – but whether this constitutes a process measure (poor nursing practice in failing to transfer patients to chairs etc.) or an outcome measure (resident's loss of physical capacities due to inadequate maintenance and physiotherapy etc.) is a less than clear-cut decision.

The point was made in passing in an earlier chapter – process and outcome are relational rather than absolute constructs. Their utility as a way of conceptualising a research task is not, however, necessarily adversely affected by this fact. The question as to what constitutes a 'real' outcome measure thus loses much of its edge; the answer becomes essentially 'one which is useful for current purposes'. Moreover, as was demonstrated in Chapter 5, it was not necessarily the

[7] At this point, one might argue that this is in effect an output measure, as the distinction between outputs and outcomes has gained increasing salience in recent years. Some discussion of outcomes as opposed to outputs occurs later in this chapter. For present purposes, however, the terms output and outcome could be used interchangeably – regardless of the name, the argument here remains the same.

construct or item itself which determined whether or not we were deal-ing with an outcome measure, but rather the way in which the meas-urement task was approached. In the case of the outcome standards regulatory programs progressively implemented in the Australian res-idential care system from 1987, it was the regulatory process which determined the outcome focus of the activity. Thus, while the stan-dards themselves were broadly based and defined in terms most com-monly associated with process measurement (*The dignity of residents will be respected by nursing home staff*), the regulatory process proceeded in terms of the outcomes for residents (Did the residents feel that their dignity had been respected? Did their families?). [8]

Cure versus care

Given that aged care services are generally aimed at caring for people with chronic or continuing disabilities, cure is not an appropriate out-come measure. One logical solution to this dilemma is to attempt to develop outcomes based on 'care' rather than on 'cure'. Within this category two distinct approaches can be identified – the one concerned with objective and specific indicators of good quality care, and the other more akin to subjective measures of quality of life or well-being.

The more specific, objective approach involves the identification of agreed indicators of good quality care. These are well exemplified by the use of sentinel health events – for example, the presence or inci-dence of decubitus ulcers or incontinence. The assumption underlying such an approach is that where there is good quality care, certain clini-cal indicators will have a comparatively low incidence rate; an approach akin to measuring post-operative infection rates in acute hospitals.[9]

This approach has given rise to a variety of scales and indices pur-portedly measuring quality of care, although many of these contain (quite deliberately) a range of items measuring structure and process, as well as those concerned with outcomes.[10] For those unfamiliar with

[8] This point has been made in more detail in Chapter 5 and will not be laboured here.

[9] A complicating factor for those wishing to apply such approaches developed in an acute care context to chronic health care facilities occurs in relation to the use of inci-dence rates. In chronic care facilities, prevalence rates have often been found to be a more appropriate construct (Zimmerman *et al.* 1995). While a methodological rather than conceptual point, it provides a rather nice illustration of the translation errors which can occur (and all too frequently remain undetected) when a method developed on the basis of one set of assumptions is transposed to a related but distinct service delivery field.

[10] See Sainfort *et al.* (1995) for a review of 24 models of quality of care in nursing facilities employing this measurement approach. While not all models in this analysis incorpo-rate outcome indicators (according to the authors' classification), the majority do so.

this literature the approach is well exemplified by the Quality Monitoring System (QMS) developed by Zimmerman and his colleagues (1995). From a preliminary list of 175 quality indicators (QIs) organised into 12 care domains, 30 were ultimately selected on the basis of substantial pretesting and clinical review for use in a multi-state demonstration trial. The project, while still in its developmental stage, reported promising findings pertaining to both validity and accuracy. The twelve domains were as follows:

Accidents
Behavioural and emotional patterns
Clinical management
Cognitive functioning
Elimination and continence
Infection control
Nutrition and eating
Physical functioning
Psychotropic drug use
Quality of life
Sensory function and communication
Skin care

A few examples of the actual quality indicators being employed in this process will serve to complete this brief illustration of the approach. Under the quality of life domain two indicators are employed, relating to the prevalence of daily physical restraints (classified as a process measure) and the prevalence of little or no physical activity (classified as an outcome indicator). Under behavioural and emotional patterns the three indicators are prevalence of problem behaviour towards others (an outcome measure), prevalence of symptoms of depression (an outcome measure) and prevalence of symptoms of depression with no treatment (classified as both an outcome and a process measure).

The strategy has demonstrated utility in quality of care appraisal in American nursing facilities. The question for present purposes, however, is to what extent indicators such as 'the prevalence of little or no physical activity among residents' or indeed 'the prevalence of symptoms of depression' can be said to represent the outcomes of an aged care facility in any meaningful sense of the term.

It is perhaps past time in this discussion to scrutinise exactly what is meant in contemporary discussions by the term 'outcomes'. Over a 30-year period the policy and data contexts have certainly changed the possibility of definitional change should be considered too. Yet there is little evidence of alteration or disagreement.

From Donabedian we have the straightforward offering that outcomes refer to as a 'change in current or future health status that
can be attributed to antecedent health care' (Donabedian, 1980).
Zimmerman *et al.* (1995: 110) suggest that in the case of long-term
care it might be 'more relevant to think in terms of a change in or continuation of health status'. The Australian Health Ministers Advisory
Council defines a health outcome as 'a change in the health of an individual or group of individuals which is attributable to an intervention
or a series of interventions' (AHMAC Sunshine Statement cited in
Eagar (1995: 25)).

There are two basic elements in these definitions. One involves the
notion of change, or in the case of Zimmerman's adaptation with an
eye to chronic care issues, the absence of change. Perhaps one might
summarise the common ground here as concerned with a difference in
health status with regard to that which would have been expected in
the absence of the intervention. This formulation allows us to include
both positive and negative changes, as well as the absence of change, as
potential outcomes of a health intervention. After all, prevention of
deterioration with regard to personal mobility may be quite an important care outcome in a chronic care facility – a change in status is not
necessarily the issue.

The second element evident in each of the definitions is that of attribution – the change (or absence thereof) must be attributable to the
intervention under scrutiny. In order to make that attribution it is necessary to predict with some confidence the likely state of the individual
in the absence of that intervention. As was argued earlier in this chapter, the presence of multiple physical and mental morbidities involving
a mix of episodic, chronic and acute health problems characteristic of a
frail aged clientele makes exactly this kind of prediction difficult.

The extent to which indicators such as 'the prevalence of symptoms
of depression' or of 'little or no physical activity' can be regarded as
attributable to the care provided and hence as some form of outcome
measure is clearly minimal. Depression may indeed be an outcome of
incarceration in a poor quality nursing facility (or indeed, as a result of
admission to a high quality nursing facility). It may equally well result
from a range of other factors to do with the individual, the facility, his
or her wider social network, or various personal or environmental
effects.

Indeed, Sainfort *et al.* (1995) in their meta-analysis of 24 quality of
care studies reported a consistent (albeit counter-intuitive) correlation
between poor quality care and the proportion of qualified staff
employed in nursing facilities. As the proportion of qualified staff
increased, the quality of care rating achieved by the facility was lower.

The explanation lay not in the staff themselves – or for that matter in the quality of care provided by the facility. Rather it lay in the fact that higher proportions of qualified staff were employed in facilities with higher proportions of intensive or high dependency nursing beds, and that despite the risk adjustment weights[11] built into most of the quality measures employed, facilities with a more dependent resident clientele consistently scored lower on various of these 'outcome' indicators. This is not to suggest a generic problem with the inclusion of such items in quality of care studies. It does, however, serve to question whether these approaches can claim to be measuring the outcomes of care.

Quality of life

The other dominant strategy in the health and policy fields has been the development of broadly based measures of quality of life, or, of particular relevance here, what have come to be referred to as 'health-related quality of life' measures. These multi-dimensional indices are intended for use across a range of conditions and in a range of contexts, and are thereby intended to avoid many of the problems of specificity associated with the 'quality indicators' approach described above. There are numerous such instruments. The SF-36 (Ware and Sherbourne 1992) has gained considerable acceptance in Australia in national data collections, but other commonly used measures include the Nottingham Health Profile (Hunt *et al.* 1981) and the Sickness Impact Profile (Bergner *et al.* 1981).[12]

Such indices have the advantage of greater specificity than more general quality of life measures, allowing a more detailed focus on the domains deemed to be relevant to health and related interventions. At the same time they are more readily generalisable than disease-specific instruments which offer limited utility for a clientele frequently characterised by co-morbidity.[13]

These indices have in general been extensively tested with regard to validity, reliability and cross-cultural applicability. They have been developed and employed by highly respected academics, and form the basis of a plethora of publications in prestigious journals. The question

[11] Statistical adjustment techniques intended to control for confounding factors associated with a preponderance of high dependency residents.

[12] There are a range of instruments, with greater or lesser degrees of specificity and strengths and weaknesses in various domains, which are employed as measures of outcome in a range of health and health-related interventions. For a review of these approaches see Sansoni (1995).

[13] For example, the Arthritis Impact Measurement Scale (Meenan *et al.* 1980).

to be asked here does not concern the legitimacy of the approach, but rather its appropriateness to the study of service use by a frail and disabled aged population.

The literature yields conflicting positions on their utility for this purpose. Eagar (1995: 28) comments with regard to palliative care, for example, that outcomes simply cannot be measured using before and after measures. Nicholas and Sharp (1995), on the other hand, report discernible change using the SF-36 to assess the outcomes of a pain management program for a group with chronic pain, although the average age of this group was 47.5 years. Perhaps more significantly, Nicholas and Sharp comment in this same paper on the limited use of health-related quality of life measures in relation to a 'pain patient population'.

In a comprehensive review of community care interventions aimed at the elderly, Fine and Thompson (1995) concluded that there was a general lack of consistency concerning the outcomes of such interventions, as indeed there was considerable variation in the ways in which 'outcome' was operationalised. For those studies which employed quality of life type measures, there was some evidence of improved quality of life where intensive levels of support (usually provided under a brokerage model) were employed to assist highly dependent elderly persons. There was some evidence of improved health status. In other studies there are not. The findings on studies exploring lower levels of provision to high-need clients were even less encouraging.

In some ways this latter point is hardly surprising. For people in difficult circumstances a modest amount of help is unlikely to improve their quality of life, be it health-related quality of life or not. But does that mean that there has been no outcome or effect for the clients themselves?

What can we reasonably expect from a before and after study employing a technically respectable health-related quality of life measure in an attempt to determine the outcomes of an aged care service? In instances where a client, or a client and carer, is struggling under difficult circumstances the provision of a well-organised system of home-based care within their financial means could be expected to produce positive results on a before and after measure, particularly if the instrument was administered immediately before the client(s) were assessed for service, and in a relatively short follow-up period. The longer the follow-up period, of course, the more potential for extraneous life events to impact on such measures. The lives of very frail and very elderly people are often redolent with losses of one sort or the other. Loss of friends or family members through death, deteriorating eyesight, hearing, mobility or mental function, a worsening of financial circumstances, the need or perhaps the inability to replace or repair major household items – all of these things can adversely affect scores on health-related quality of life scales in ways which have nothing to do with the system of care provision.

It is, of course, a common problem for the social scientist – people cannot, generally speaking, be examined and tested in isolation from their social context. But here is a study population who is significantly more likely to encounter adverse life events, and significantly less likely to have the resources (physical, mental or material) to deal easily with those adverse circumstances and events.

There are other methodological problems with a before and after design for this population group. A significant proportion of highly dependent aged persons – the group on whom aged care services are increasingly concentrated – are not physically or mentally capable of completing such instruments. Loss from the sample through death or increased incapacity (thereby precluding retention in the sample for post-test measures) presents more than a problem of sample size attrition (often substantial).[14] If those who are dead or who are no longer capable of completing the post-test phase are disproportionately representative of the clients in more difficult circumstances (as seems likely), then projects reporting a comparison of pre- and post-intervention scores will be a more accurate portrayal of the impact of the intervention on those clients who were in more favourable circumstances to begin with.

As social scientists we were raised on the primacy of the experimental method, or as epidemiologists persuaded at an early age of the advantages of cohort studies and case control designs. But I would argue that the nature of the client population under scrutiny here renders the assumptions which underlie the unquestioned supremacy of these methodological approaches less compelling.

What is the potential for matching in preparation for a case control study 100 admissions to a particular aged care facility? Given the variable trajectories and the variable capacities of residents on a day-by-day basis, on which day do we match? If random assignment to control and experimental groups is to be achieved (not a politically possible strategy in Australia, but certainly in the United States some

---

[14] Kane and Kane (1987), in their review of long-term care policies, used this problem of sample attrition as one of the indicators of 'poor quality research' which led them to place less weight on the findings of those research projects in their meta-analysis. While one can sympathise with the methodological principle, one can only speculate on what practical implications such exclusions may have had for their overall findings.

quasi-experimental designs have been successfully employed in various demonstration projects),[15] then quite a sizeable study population will be necessary in order to establish some control over the considerable variations which characterise the client populations.

A group of asthma patients may be readily appraised at the beginning and end of an intervention, test scores on various indicators of severity and medication incorporated into the design, and all with little danger that the number of relevant variables will rapidly exceed the size of the study population. For a highly dependent and frail aged population living at home we have not only indicators of physical and mental capacity (which may fluctuate on a daily basis), but also the domestic environment, the roles played by family and friends in terms of both instrumental and affective support, income, and exposure to key life events. All of this before we attempt to measure the nature of the intervention (necessarily also variable if it is to meet contemporary standards of good quality care as flexible and designed to meet the varied needs of elderly clients).

So far, I have advanced my argument in general conceptual and methodological terms – but it is to the immediacy generated by specific case histories which I now turn. Consider the following three case histories, drawn from a detailed study of a brokerage project undertaken on the south coast of Queensland. The project involved pre- and post-test measures, the collection of both quantitative and qualitative information, and a series of interviews with service providers both within the service itself and from parallel agencies working in conjunction with the brokerage project (Gibson *et al.* 1992).

Case study 1

Mrs B was 72 years old; she suffered severe arthritis, particularly in her hands and knees. She had Meuniere's Disease, and suffered from severe vertigo and falls, both symptoms of the disease which are exacerbated by stress. She was the primary carer for her 70-year-old husband.

Mr B had severe diabetes and kidney failure, and had been in and out of hospital many times over the five years prior to the initial interview with this couple. His diabetes required constant monitoring, and the kidney failure necessitated a regime of body fluid cleansing performed by slowly draining two litres of fluid through a tube into Mr B's peritoneal cavity, then draining away the fluid, with the whole process being repeated at strictly six-hourly intervals.

---

[15] See, for example, the extensive review published by Kane and Kane (1987).

Mrs B had to wear gloves and a face mask for the procedures, and sterilise all components employed, due to the very real risk of peritoneal infection. She found this difficult given the arthritic condition of her hands; the whole process took her two hours. This time-consuming and exacting task had to be performed through the night, consequently Mrs B never had more than six hours of sleep per night, broken into two shifts.

Mr B also required assistance with moving about the house, dressing, eating, showering and toileting. He was almost totally blind and in the early stages of dementia. In the eight months prior to interview his condition had been deteriorating, to the point where he required constant supervision as he would persistently attempt to open the drain bag for his kidneys if left unattended.

Apart from the nursing and personal care which Mrs B provided for her husband, she was also responsible for the housework, meals, shopping and so on. The shopping in particular was difficult as she had to take Mr B with her, and he tended to get out of the car and wander (despite his blindness) if left in the vehicle. There was no assistance from family and friends.

The community options project put in place five hours a week of home help services, some assistance with gardening and home maintenance, blind aids, and three visits a week from a domiciliary nursing agency to help undertake the peritoneal drainage. Moves were also under way to provide in-home respite care once a week while Mrs B went out to do her shopping.

Mrs B described the eight months prior to the involvement of the community options service as 'traumatic' and was very happy with the service provided. She was looking forward to obtaining the in-home respite to allow her to undertake her weekly shopping without having Mr B accompany her, but there was no doubt concerning her gratitude for the assistance being provided. However, by the six-month follow-up interview, Mr B had died.

Case study 2

Mrs D lived alone. At 90 years of age she could walk with the aid of a walking stick, albeit very unsteadily and bent over to one side. She was severely deaf. At the time of the first interview she could not hear the interviewer's knock, and was only eventually made aware of her presence by the interviewer opening the door and yelling at full volume. Although an interview appointment had been made and agreed to by Mrs D, she had no idea of why the interviewer was there and no recollection of the appointment. Due to her deafness, it took the interviewer (fortunately a speech therapist experienced in rehabilitation therapy) some 10 minutes to explain the reason for her presence; communication was achieved by speaking very loudly some 15 centimetres from her left ear.

Mrs D could not shower, eat or dress without assistance. She had difficulty getting to the toilet which was at the back of the house and down two steps. To overcome this problem she used a bucket which she emptied herself once a day. She could move around the house, but could not go out without supervision and assistance. She had no children and little by way of an informal network; she was, however, receiving a substantial amount of formal support – personal care and nursing assistance, delivered meals, home help, and assistance with gardening.

The first interview was successfully completed, albeit with some difficulty. Mrs D denied any knowledge of the community options program providing the package of care which she was receiving, or the co-ordinator who had arranged it and remained in contact with her. She was aware that she was receiving help, but thought it was something to do with the doctor or the church. When the time came for the six-month follow-up interview several attempts to obtain an interview failed. This was in part due to her profound deafness, and in part due to her inability to understand what the interview was about.

Case study 3

Mr and Mrs T were both seriously ill with cancer. Mrs T, the actual client of the brokerage service, was not conscious for most of the interview. While Mrs T was bed-bound, her husband was still mobile, albeit in severe pain as a result of tumours in his spine. Both were on heavy levels of medication. Their daughter had left her job in Brisbane to look after her parents. She had also left her young children in Brisbane in the care of her husband; he had a neurological condition which had progressed to the point where he could no longer work.

The household was receiving quite extensive domiciliary nursing assistance, including three hours of in-home respite twice per week. For a limited period they also received night nursing twice a week.

The daughter was very appreciative of the assistance which she was receiving, but felt that she needed more respite care assistance in order to allow her to continue coping with what was essentially a 24-hours-a-day-seven-days-a-week caring responsibility for two very ill people. She also said that she would like to be able to see her husband and children in Brisbane for two days a week. When she had used hospital-based respite care over Christmas, her mother's condition had deteriorated so seriously that it had taken several weeks to stabilise her condition when she returned home.

Health-related quality of life?

In the context of specific case studies such as these, it is not difficult to see that reliance on before and after measures, whether they be of quality of life, health-related quality of life, or morale scales, are unlikely to provide a reliable indication of the outcomes of the brokerage intervention for the individuals involved. The circumstances with which these individuals are confronted are well outside the realm of everyday life experiences. They are in the majority of cases perfectly capable of expressing appreciation for or satisfaction with a service or assistance, but to expect such an intervention to significantly affect quality of life (health-related or not) or morale scores in such circumstances is both inappropriate and unrealistic. Assistance may indeed be expected to help a woman caring for two parents dying from painful cancers, living away from her young children and ill husband to cope with her situation. It is also likely to be recognised by the recipient as providing support – but it is less than likely to lead any reasonable person to a recognisable improvement on a health-related quality of life scale over, for example, a six-month period.

Finally, periods of severe stress simply do not always lend themselves to reliable client reports. The point is well illustrated by the words of another client of the community options project, who was reflecting during her first interview (on becoming a client of the service) how the package of care which she was receiving had come to be decided:

> I wasn't coping because I had been in hospital for the best part of a year, and then looked after by my daughter in Melbourne. When I came back I didn't know what was which . . . I think my daughter took it out of my hands really. I've got it all conglomerated in my mind. There were so many people involved. I can't remember. Perhaps I wasn't thinking properly then. My dog died and that was very sad.

Outcome versus importance

All of this is not to suggest that there are not important things to be measured in programs which serve severely disabled frail older people. Satisfaction with care, an improved sense of being able to cope, or simply having access to one or two nights a week of unbroken sleep can all be critical indicators of the value of such a program to individual clients at particular points in time. For one 70-year-old carer 'Knowing they're there is a comfort. Just to know I can call on them.' It is simply that outcomes – measures which have high reliability and can be administered in test–retest situations, or routinely collected through government statistical collections – may not be the best way to go in picking up the impacts of a service for people in these kinds of circumstances. We may be able to measure outcomes for such programs, but we may not be measuring what is important.

Outcome versus output

It has become quite common in recent government reports in Australia and elsewhere to cite the importance of a client rather than a program focus, and an emphasis on accountability via outcomes rather than inputs. In these same reports the difficulty of gathering such information is often recognised. Quite commonly, outputs are described not only as of value in their own right, but also as an acceptable interim alternative indicator while the still elusive outcome measures are developed and incorporated into national data systems.

Such a strategy is quite exemplary. While governments generally know what their expenditure is on a particular program, the development of data and administrative systems which allow the number of units of a service to be reported, whether these be hours of nursing care, respite bed days utilised, or meals delivered, are obviously an important component in maintaining a reasonable level of accountability. Where public money is being spent it seems perfectly reasonable that an agency, whether government run, or part of the voluntary or private-for-profit sectors, might be expected to report on the quantity of service provided for the resources utilised. It is when the outcomes of, for example, 50 hours of domiciliary nursing for a particular client become the focus of investigation that many of the difficulties discussed above come into force.

Quality or outcomes?

It has been argued that despite their intrinsic appeal in many fields, outcomes may have less to offer for those concerned with chronic health care services in general, and aged care in particular, than they do in fields such as acute health care and education. In both acute health care and education the concept of what constitutes an appropriate outcome, while not necessarily a simple set of issues, poses far fewer problems for those attempting to define outcomes for a care system aimed at the very dependent frail aged.

The outcome movement in its contemporary form is being heavily driven by national governments in pursuit of systems of accountability under conditions where they are no longer involved in direct provision. Their role in regulation and accountability is thus a more central function, and in terms of their responsibility to the public, a critical one. National statistics on the outcomes of our health and welfare systems are certainly one way of attempting to demonstrate the effectiveness and appropriateness of those systems to the general public, and to the various lobby groups and interest groups (including the political opposition of the day) that public money is being spent faithfully, wisely and well.

As we have seen, however, the extent to which such outcomes can be appropriately defined and measured with regard to aged care is open to question. While accountability has become almost an explanation sufficient to itself, the question of what is truly expected of outcome measurement in aged care – that is, apart from its fashionable nature, what it is we are actually trying to achieve – is one perhaps worthy of more detailed consideration.

In any regulatory system there is the question as to whether the function or orientation is one of maintaining or improving quality (an educative function) or one of policing (a punitive function). While a punitive system aimed at policing miscreants may be best served by concrete objective non-debatable outcome measures, the aims of an enlightened aged care system should surely be more directed towards improvements in quality of care. In the context of a high quality national aged care system, the likelihood that inappropriate care will remain unnoticed and unrebuked diminishes substantially. In the context of a national system of care which provides an adequate level of supply so that people are not forced to accept poor quality or inadequate services as an alternative to no assistance at all, we will be less likely to find frail aged persons using poor quality or inadequate services.

It is my contention that while the pursuit of high quality care will inevitably involve the pursuit of better outcomes (and processes and inputs, as well as adequacy and appropriateness of services), it will not necessarily be displayed in terms of aggregate collections of 'hard' objective indicators. Until we can persuade the Treasuries and Finance departments of the world that good outcomes for frail aged people are not necessarily going to be demonstrated by outcome indicators, we remain in some danger of the more measurable driving out of the more important. And perhaps even more dangerously, the corollary – that if it is not readily measurable in this way, then it cannot really be of importance.

CHAPTER 9

Whose Rights? Whose Responsibility?

Introduction

As we saw in Chapter 6 the rights of aged persons, particularly those in residential care, emerged as a critical issue in the reform of the Australian aged care system during the late 1980s. Elsewhere, of course, they had been an issue of concern for some time; user rights having been an important component of the American residential program, for example, for two decades. Yet while residents' rights have been the subject of much public concern, they have rarely been the subject of critical scrutiny. In the aged care context an attack on residents' rights is virtually a secular heresy, to be expected from the occasional poorly informed or ill-motivated nursing home proprietor, but not an appropriate topic for academic debate.

Some critical attention has been directed towards the *viability* of implementing user rights models in the case of an extremely dependent population, but virtually none has been directed towards the *desirability* of doing so. Yet the classical theories of rights are predicated on assumptions of human rationality and human agency which are frequently lacking in the case of extremely frail older people. In the first section of this chapter, I examine the rationale underlying this emphasis on aged persons' rights. Why such an emphasis on residents' rights? And what is actually meant by rights in that context? In the second section, I explore the contributions of political and moral philosophers on theories of rights, to identify specific lessons of relevance to aged care. In the third section the adequacy of rights per se to the task at hand is

166

subjected to critical scrutiny. The final section distinguishes between the rhetorical and practical utilities of a rights-based strategy.

Why residents' rights?

In 1988 the Australian government commissioned a consultancy to identify the major rights issues in residential care, a process involving extensive community consultation via public meetings, calls for written responses, a national phone-in and two major reports.[1] Neither was this the first indication of such an interest; as was outlined in Chapter 6, references to residents' rights may be found in reports and inquiries spanning the last decade. The United States has a longer history of residents' rights; advocacy services, ombudsmen and community visitors schemes date in some states from the 1960s, and continue to be viewed as an important component of the aged care system. On the other hand, such strategies have not played a central role in the United Kingdom.[2]

The question as to why residents' rights emerge as a policy agenda item at a particular time in a particular context is not central to my argument. In passing, at least a partial explanation may be constructed in terms of cultural and political specificities. The United States has a long-established, active consumer rights movement. It has a health care system with a large private sector and a tradition of litigation. Scandals in the nursing home industry have been plentiful (Mendelson 1974). Taken together, these elements provide a rich context for an active aged rights movement. Conversely, Australia has a younger, less experienced and less well-resourced consumer movement, a large public sector-funded health care system, and virtually no history of resort to litigation, although several nursing home scandals were revealed during the 1980s. Britain is different yet again. The nursing home industry is heavily publicly funded, there is again a lack of frequent recourse to litigation characteristic of the United States; the consumer movement would appear to have historically focused its energies on advocacy at the policy-making level (viz. Aged Concern) rather than on user rights strategies at the grassroots level.[3]

The central preoccupation of this section is with why residents' rights have gained currency as a self-evident good in countries with

---

[1] For the final report of this process see Ronalds *et al*. (1989).

[2] The subject has, of course, been one of increasing interest in the United Kingdom, with various charters emerging across a broad range of contexts. For a recent review of initiatives with regard to community care, see Thornton and Tozer (1994).

[3] For a review of recent developments concerning consumer-level involvement in community care, see Thornton and Tozer (1994).

such diverse aged care and consumer movement histories. Why do residents' rights deserve our uncritical acceptance? And why does an attack on residents' rights constitute, at least on first consideration, a secular equivalent of heresy?

To address such questions a clearer formulation of what is meant by residents' rights is required. Expressions of what rights should accrue to residents can be found in statements by individual nursing homes, industry associations, academics, professionals and policy-making bodies across different countries. Clearly, views on the nature of residents' rights will vary according to the source. Equally clearly, an adequate starting point for the present task requires some minimal level of claim to represent a consensual view.

A detailed analysis of a variety of such sources is one potential strategy. Arguably, however, it is an unnecessary one for present purposes. I am concerned here not with the specific content of particular rights statements, nor with their applicability in particular national or organisational contexts, but rather with a broad categorisation of these rights. For this purpose it would seem adequate to employ any recent major national statements of what is and should be involved in ensuring residents' rights. The Ronalds Report (1989) to the Australian federal government has the advantages of a relatively recent genesis, and a basis in both extensive local community consultations and the experiences of other nations.

The key principles and recommendations of the Ronalds Report were summarised in Chapter 6. The emphasis of that earlier discussion was, however, on strategies and recommendations and implementation, rather than with the specific nature of the rights to be ensured. It is this latter aspect – the specific nature of the rights to be ensured – that is the subject matter of the present chapter.

Of the six fundamental principles put forward in the introduction to the report, three are predominantly concerned with the specific nature of the rights to be ensured, rather than with the strategies to facilitate the rights process.

- The principle of 'individuality in a communal setting' emphasises the right of individuals to be treated as individuals, while recognising that some conflicts will inevitably emerge between individuals in a communal setting.
- The second principle of 'provision of information' specifies the need for information if residents are to make informed decisions about their own lives.
- The principle of 'consultation and participation' invokes the residents' right to be involved in and consulted over decisions which affect their lives.

A more specific level of analysis aimed at the rights proposed by Ronalds in the Charter of Residents' Rights and Responsibilities reveals a similar thrust – the predominant concerns are with the right to be treated as an individual, with respect and dignity, and the right to make informed decisions on one's own behalf.

The 1987 Nursing Home Reform Amendments enacted by the American Congress demonstrate a similar preoccupation with the rights of the individual. The amendments require each nursing home to protect and promote the rights of each resident, and divide neatly into two types. One set, of less interest here, is concerned with protecting the individual and his or her property (protection of personal funds, protection against Medicaid discrimination, protection regarding abuse and the use of restraints). The second set is concerned with the traditional libertarian rights (rights to self-determination, personal and privacy rights, rights to information, and rights to visits) which are central to this chapter.

These then, are rights in the classic liberal tradition, emphasising human agency, self-assertion, self-determination, freedom of choice – in short the pursuit of individual liberties. They focus on the rights of human beings to make choices and act on their own behalf, to retain their independence of thought and action. They are not legal rights, in the sense that they are rights which exist by virtue of law. Even if not enshrined in the positive law of a particular nation or state, they would still be held to exist. This does not, of course, preclude the use of legal sanctions or a legal framework in an attempt to guarantee them. But it is to argue that they do not have their basis in law per se. It is the concept of rights premised on a commitment to individual liberty which forms the core of current demands for residents' rights.

Few people would choose to argue with such rights. They are, at least intuitively, beyond dispute. The right of residents in nursing homes to make their own decisions where possible, to be treated as individuals, with respect and dignity, to retain privacy, and to access personal information could hardly be said to be controversial. What, then, is the nature of the problem being posed in this chapter? It is on the use of rights, as a concept and a strategy, and their applicability in an extremely frail and dependent population, that I wish to focus critical scrutiny.

These statements of residents' rights could easily be framed in other ways. So, for example, in the language of duty or obligation: nursing home proprietors and staff have an obligation to treat residents as individuals, to allow them to make their own decisions about their life and their care, to allow them privacy and so on. Or alternatively, in the language of goals: it is the goal of this institution to treat its residents as individuals with respect and dignity, to allow them to make their own decisions, and to allow them personal privacy. As propositions, each type of statement – those oriented towards rights, towards duties and towards goals   is concerned with the same basic issues. They all constitute, if you will, basic value statements about what it is or might be to provide good nursing home care to aged residents.

What then are the implications of constructing such values in terms of rights? What is the justification underlying the use of a rights strategy? And what, most significantly in policy terms, are the consequences of employing such a strategy?

These are difficult questions. We can go no further without a clearer definition of what is meant by a right. Such formulations have not been a major preoccupation of those writing and working in the field of residents' rights. They have, however, occupied the minds of political theorists for centuries.

Defining rights

Modern rights theorists frequently used Hohfeld's (1923) account of the ambiguities implicit in the notion of rights as a point of analytic departure. While his formulations were aimed at legal rights, they have been found useful in developing broader theories of human rights (Waldron 1984: 7). In particular, the notion of a *claim right* has particular utility in the current context.

The classic formulation of a claim right contains at least three elements – A (the right holder) has a right X (the object of the right) against B (the person who has the correlational duty). Gewirth (1984: 93) adds a fourth element – A has a right X against B by virtue of Y – including, thereby, the justificatory basis for the right. Such rights may be held against a particular individual or against, in principle, everyone. They may be contingent upon a particular transaction, or they may be held as a fundamental right common to all members of that society. Moreover, as Waldron (1984: 6) notes, the claim right may involve B in a range of activities from not preventing A from engaging in X to positively assisting him or her to do so. 'The class of claim rights therefore includes rights to active assistance, as well as rights to negative freedoms.' This point may gain particular salience in the case of a highly dependent population, where that class of rights usually regarded as rights to negative freedoms (to make one's own decisions, to exercise freedom of choice etc.) may require active facilitation and assistance, rather than the absence of interference.

It is then, to return to our present example, the duty of the nursing home staff to ensure that the dependent residents are treated in certain ways in their daily lives. Are right holders, then, no more than the objects of other persons' duties? If so, then the dependency level or cognitive functioning of the right bearer will not be at issue where the right can be clearly formulated by others (the right not to be physically maltreated), but will remain so where the right involves individual choice (the right to choose a meal). In this latter case, at least, the duty bearer cannot discharge his duty without some degree of assertion by the right bearer, in this instance, the specification of his or her choice.

The capacity to assert individual choice, then, is an additional requirement in the specification of that class of rights involving self-determination and freedom of choice. Moreover, for members of a highly physically dependent group who are nonetheless cognitively capable of making such decisions, it will not be sufficient for the person charged with the appropriate duty to not interfere with the individual's freedom of choice (the usual formulation of a liberty right); there will also have to be active assistance for the right bearer to exercise that right. For those individuals cognitively incapable of such decisions, rights of this kind can clearly not be discharged by those bearing the correlative duty.

Where the capacity to assert individual choice is not at issue in defining the right (the right not to be physically maltreated), the duty bearer may discharge his or her obligation regardless of the physical and cognitive capacities of the right holder. Note that on Hart's classic theory of the relation between a right and a correlative duty, the capacity of the right bearer to choose whether to waive that right is central, and explicitly precludes from consideration as rights any duties which we owe to those incapable of such a waiver, viz. animals and babies (1984). The so-called 'interest' theory of rights, indeed, had its origins in an attempt to extend such analyses to circumstances where the right in question was not subject to waiver, owing either to the nature of the right itself or the capacity of the right holder.

On Hart's formulation the requirement to choose whether to assert the right is not met in the circumstances under discussion. The alternative interest theory appears to offer some advantage as there is no requirement to exercise choice. The right protects an individual's interest (not to be physically abused) and the bearer of the corresponding duty is bound simply to protect that interest.

What then, in this latter formulation, distinguishes a right from a duty? What additional element is at work? There is no doubt that the notion of rights is used to imply a special importance, to confer a certain status on the claims of the right holder; it involves an appeal to an over-riding set of obligations. For example, the special force of rights can be demonstrated by the power they confer on the individual even in the face of conflict with some collectively held social goal. Rights may thus be held to apply to a special category of interests which must be granted some level of priority. Dworkin's famous analysis of rights as 'trumps' captures this representation.

Hart's analysis would suggest that talk of rights in such a context is indeed little more than that – a loosely defined appeal to the language of rights in order to confer power on an important moral obligation. But on the interest theory at least, a duty of the kind described above is indistinguishable from a right. The individual in question is certainly not in a position to press that right, which may nonetheless be held to be a right, and pressed by others on his or her behalf.

The ascription of externally formulated rights to cognitively incompetent individuals, and the necessity to involve a third party in claiming those rights, defines the second stage at which the question of individual assertion emerges.[4] By definition, the general class of claim rights can be claimed. A right is not held at the discretion of the duty holder, but can be asserted by the claimant. For both classes of rights described above – those which involve individual assertion to be identified and those which do not – there is a requirement that the right can be asserted by or on behalf of the individual holding the right.[5]

There is thus a role for a third party who, while not the right bearer, may as regulator or advocate, family member or functionally competent co-resident, assert that right on behalf of a demented or semi-conscious resident. In the absence of such an agent, the absence of any sanction or response if the duty bearer does not meet his or her obligation would render the notion of a right meaningless. The extent to which a right can be effectively claimed even by a cognitively highly competent member of an extremely physically dependent group is taken up in the more detailed examples in the next section. In theory, at least, such a group is in a position to assert a particular right.

The issue of a third party as claimant on behalf of a right bearer is not one which has emerged in the rights literature. More commonly, the third party recognised is that of a beneficiary of a right, as distinct from a right holder and a person owing the correlative duty (Hart 1984; Lyons 1969). The common exemplar in these discussions is indeed that of aged persons. (I have agreed to look after X's aged mother; I owe X a duty to look after his mother; X has a right to expect that I do look after his mother; his mother is a beneficiary of that right but not the holder thereof. Or alternatively, I as nursing home proprietor have agreed to provide care to X's mother; I therefore have a duty to X etc.)

[4] For an elaboration of this argument in relation to the rights of the young, as well as those of the old, see Goodin and Gibson (1997).
[5] See Joel Feinberg (1980) for a discussion of the centrality of notions of claims to those of rights.

Yet I hold that there is no logical basis in these examples from excluding X's mother as a right holder (and some logical advantages in 'dealing direct', as not all older women have sons, many pay their own nursing home bills and so on). The model proposed here, whereby the holder of the right is not necessarily the claimant of that right, is at least a plausible alternative construction, and less obviously dismissive of the competences and capacities of a relatively heterogeneous aged population.

Let us conclude on three summary points. First, the capacity to assert oneself as an independent individual is central to that class of rights which may broadly be described as concerning individual freedom of choice. Second, the capacity to assert that right if the correlative duty is not performed is central to all claim rights, although not necessarily involving the right holder as the active claimant. Third, that the more traditional formulation of the role of a third party in this literature (which separates in similar instances the right holder from the beneficiary of the right), while having utility for particular arguments, does not in any way preclude the separation, where necessary, of the right holder from the claimant of that right.[6]

Rights for the frail aged?

The argument to be considered here contains two elements. The first concerns the extent to which the right to self-determination and choice is of itself viable and desirable in a specific social context – that of very frail aged persons in nursing homes. The second focuses on an implicit and sometimes explicit corollary of the first – that the consequences of self-determination and choice will be improved quality of life among nursing home residents. It should be noted from the outset that the point of contention here is not with whether or not freedom of choice (a choice of food, a choice of room, a choice of activities or whatever) if offered to residents contributes to quality of life – there is ample evidence to show that it does.[7] What is at issue is the nature of the consequences attendant on asserting one's right to choose.

Frail older people are themselves an extremely heterogeneous group. There are individuals who are capable of exercising rights, and who may or may not wish to do so. There are also those who suffer

---

[6] Note that this alternative construction of a third party as claimant or advocate has parallels in other arenas where an individual, although cognitively competent, is not professionally competent, e.g. the use of lawyers to claim or assert legal rights before a court of law.

[7] See, for example, Freytag (1986), Ronalds (1988), The National Citizens' Coalition for Nursing Home Reform (1987) and B. Davies and M. J. Knapp (1981).

from dementia, whose capacity to make meaningful choices and thus to self-determination is seriously impaired, and not infrequently absent. There are others who for reasons of physical frailty and disability may lack either the interest or the capacity to choose or to make decisions. Moreover, all of this will be compounded by the type of decision in question. A demented resident may be quite well placed to make a decision about whether she or he continues to play a game of carpet bowls; she or he may not be so well placed to make a decision concerning the management of her or his financial affairs.

For present purposes it is useful to take two 'ideal types' or 'test categories': that of the physically disabled but mentally alert resident, and that of the physically active but demented resident. First, take the case of a mentally alert but physically disabled resident who wishes to assert her rights on the matter of not having to eat fish, which is always served on Fridays and which she dislikes. The home does not offer routinely a choice of meals. While being fed her meal, the resident tells the personal care assistant that she does not like fish. The personal care assistant, trying to get four residents fed and supervise several others needing assistance, responds by saying that it is good nutrition and the meal for the evening, and continues feeding the fish to her. The resident then refuses to open her mouth for the fish, the remainder of the meal is not consumed.

The personal care assistant may respond in a variety of ways. She may forget about it. She may be annoyed that the resident is being difficult. Or she may decide that the resident has a right to a choice, and arranges with the kitchen for a simple alternative (an egg and cheese salad which can be easily prepared ahead of time by the kitchen staff) to be provided on subsequent Fridays.

In this scenario the personal care assistant would then be fulfilling her duty to facilitate the resident's right to choose. But what of the instances where the matter is ignored or forgotten? Let us assume that the resident then asks to see the director of nursing, and complains about not liking the fish. The director of nursing, supporting the resident's right to choose, organises an alternative meal. She also points out to the personal care assistant in question that she responded inappropriately to the resident. For the subsequent period, the resident must deal with a personal care assistant who is annoyed with her, and who can demonstrate her annoyance in a variety of ways – feeding her a little carelessly, taking the food away before the resident has really finished, not providing back rubs when time is a bit short, or being slow to answer call bells. The physically frail resident is highly dependent on services, many of which are at the discretion of carers, and which are very important to quality of life. The resident may be in a position to assert her rights through contacting a higher authority – the director of nursing, or, if that were unsuccessful, an advocacy service – but she is not in a position to protect those rights in the longer term, owing to her ongoing physical dependence on the very nursing home staff with whose behaviour she is expressing dissatisfaction. If they do not choose to fulfil their duty there is little in real terms that the resident can do about it, other than removal to another nursing home where the same cycle may re-occur.

In the fieldwork associated with the Nursing Home Regulation in Action Project (described in chapters 5 and 6), examples of this kind were observed. One resident, whose call bell had gone unanswered for some time, was asked by another resident: 'They're mad at you, too, huh?' And the vulnerability of very disabled older residents was well illustrated on another occasion in a Chicago nursing home. As I entered a room where a resident lay moaning loudly, a staff member followed immediately on my heels. The resident looked up at us as we entered and cried 'No, No. Please don't hit me'.

How real can residents' rights be in these and related contexts? Only, I would argue, as real as the willingness of the staff member to fulfil the appropriate duty. For people in such circumstances the feasibility of asserting one's rights must be seriously questioned.

What of the second category of resident? What are the circumstances of a demented resident with regard to choice and self-assertion? Again taking a simple dietary example, a resident is observed not to eat his fish. He does not request an alternative. The food may be either taken away uneaten, or the resident may be encouraged to eat, to which he responds by knocking the plate away. The aide in question then has to clean up the resulting mess.

How are the rights of this person to be interpreted? Is he simply not hungry? Does he dislike the fish? Consistent observation by a staff member over time, or perhaps an inquiry to a mentally alert resident who frequently eats with him, could reveal in fact that he never eats the fish, that he is always extremely hungry the morning after the fish meal and so on. It is quite possible to conclude therefore that he does not in fact like fish, and that his right to a choice of food is not being met. If the staff member does not work this out, however, the resident's rights will not be met. An outsider may become involved, a family member may visit during that meal and, knowing that the resident does not like fish, inform the director of nursing. Let us assume that the resident is then offered an alternative meal. After a few months, due to staff changes, this information is lost, and the resident is served fish again. The situation may be corrected again by another chance encounter, or it may not.

The resident may well have a right to an alternative meal; the fact that he is not in a position to communicate the relevant interest, let alone assert that right, will invariably reduce the likelihood that the right will be met. Moreover, if the event has been connected with a complaint, either from a relative or a community visitor or a standards monitor, the resident's vulnerability may be compounded in the ways illustrated by the preceding example.

Our fieldwork on the Nursing Home Regulation in Action Project demonstrated that these issues do not go unnoticed by residents. Residents are concerned that they will be targeted if they complain. They are aware of their own vulnerability.

The two illustrations used in the preceding discussion concern a rel- atively innocuous issue such as food preferences. What if the example were more serious, such that the resident was left lying in a urine- soaked bed? The discomfort for the resident, the associated quality of care issues, the criticism of the staff and management of the nursing home and the potential negative consequences for the resident would all be likely to escalate. This would still constitute a relatively straight- forward case.

More complicated instances are not uncommon in the care of very frail persons resident in nursing homes. Take an example of an 82- year-old resident suffering from dementia who has an intense dislike of restraint. She has, however, developed a balance problem which has resulted in two falls in the past two months. As yet, no serious injury has resulted, but the likelihood of a broken hip or pelvis must be con- sidered if the falls continue.

What are the rights of the resident in this regard? The resident clearly has an interest in freedom of movement; in fact she becomes distressed when restrained. She also has an interest in not having bro- ken bones. Who is in a position to decide what the dominant interest of the resident is – a necessary prerequisite to protecting that interest? Is the right to freedom of movement or the right not to be injured to be accorded priority? An experienced director of nursing may declare that the risk is small compared to the distress associated with restraint. The daughter who has seen and been upset by extensive bruising down her mother's hip and leg may forcefully request the use of restraints for her mother's safety. The director of nursing may then have to consider possible litigation if a subsequent fall results in serious injury. The demented resident still does not want to be restrained. Who is to determine what is in the resident's interest? Will the resi- dent's interests, however determined, be likely to be the ones at issue?

If rights are the strategy by which we protect interests, how useful are they as a concept when the interests of the individual are not clear?

And if the prior concern with rights is the right to freedom of choice, what is their utility in an instance where someone else is making the choice?

These arguments can as easily be applied outside the residential care context. Take the case of an extremely physically dependent man being cared for by his wife. If the domiciliary nurses come three days a week to bathe the husband, and yet both husband and wife would dearly like him to be bathed daily, what are the rights of the couple? Is a daily bath beyond the rights of a frail, disabled older person? If not, what are the options open to the aged couple when the agency responds that they do not have the resources available to provide the service? Or outside of resources, what if the request is that the service be provided in the morning to allow the couple to take an afternoon drive? What rights can be asserted in this situation? If the agency practice is not to schedule visits in this way it simply does not happen. The agency does not opt to meet an obligation of choice. Let us assume that an advocacy service gets involved in this issue. After a significant bloodbath it is agreed that the agency should provide the service in the morning. What is the likelihood that this couple, when their need for assistance increases, will obtain additional help from that agency in a climate of competing demands on quite limited agency resources?

Notions of 'need' dominate the language of community service providers. They must ration their resources, decisions are at their discretionary judgment and quite often difficult to make. It would hardly be surprising if such subjective appraisals favoured 'good' clients; those who contact advocacy and complaints services are unlikely to fall into this category. 'Difficult' clients may well be treated with caution in formal terms, but even so discretionary elements of service provision – the smile, the gentle handling of painful conditions, the extra visit when things are difficult, the extra thinking about the particular complex problem that yields the 'smart idea' about a solution – all of these things are less likely to be provided to those who are difficult or otherwise unappealing clients. And asserting rights is one way to fall into that category, especially when the dominant societal expectations of 'aged person' and 'service recipient' coincide to suggest an 'ideal' or typical client characterised by passivity and gratitude.

Collective assertion of rights

The role of dependent client in the community sector thus shares, at the individual level, some of the difficulties which characterise the frail resident in a nursing home. In one sense, however, the resident may have an advantage over the community client. Many of the issues raised to date pertain to the client as an isolated individual consumer. Yet one of the main lessons from the consumer movement, and one of its major strategies, has been that while any one individual may have limited power as a consumer, aggregations of relatively powerless consumers may significantly affect the actions of the more powerful providers. Nursing home residents by virtue of their physical proximity may be better placed to exploit this strategy.

In nursing homes the classic strategy to empower consumers is by way of residents' committees. Long established in the United States, residents' committees expanded in Australia only in the early 1990s (see Chapter 6). While American evidence suggests that such committees are active and viable mechanisms for providing input into nursing homes, it also demonstrated that many were not in practice. The Australian evidence also suggested that the majority of such committees are indeed ineffectual in the context of the present discussion. Certainly, at the empirical level, the presence of a residents' committee did not significantly increase the likelihood that the facility in question had higher quality care.[8] Given the issues discussed and the ways in which the committees function, this is not surprising; frequently they were more a conduit for the nursing home management to communicate with residents than a channel for complaint and requests for institutional change.

The question which we must ask, however, is to what extent this 'failure' of residents' committees is a problem for residents themselves, or whether it is a failure in terms of the ways in which we have formulated the problem and in its turn the solution. Let us review the expectations that we place on residents' committees.

As a starting point there is the reported concern of a non-government sector management body, whose representative commented that they had hoped the residents' committee would provide information that was useful at a policy level, but that the residents seemed only to be interested in more mundane day-to-day issues (Brown and Halladay 1989). Earlier in this book I commented on the fact that many residents' committees were interested in only 'trivial concerns' – planning the next fete or where to go on next Saturday's outing rather than in more serious issues. What does this say about our notions of residents' rights? What if the rights they choose to exercise are those concerning next week's fete, rather than censuring a bad-tempered staff member? What moral force underlies the position of policy analysts or management bodies in claiming they should focus on the more 'serious' issues – that is the more serious issues from their (dominant) perspective?

---

[8] Braithwaite *et al.* (1993).

Do the residents' rights extend to the right to choose which interest they would assert their rights on? This argument could be recast in terms of 'false consciousness', that residents simply do not realise what is in their best interests. But the question remains as to whether it is appropriate to force that particular role on them.

This is more particularly the case given that the proposed vehicle for the collective assertion of rights, the residents' committee, is itself in an ambiguous position within the nursing home. The committee typically has no formal role within the nursing home management structure. It has no formal right of sanction. It has, in fact, no formal power. The residents' committee is dependent on the director of nursing to take notice of and respond to their suggestions. Her response is discretionary. The residents may choose to involve an advocate or a complaints facility if their complaints are ignored – but to do so leaves the key players on the residents' committee at least potentially vulnerable to the annoyance of nursing home staff and management.

Arguably, these key players are likely to be among the more able aged in the nursing home, and hence somewhat less vulnerable in terms of dependency. However, to act against the nursing home management, perhaps solely or partly on behalf of their even more powerless co-residents, requires them to put their own position at some degree of risk. And to do so presumably in full awareness that their own level of dependency may increase (gradually or acutely) as their own health deteriorates. This then is the relatively powerless protecting the powerless.

Such a situation is exacerbated where the residents' committee has no formal role in either the management structure or the regulatory process. In Australia there is no formal requirement to involve residents' committees in the standards monitoring process at either the inspection or negotiation stages, although the whole standards monitoring process is, as I have noted earlier, heavily resident centred.

The nature of aged care services

The focus of this discussion has been on the client of aged care services, and, I would argue for a chapter on user rights, appropriately so. There are some elements of aged care services themselves, however, which are particularly relevant to the question of consumer rights, and which differentiate aged care services from many of the areas which spawned successful and active consumers' rights movements.

The first of these issues is temporality. The consumer movement has frequently been concerned with issues of either one-off or episodic consumption – the occasional purchase of a commodity such as a washing machine or the regular purchase of items such as powdered milk. Even in the consumer health field the preoccupation has generally been with the management of episodic relationships – the doctor–patient relationship for example. In the case of residential care the service providers against whom one might be asserting one's rights may well be an integral part of one's life for the remainder of that life. The resident may literally live with the consequences of any action taken. For home-based care the difference may be less stark, but the reality of ongoing dependency means that the relationship with caring agencies and their staff will be a continuing one, and future access to services is likely to be influenced by present behaviour.

Second, the pattern of supply and utilisation in residential aged care undermines the potential for consumer action. As Broom notes in relation to general practitioner services, an over-supply of services ensures that consumers have the possibility of changing service providers, but the same over-supply has negative implications for escalating government expenditure (1991: 18). Current policies ensure close to 100 per cent occupancy in Australian nursing homes and hostels, and this tight control over levels of supply necessarily reduces the capacity of residents to 'vote with their feet'; a problem exacerbated by the frequent importance of locality to maintaining regular contact with family and friends, and the documented negative physical and mental health consequences attendant on moving frail older people between institutions. While a change in home-based care provider may not involve quite that degree of upheaval, some elements remain constant. In particular, the rationing of home-based services also means that alternative sources of care are likely to be limited (or non-existent) within the relevant geographic region.

Exit, or even implied exit, is thus a much less salient force in aged care services – the alternative options are simply often not available. This situation is simply compounded by the ongoing nature of the service relationship characteristic of chronic care facilities described above.

Third, there is an issue of relevance to the wider consumer health movement which impacts with particular force in areas such as aged care and disability services. Adequate consumer participation and representation in any arena requires adequate resourcing (Broom 1991). While some provisions have been made with community visitor schemes, advocacy and complaints units, the question of resourcing at, for example, the individual nursing home or community care agency level has not been seriously considered. Yet an adequate and active residents' committee in a nursing home with a very frail resident population (and Australian nursing homes do increasingly have very frail resident populations) may only be possible under an allocation of significant resources by nursing home management.

These qualities inherent in the structure of aged care services, when taken together with the circumstances of the vulnerable client populations discussed earlier in the chapter, lead to the question of where the responsibility for maintaining quality of care should lie. To what extent is an emphasis on residents' rights an attempt to make residents take part of a responsibility which is more appropriately borne by the nursing home proprietor or the director of the service, by the staff as professional providers of care, and by the government as the funding body and regulatory agency? Assuredly, we must recognise the rights of residents and home-based service users to freedom of choice and self-assertion. But whose responsibility is the assertion of those rights? And to what extent do user rights models seek to implement a policy which requires the powerless to police the powerful?

Rights talk, right behaviour

These arguments do not apply only to very frail older people in residential care. Indeed, neither are they limited to the circumstances of frail older people in general. The questioning of the appropriateness of user rights-based models is relevant wherever a highly vulnerable population is involved. As is argued in more detail in the next chapter, vulnerability will be maximised where the individual need for assistance is high, where alternative sources of assistance are limited, and where provision of that assistance is in some way at the discretion of the service provider (Gibson, 1985; Goodin 1985b). The situation of a frail nursing home resident provides an apt exemplar of that model.

Frail aged residents of nursing homes are highly vulnerable. It is indeed that vulnerability which makes the rhetoric of user rights appealing. The classic construction of rights is, after all, to protect the rights of the individual against the generalised good or will of the larger community. While this conception does not translate directly to aged care, there is an emerging sense in which the issue of rights for aged persons has come to revolve around the notion of protecting the interests of the powerless against the potential abuse of the powerful. The central problem emerges when there is an expectation that those interests will be protected by aged persons asserting their rights, when it is their very vulnerability which makes that assertion unlikely.

User rights strategies cannot offer a viable strategy for enforcing the moral obligations or duties held by service providers in the case of highly dependent populations. Yet the rights model does have some undeniable strengths which should undoubtedly be preserved. In discussing the moral and political theory of rights, I drew attention to the potency of rights over the centuries as an ideological strategy, protecting the 'natural rights' of man (*sic*). The claim that 'the aged have rights too' appropriates this strategy to assert a primacy and legitimacy that could never be accomplished by reference to mere duty or obligation. The uncontestable value of the rights strategy lies in its linguistic and ideological appeal, both to the community at large and to the nursing home industry itself. 'Rights talk' is a particularly potent weapon in the battle to achieve better quality of care and better quality of life for those in nursing homes, as indeed for any seriously disabled members of the population.[9] The rights model acts simultaneously to promote the value of the social group (viz. a group worthy of and deserving rights) and the inappropriateness of behaviour which denies those rights.

The potential of the rights strategy can be further recognised if we question why our society has long regarded it as acceptable practice for nursing home residents not to have freedom of choice and self-assertion. Why have the kinds of practices which have persisted been permitted to exist for so long? To argue that these are institutional practices is insufficient. Children's orphanages at the beginning of this century had similar practices – they have not persisted as acceptable patterns of 'care' into the 1990s. Arguably, the issue is intrinsically tied to questions of perceived social value. Lack of choice and lack of control may be more acceptable if the group in question is perceived as being of limited social value. Moreover, breaches of acceptable practice will be more strongly sanctioned where the group in question is a more highly valued one. There is little doubt that old age is not a highly valued life stage in contemporary industrial society. As a consequence, the allocation of additional resources to ensure that a relatively powerless and poorly valued social group will be provided with greater choice and personal freedom becomes less likely. In a highly competitive society, the freedom and independence of frail older people are unlikely to emerge as a highly valued social good.

Further evidence of this point can be gained by considering the sanctions which accrue to breaches of individual freedoms in old age. Consider the frequency with which unnecessary physical restraints have been used on nursing home residents in the United States, in comparison to the proportion of active three year olds who are similarly restrained in child care centres. Who could deny the relative

[9] See Melden (1959)

severity of the public outcry concerning unnecessary restraint of an 86-year-old resident of a nursing home, compared with the instance of a three year old being strapped into a high chair all day?

Conclusion

Any recognition of the power of 'rights talk' for changing societal attitudes and expectations is critical for those concerned to improve the quality of life for aged persons. Rights talk helps to change attitudes in the wider community – and thus to change ideas of what can and should be expected in the care of older relatives and friends. It helps change the attitude of older people themselves, who too often appear willing to settle for much less than they could reasonably expect. It also helps to change the attitudes of those in the industry to what constitutes acceptable codes of practice and standards of behaviour – to what constitutes 'right conduct' in the care of the frail aged.

To the extent that the residents' rights movement has the rhetorical power to modify societal expectations concerning the care of the aged then it is indeed a potent weapon. But we have seen that there are serious limitations imposed by the vulnerability of highly dependent populations. The major danger in the residents' rights movement is encapsulated by this point. The (undeniable) value of user rights strategies lies heavily in their rhetorical, rather than their practical, utility. The capacity for highly dependent people to actually assert their rights in the nursing home or related context is seriously limited. Yet the need to protect those rights is critical. If nursing home policies, practices and regulatory strategies are developed on the assumption that residents can indeed reliably assert such rights in a meaningful way, then they will be proceeding on a premise which is fatally flawed. The rights of residents in nursing homes and those of other dependent groups are indeed worthy of respect and protection – it is not however the responsibility of the relatively powerless to assert them.

CHAPTER 10

The Problem of Dependency: Construction and Reconstruction

Introduction

Dependency and the debates surrounding it have a long and often honourable history, ranging broadly across the fields of social theory and social policy. Dependency has been a particularly ubiquitous presence in the analysis of ageing. This is hardly surprising in a field where the key issues have been retirement and income security, morbidity and mortality rates, disability levels, the use and costs of community services and residential care, the role of informal care, and more broadly defined areas such as quality of life, social integration and 'successful ageing'. Indeed, it is here that the myriad of uses and multiplicity of meanings associated with dependency might be expected to be most keenly felt. I wish to argue, however, this very range of uses can be employed to add clarity rather than confusion to our understanding of the concept 'dependency'. Old age can provide the theorist with a crucible in which the various elements and forms of dependency can be melted down in order to identify an essential conceptual core.

This chapter is structured around three core questions. First, what is the nature of the concept dependency? Second, what is actually meant by reducing dependency in a context where the population under scrutiny is by definition a 'dependent' group? Third, what is really wrong with dependency – or rather, what gives it that unremittingly negative aura?

In this and the final chapter of this book the answers to those questions are used to explore the extent to which current Australian aged care policies (and by implication many of the similar policies being enacted internationally) are accomplishing that veritable icon of aged care policy – 'the reduction of dependency among the aged'.

What is dependency?

While some authors have taken dependency to be a relatively particular and unambiguous concept, a number have recognised various kinds of dependencies. In 1972 Clark published one of the earliest typologies, categorised in terms of the underlying causes of dependency. It separated categories such as developmental dependency, dependency of crisis, non-reciprocal role dependency and neurotic dependency, all more or less associated with the characteristics of the individual under scrutiny.

A decade later Alan Walker (1982) published an influential article on the social construction of dependency, which, while again pointing to the problems associated with lack of consistent usage, introduced and emphasised the role of the social context in the experience of dependency. His five-fold categorisation included life-cycle dependency, physical and psychological dependency, political dependency, economic and financial dependency, and structural dependency.

In the 1990s Nancy Fraser and Linda Gordon (1994a, b) offered another classic contribution to the dependency literature when they pointed to the changing historical and cultural meanings associated with the term, arguing that dependency was an ideological, as well as a social, construct. Their analysis employed four 'registers of meaning' – economic, socio-legal, political and moral or psychological – pertaining to the concept of dependency.

On the basis of such a brief review, we have already identified three levels of analysis for dependency (individual, social and ideological) as well as a number of fields (developmental, psychological, physical, political, economic and structural etc.). Other discussions and debates have raised aspects or elements not included in any of these typologies. These are descriptors and attributes such as 'natural' dependencies, 'legitimate' dependencies, dependency on the family versus dependency on the state and so on. While each of the three categorisations outlined by Clark, Walker, and Fraser and Gordon (and other similar ones) has demonstrated utility for a variety of descriptive and analytic purposes, they certainly do not capture the full range of contexts and uses associated with the term.

Dependency is simply not a one-dimensional concept. Thus, attempts to systematise dependency into several mutually exclusive categories will inevitably fall far short of a comprehensive coverage of the use of the term. This is not necessarily a disadvantage, however. Authors intent on developing a sophisticated theoretical analysis of a particular social construct (Walker on old age; Fraser and Gordon on 'welfare mothers') do not typically start their project with a review of various uses of the term from a range of irrelevant fields; nor would they be well advised to do so. Such analyses take as their point of departure the basic elements of dependency as they have emerged in their particular field; the classificatory scheme is a device for the argument, rather than the subject matter of the analysis itself.

In contrast, my purpose in the first section of this chapter is to focus attention on the diversity of uses associated with the term. The theoretical analysis attempted here requires the leverage provided by a mass of complicated details, rather than the elegant convenience provided by a four- or five-fold categorisation. Indeed, my intention is more illustrative than classificatory – to establish the multi-dimensional nature of the term, and the range of elements and attributes involved in it.

What kind of dependency?

Categories such as economic dependency, political and legal dependency, psychological dependency, emotional dependency, and dependencies arising from mental or physical disabilities are readily recognised as discrete 'kinds' of dependency. They have intuitive appeal, and are the bases for most categorisations in the existing literature. While not consistently recognisable as cause (as is the case with Clark's categorisation) or as content (as is the case for Fraser and Gordon) or even as a mixture of the two (Walker), they broadly define the general areas in which dependency relations are seen to operate.

Economic dependency embraces all forms of reliance for economic support, including dependence on income security payments or on another family member. Political and legal dependencies involve that class of dependencies associated with the absence of legal or political citizenship, such as the right to vote or the right to own property.

Psychological dependency generally refers to inadequate or flawed personality development, but is not limited in its application to the purely psychological. This kind of dependency has also emerged as an important dynamic in the explanation of patterns of entrenched urban poverty in the culture of dependency literature, that is, the failure, exemplified by the black urban 'underclass', to develop and maintain 'normal' patterns of adult economic independence.[1] Emotional dependency, on the other hand, involves the 'normal' patterns of reliance on affective support, such as that provided in spousal, parent–child, or friendship relations.

---

[1] I refer here to the writings of Mead (1992), Moynihan (1973) and Wilson (1987), among others. This literature is discussed later in the chapter.

The final two categories, dependencies arising from mental and physical disabilities, include both dependencies associated with temporary or episodic ill-health, as well as those associated with chronic illness and physical or intellectual handicap.

Dependent on what?

A second dimension concerns the source of support or assistance, put simply, dependency on who or on what. In most analyses, although not in all, dependency is at least implicitly recognised as a relational concept. Dependency on family members or on the state are the more commonly analysed; in much of the relevant literature, dependency appears defined almost exclusively in one or the other (or both) of these terms.

There are, of course, other categories which could come into play here. Dependency on the third or voluntary sector in providing human services is one, as is the support and assistance provided by non-family individuals outside the framework of voluntary organisations. Examples include reliance on a friend or neighbour to deliver shopping or perform errands, and reliance on paid help, for example, on a staff member to remove a bedpan in a nursing home, or reliance on the spontaneous charity of individuals through donations of cash or in kind.

Dependent for what?

Yet a third dimension involves categories of dependency classified in terms of what one is dependent on another for – the nature of the services or assistance being provided. Most of the categories here are relatively straightforward, including being reliant for financial resources, for domestic assistance, for personal care in periods of ill-health or disability, and for emotional and psychological well-being.

One can also be dependent on others to undertake caring responsibilities, however, although this is perhaps less commonly recognised as 'dependency'. Examples would include the mother who relies on a child care centre to undertake the caring role on her behalf for a defined period of the day, or the father who relies on his wife to provide that care. Similarly, you might be dependent on others to provide assistance to an ill or disabled family member, where you are unable, due to other commitments or physical capacity or disinclination, to undertake that care on your own behalf.

In addition, of course, there are a range of arenas where we are dependent on others not to act in particular ways – not to violate our basic human and civil rights, not to abuse us physically or emotionally, not to steal or destroy our homes and possessions, and so on.

Causes of dependency

A fourth way of looking at dependency concerns its causes. Physical and mental disabilities are two obvious potential causes of dependency, as are psychological or emotional inadequacies. Unemployment frequently leads to dependency, but as an inadequate income may induce dependency even among the employed, poverty can thus be listed as a separate (albeit related) causal agent. Employment can itself function as a cause of (non-financial) dependency, as employment responsibilities can render one dependent on others to perform a range of functions, including caring for dependent family members, or ensuring that various domestic tasks are completed.

References to dependency due to caring responsibilities first appeared in the feminist social policy literature, and are well illustrated by the economic dependency of married women caring for young children on a male breadwinner. The point is a more general one, however; caring responsibilities whether they be for children, aged parents, or persons with a disability, all may render the caring individual dependent on a range of financial, domestic or other kinds of assistance in order to continue to provide an adequate level of care and perform the other tasks and functions necessary to his or her survival and well-being.

The life-cycle stage is sometimes cited as a cause of dependency, for example, the dependencies resulting from childhood, adolescence or old age. Dependency may also be a consequence of particular legal and political systems. A legal system may cause dependency by not providing a class of individuals with basic citizenship rights, for example, in the cases of coverture or slavery. Similarly, a political system may not fully endow a class of residents with citizenship rights, such as the so-called 'guest workers' in contemporary Germany.

Attributes of dependency

There are also normatively derived categorisations of dependency. These are less types of dependency than labels (often evaluative) which have frequently been associated (implicitly or explicitly) with the term.

Legitimacy is perhaps the most common such attribute, referring to whether or not the particular dependency is regarded as an acceptable one. This acceptability may be from the perspective of a particular individual, or the broader society or some subset thereof. The legitimate dependencies of old age, for example, might be contrasted by some with the laziness of the deliberately unemployed.

Temporality distinguishes permanent dependencies (people with chronic disabilities, or the long-term unemployed) from those who are linked to temporary circumstances (ill-health or a short period of unemployment) or life phases (childhood).

One may also find reference to 'natural dependencies' that appear to be based in implicit assumptions rather than any more objectively ascertainable criteria. The term is sometimes used in association with life-cycle stages, and with regard to periods of ill-health and disability, as well as with regard to the 'natural dependencies' of the family.

Other aspects of dependency which appear to influence the meanings attached to the term concern the degree of responsibility which attaches to the individual for his or her position. Here we find notions concerning the choices open to the individual (being unemployed in a period of very low unemployment may be a choice in a way in which being unemployed during a period of very high unemployment is not) and the actions and events which led to the current situation. Hence, for example, we have the different public perceptions which are attached to the dependency of AIDS victims who are haemophiliacs, in comparison with those attached to AIDS sufferers who are intravenous drug users.

Lastly, there is the issue of dependency as a relational concept versus that of dependency as an individual attribute. While dependency is most frequently analysed as a relational concept – that is, as involving a dependency on some person or thing external to the individual – in some of the dependency literature it is explicitly viewed as a characteristic internal to the individual him or herself.[2]

Of taxonomies and typologies

The various categories and representations of dependency described here are quite broad ranging, but still are neither exhaustive nor definitive. There are a number of other uses which I have excluded as peripheral to the concerns of this book: dependency in development economics, the drugs of dependence literature and the environmental literature concerning sustainable development. Looking a little more broadly again, there is also the dependency members of any developed society have on the continuing existence of the market for the supply of

---

[2] As in the work of Margret Baltes and Susan Silverberg (1994) in developmental psychology, and that of Moynihan (1973) and Jencks (1992) in the culture of dependency literature, both of which are discussed later in this chapter.

their basic goods and services, and hence for their own continuing existence.

Furthermore, the five dimensions of dependency just described (*What kind of dependency? Dependent on what? Dependent for what? Causes of dependency; Attributes of dependency*), and the categories within those dimensions, are not mutually exclusive. So, for example, economic or financial matters can appear as one of the broad areas of dependency, as one of the 'causes' of dependency, and as one of the forms of assistance which characterise the dependency relationship. And within the 'attributes' of dependency classification, notions of responsibility and blame overlap and impinge on those of legitimacy and 'natural' dependencies.

In fact, far from being mutually exclusive, each of the five dimensions can and does interrelate, combine and recombine in a variety of ways. So, a university student on a government scholarship could be seen to be receiving economic support from the state due to his or her life-cycle stage – we would probably regard such a dependency as for economic support and because of a life-cycle stage. However, a physically disabled student receiving such a scholarship plus government financial assistance with continence aids is not so easily classified. To be sure the second component of financial assistance is still economic support from the government, but the purpose is to allow self-care, and the cause is in part a physical disability, although also due to the life-cycle stage or perhaps the absence of adequate financial family support. When it comes to the broad area within which this dependency relation could be said to operate, there is no clear choice to be made between the physical disability and economic categorisations.

The various dimensions of dependency described do involve some degree of duplication in terms of their categories, but the categories do not always map onto each other in the same way. This means that categories which appear in more than one dimension are not necessarily reducible to each other. For example, where poverty leads to a need for economic assistance it is relatively easy to say that this falls in the economic or financial sphere, and the distinction of 'cause' and 'kind' has little relevance. However, in the case of physical disability leading to a need for economic assistance, or a caring responsibility leading to a need for both economic assistance and help with domestic labour, the distinctions between 'cause' and 'kind' emerge as much more salient.

The aim in this section is not to classify dependencies into one type or the other, but rather to sketch the diversity of the concept, and the complexity. Although the dimensions may not be exhaustive and the categories not mutually exclusive, the discussion serves to illustrate that the topics covered and perspectives brought to bear on the study of dependency are diverse. In attempting to identify core elements which can be employed to examine the capacity of our social policies to reduce dependency among the aged, it is useful to consider at the outset the range of issues involved, the variety of assumptions from which the debate has proceeded, and the diversity of perspectives which have been brought to bear, when the subject of dependency has been aired.

Reducing the dependency of the elderly?

Dependency is a term with a variety of meanings employed in a variety of contexts. While all its uses aren't pertinent in the current context, in this chapter the focus will be a fairly broad one, at least in the initial stages. Yet, this is a book about old age. More specifically, it is a book about old age and the kinds of social policies we employ, and should employ, to assist frail and disabled older people in contemporary society. The desirability of reducing dependency (and promoting independence) among older people is a key touchstone in contemporary international debates on aged care policy. But just what kinds of dependency are we talking about, and in what ways are these various dependencies actually amenable to change?

The answers to these questions can vary according to the way in which we view dependency. In particular, a survey of relevant literatures yields different perspectives on both the question and the likely answers. While dependency has, as we have seen, been a topic of relevance in many fields, those of most direct relevance here are the social welfare, culture of dependency, ageing and disability literatures.

The social welfare literature

The sense in which dependency has been analysed in the broader social welfare literature has generally concerned financial dependency on the state. There has been an assumption that social welfare should adequately protect those experiencing legitimate dependencies in a society, and there has been a concern as to whether such public assistance would mitigate against self-reliance, self-help and family support. Such debates can be traced to the emergence of the British Poor Laws, and can also be found to surround the emergence of social welfare legislation in the United States and Australia. Moreover, the debates continued through the intervening decades to the present day, as exemplified by the case of welfare mothers in the United States.

The argument is in essence one about financial incentives. If the government provides an adequate standard of living without requiring individuals to work, then there will be no incentive to work, and in the attempt to provide for a group of persons with 'legitimate' dependencies a cast of parasitic, publicly dependent people will have been created, and overall levels of dependency thereby increased. The debates and the evidence around this question have been canvassed at length elsewhere, and will not be repeated further here.[3]

Within this tradition, dependency was generally and uncritically assumed to be synonymous with public dependency (i.e. reliance on the state) for purposes of financial support. Dependency could thus be unproblematically 'reduced' by decreasing the numbers of persons reliant on the public sector. In general, it was the 'illegitimate' rather than the legitimate dependencies which should be so reduced, and there was little recognition of the problems inherent in the categorisation of certain dependencies as 'legitimate' and others as 'illegitimate'.[4]

The late 1970s and early 1980s saw the development of a more sophisticated approach to understanding dependency, largely emergent from an essentially British feminist social welfare tradition.[5] The thrust of these analyses was that much social policy presumed a gendered division of labour, such that women's economic dependency on men was both assumed and reinforced by the existing system of social provision. This work consistently presented a different and more differentiated account of dependency to that which had hitherto characterised the social welfare literature. In particular, it drew attention to the existence of dependency within the private as well as the public sphere, and the role played by the family wage system as an underlying cause 'creating' women's dependency. There was also, however, a notable and interesting conflict among feminists as to the way in which women's dependency was 'structured' by the welfare state, and the meaning which attached to that dependency.

The early accounts cited above emphasised the assumed dependency of women inherent in our system of welfare provision – that welfare payments for single mothers, for example, simply assumed that a woman with children would be financially dependent on a man, and that only if there was no man available would the state step in and

---

[3] For early examples see Malthus (1826), Emerson (1841), John Stuart Mill (1848), Herbert Spencer (1894) and Beveridge (1942), more recently Titmuss (1958/1976, 1968), Rein (1970) and Goodin (1988).

[4] There are notable exceptions to these generalisations. Writers such as Richard Titmuss (1958/1976) and subsequently Martin Rein (1970) pointed to the normative assumptions in such analyses, and others such as Goodin (1988: chapter 12) provided explicit recognition that a reduction of (public) dependency so defined was likely to result in an increase in dependency within the family.

[5] See for example the work of David and Land (1983), Land (1978; 1985), McIntosh (1978; 1979), Rose (1981), Tulloch (1984) and Wilson (1977).

support that dependency. This was critically viewed as reinforcing women's dependency both on men and within the family, first by viewing it as a natural and legitimate dependency, and second by providing women with only unattractive and stigmatised forms of support – welfare payments – as an alternative.

These analyses drew on and intermeshed with earlier and contemporaneous feminist analyses of the family which emphasised the ways in which the family was centrally responsible for the continued oppression of women (Barrett 1980: Chapter 6; Barrett and McIntosh 1982/1991; Firestone 1979; Oakley 1974 and Segal 1983). Individualism, isolation in the home, unequal sexual power, responsibility for domestic labour, caring responsibilities, a disadvantaged base from which to engage in the labour market – all of this and more was said to reinforce in both ideological and institutional ways women's dependency both within the family and more broadly within society.

Such analyses were also connected with the emerging construction in the 1980s of welfare as a form of social control – the very structure of the welfare state was viewed as increasing the control exerted over women, and the oppression and dependency experienced by them. Some authors suggested that the form and nature of the state's control over women was directly oppressive (see, for example, Bryson 1983; Cox 1983 and Nelson 1990). In other related accounts the role of the state in requiring, creating and maintaining particular forms of women's dependency largely via their continued oppression within the family is viewed with equal disfavour (Abramovitz 1988; Barrett 1980 and Gordon 1990). In its most negative form, these analysts refer to a virtual shuffle between dependence on the state or dependence on men, with dependency on one or the other emerging as all but unavoidable (Zinn 1984).

While sharing many of these perceptions of the patriarchal welfare state, there have also been the somewhat contradictory propositions put forward by authors such as Carole Pateman (1988) that dependence on the state is frequently preferable to dependence on a man, or Frances Fox Piven's argument that the welfare state has actually led to increased independence for women (1990). Certainly, in the debates that surrounded the introduction of the Child Support Scheme in Australia, women's preference for reliance on the state rather than former husbands or partners (and the greater associated independence) was put forward as an important issue by feminist activists.

These feminist accounts added significant sophistication to the mainstream literature as it existed in the 1970s and 1980s. They focused attention squarely on the reality of dependency within the family, and specifically on women's dependence on men. Dependency within the private sphere became a legitimate object of analysis. Moreover, the movement between spheres – from dependency on a male breadwinner to dependency on the state – was also recognised and with this came at least a tacit recognition that simply transferring dependency from one sphere to another did not necessarily change the fact of that dependency. Finally, feminist writers revealed and critically analysed the normative bases underlying various accounts of dependencies – most particularly notions of naturalness and legitimacy.

Implications for reducing dependency

In applying these analyses to the problem of reducing dependency among frail and disabled older people, the solution to be taken from the earlier analyses in this field could be as simple as reducing the number of aged persons dependent on publicly funded care. Assuming that the need for assistance (i.e. the number of dependent frail and disabled older people) remains constant, this would involve an equivalent increase in dependency within the family, or on privately provided assistance for those in a financial position to adopt that alternative. Such a reduction in public dependency is quite easily accomplished by a reduction in supply, either directly (there will be x fewer nursing home beds) or by tightening eligibility criteria to exclude certain segments of the potential client population (only persons at a particular level of dependency, or those who have limited financial resources, or those who meet both these criteria, need apply). In any case it is only public dependency, not the number of dependent individuals (and certainly not dependency within the family or on privately paid assistance) which is reduced by such strategies.

There is also the question of which of these dependencies (on the state, the family or on privately paid assistance) is most acceptable to the individual. There is, of course, no universal answer to that question, which must involve the preferences and circumstances of individuals. There are, however, some general principles concerning which dependencies are most subjectively acceptable to individuals (what's wrong with dependency?), to which question I return in the third section of this chapter. On the material reviewed to date the total sum of dependency among the aged would appear likely to remain unchanged using strategies derived from the social welfare literature, although the auspices (dependent on whom) and the individual experience of dependency is certainly likely to be influenced by the style and quantity of public provision, and the eligibility criteria which determine access.

The culture of dependency literature

The culture of dependency literature dates from Moynihan's often-cited introduction to his 1973 book on the politics of a guaranteed national income – 'the issue of welfare is the issue of dependency'. Moynihan went on to outline the undesirable personal attributes associated with dependency, and its 'abnormal' status for adults. These ideas have been taken up, developed and modified by a range of writers, but perhaps most notably by Charles Murray (1984), Lawrence Mead (1986), William Julius Wilson (1987) and Christopher Jencks (1992).

Although there is disagreement as to the causal mechanism (with the more conservative writers arguing for biology, psychology and family pathology, and the more liberal for social and economic context) there are nonetheless some generalisable points to be extracted.[6] First, it is in these debates that dependency emerged as a personal attribute, in addition to the older relational sense of being dependent on the state. Second, this dependency was held to be created, in varying ways and to varying extents, by social welfare. Third, there was the notion of blame – these were not persons with a legitimate claim for support, and they were responsible for their own difficulties.

While some of these ideas were taken up in Britain by writers such as Hartley Dean and Peter Taylor-Gooby (1992), this is predominantly an American literature. As such, it combines a number of racial, sexual and social stereotypes surrounding the black urban poor, and particularly black welfare mothers, which did not go unchallenged by American feminist writers (Nelson 1990 and Gordon 1990; 1992).

More recently, under the influence of Nancy Fraser and Barbara Gordon (1994a, b), Frances Fox Piven (1994) and Jacqueline Jones in her book on the history of the American underclasses from the Civil war onward (1992), there has emerged a sustained feminist response to the culture of dependency literature. While no key developments had occurred in the feminist literature on dependency during the 1980s, this more recent (largely American) body of work has gathered momentum and depth since the early 1990s, emphasising not just the gendered and racial nature of the culture of dependency argument, but also the changing meanings attached to dependency, and the ideological components of such debates. Fraser and Gordon's (1994a, b) work offers a good illustration of this literature.

Fraser and Gordon provide a detailed historically based account of

---

[6] For a succinct indication of some of issues and differences of position within this literature, see Fraser and Gordon (1994b: 328–29), a lengthier version may be found in Dean and Taylor-Gooby (1992: chapter 2).

the changing meanings associated with dependency in four 'registers of meaning' (economic, socio-legal, political and moral/psychological). Their argument is that dependency is an ideological term, their concern is to 'dispel the doxa surrounding current US discussions of dependency' (1994b: 310), and their intent is to dislodge the force of the stereotype of 'welfare mothers':

> In current debates, the expression welfare dependency evokes the image of 'the welfare mother', often figured as a young, unmarried black woman (perhaps even a teenager) of uncontrolled sexuality. The power of this image is overdetermined, we contend, since it condenses multiple and often contradictory meanings of dependency. Only by disaggregating those different strands, by unpacking the tacit assumptions and evaluative connotations that underlie them, can we begin to understand, and dislodge, the force of that stereotype (1994b: 311–12).

This article signalled a key development in the dependency literature. It takes account, not only of the different spheres in which dependency operates, but also of the changing historical meanings associated with the term within those spheres. The self-conscious recognition of dependency as an ideological term, and the grounding of that recognition in a detailed historical analysis of linguistic and social-structural change, is another key advance. And of some interest is the inclusion of a specifically moral/psychological register of dependency, incorporating both the culture of dependency literature and a hitherto specifically feminist (or anti-feminist) literature:

> . . . a burgeoning cultural-feminist, post-feminist, and antifeminist self-help and pop-psychology literature [in which] women's dependency was hypostatized as a depth-psychological gender structure: 'women's hidden fear of independence' or 'the wish to be saved' . . . [also] . . . a spate of books about 'codependency', a supposedly prototypically female syndrome of supporting or 'enabling' the dependency of someone else (1994b: 325–26).

A particular usefulness of this incorporation lies in the social problem to which Fraser and Gordon's article is directed – the construction of 'welfare mothers' in contemporary American literature.

Implications for reducing dependency

The culture of dependency literature per se provides us with little leverage for reducing the dependency of frail older people. To the extent that dependency is viewed as an individual characteristic, it is difficult to see how mental and physical frailty are to be avoided in advanced old age. Biology is certainly not deeply amenable to modification at present; although programs on 'healthy ageing' may have some potential impact. Moreover, the frailties of old age are generally seen to have legitimacy and to be unavoidable; the ideology of blame and the negative evaluative stance are thus not present in discussions of the dependency of frail and disabled older people. Fraser and Gordon's analysis of the historical and linguistic shifts associated with dependency are similarly grounded in the negative connotations surrounding the term, and thus of limited usefulness in drawing out potential implications for reducing the dependency of the aged where it is grounded in physical and mental frailty.

There are, however, some potentially useful threads in this debate, which are even more directly articulated in the psychological and ageing literatures (reviewed below). Concerns about the extent to which a system of social provision (in the culture of dependency literature, social welfare) can create dependency within the individual (the creation of a 'dependent' personality) resonate with the notion of a dependency support script pioneered by Margret Baltes (1988) concerning the systems of care which create or increase the dependency of frail elderly people. Concerns about the ideological construction of dependency (a particular class of people, in this case welfare mothers, becoming an icon of dependency) resonate with notions of socially constructed dependency among older people by direct means – exclusion from the work force in the form of mandatory retirement – or indirect means – exclusion from various social responsibilities and activities by societal attitudes as to what is 'appropriate' for older people. Both of these issues are discussed in more detail below.

The psychological literature

The predominantly pop-psychology literature on co-dependency and the Cinderella complex referred to above has some connections to a more established and mainstream academic tradition – that of developmental psychology. In this broader and more academically sound literature, dependence or independence is explicitly an individual trait, and the transition from dependence to independence is part of the naturally occurring developmental process. Dependency is thus a normal trait in the early years of life, and progressively shed through childhood, adolescence and the young adult stage of the life cycle until the normal, mature pattern of independent behaviour is reached.

While originally a model applied to the early and middle stages of the life cycle, interest has recently been extended to the latter years of the life cycle in this literature. Margret Baltes and Susan Silverberg (1994) provide a valuable introduction to this approach in their work on dependency throughout the life cycle. [7]

This approach shares with the more popular psychological work on

---

[7] See also Hockey and James (1993).

co-dependency and the Cinderella complex an assumption that while dependency is normal at the early life-cycle stages, any divergence from these normal and naturally occurring dependencies is pathological. Dependency for adults is thus a negative state. The paradigm was, of course, predominantly and originally concerned with the analysis of development from infancy to adulthood, rather than the reverse process in old age.

The model has been extended, however, in work which specifically focuses on ageing and dependency, to incorporate 'normal' increases in dependency associated with the loss or decline of physical and mental functioning. Baltes and Silverberg argue that acceptance of dependency in old age can represent a positive adaptation strategy, if dependence in some areas is used to protect reduced resources in order to maintain independence in 'key' areas for that individual. Certain levels of dependency can thus be seen as positive (and 'normal') at latter stages of the life cycle.

An interesting correlate of this approach is the potential for the construction of unnecessary dependency via caregiving behaviour – what Baltes refers to as the 'dependency-support script' (Baltes 1988, Baltes and Silverberg 1994). The point at issue here is the psychological creation of dependency, rather than the social or structural construction referred to by earlier writers.[8] Baltes is concerned with the creation or fostering of dependency in individuals as a result of 'overcare', particularly in an institutional context. She warns that in such circumstances the reinforcement of higher than necessary levels of dependency resulting from physical or organic causes may become unnecessarily equated with 'decisional dependency'.

At this point we have undoubtedly moved into an area where the psychological and the gerontological literatures can no longer be usefully separated. But before leaving the developmental psychology literature, some general points should be made. First, developmental psychology uncritically posits natural and therefore positive dependencies at certain stages of the life cycle, with departures from these normal patterns being regarded as pathological. Interestingly for present purposes, it posits certain dependencies as positive in old age – or at least a positive adaptation to the ageing process. Second, the unnecessary creation of dependency through the 'dependency-support script', and certain kinds of dependency such as decisional rather than organic, are regarded as undesirable; this suggests that while certain kinds and levels of dependency are more acceptable than others in old

---

[8] For a discussion of the structural creation of dependency in old age, see Walker (1980; 1982), Townsend (1981) and Gibson (1985). These issues are also discussed later in the chapter.

age they should, wherever possible, be minimised. Dependency remains, therefore, a largely undesirable state. Third, while this perspective starts from the premise that dependency is an individual trait, it is evident in these discussions of the possible creation of dependency through the 'dependency-support script', that at least some elements of dependency are unavoidably relational in character.

Implications for reducing dependency

The idea of the 'dependency-support script' offers direct leverage on the reduction of dependency in old age, although it is specifically concerned with the creation of 'decisional' dependency. If care is provided in ways that reduce the individual's capacity to make decisions, then dependency is created. The way in which care is provided thus becomes an issue. This point, or at least a closely related one, emerges more generally in the ageing literature.

A second important point to arise from this analysis is the notion of positive dependencies – dependencies which allow the individual to remain 'independent' in other key areas of their lives. Here is the first indication that dependency is not necessarily negative, and not necessarily something to be arbitrarily reduced. This conflicts, of course, with the premise on which the present review is based – the search for ways of reducing the dependency of the aged. It creates the possibility, however, of reducing 'negative' dependencies while expanding 'positive' dependencies, an interesting development explored later in the chapter.

The ageing and disability literatures

Not surprisingly, dependency has long been a central issue in the ageing and disability literatures. The predominant usage, however, has been with regard to physical or mental disabilities. Curiously, the debates characteristic of the social welfare literature concerning the creation of economic dependency seemed to have relatively little salience with regard to income security for 'the aged'. This may reflect what a number of commentators have claimed as the sense of legitimacy associated with income support for the aged,[9] or more simply a lack of integration between the two literatures.

It was not until the early 1980s that Alan Walker (1980; 1982) and Peter Townsend (1981) drew attention to the social construction of dependency in old age – by which they meant the way in which patterns

---

[9] See, for example, Kewley (1980: chapters 1, 2) for an account of the notion of 'an earned right' associated with the Australian aged pension, or in the American literature Fraser and Gordon (1994a: 14).

of labour force participation, including mandatory retirement and income security provisions, structured the economic circumstances of old people in contemporary society. Their work focused on dependency in an economic sense, and largely with regard to public dependency. The concept was, however, readily applicable to other areas of dependency.

While Baltes outlined the possible creation of 'decisional' dependency as a result of the caring process, there are broader social, physical and perhaps mental ramifications. In the early 1980s, as was discussed earlier in this book, the Australian system of care was quite heavily reliant on institutions, particularly nursing homes, and lacked flexibility in its home-based care provisions. In 1985 I argued that the system of care at that time was one which created dependency by virtue of the lack of alternatives at less intensive levels of provision (Gibson 1985).

Thus, a combination of the absence of services and perverse financial incentives at the client level led to a situation where even though the care requirements of an individual may have been quite modest, nursing home care was the most obvious solution, with subsequent losses of individual independence in terms of control over one's own life. In addition, the potential for physical and mental decline associated with the non-use of particular capacities (summed up in common parlance as 'use it or lose it') increased the likelihood of a further loss of physical or mental independence.[10]

Probably the most common treatment of dependency in the gerontological and disability literatures has been, however, as a virtual synonym for disability. This is in a sense a specialist usage of the term, although the extent to which it is a characteristic of the individual or of the level of care needed by the individual has remained an unresolved tension.[11] The common measures of functional ability in old age, the so-called ADL (Activities of Daily Living) and IADL (Instrumental Activities of Daily Living) scales, provide an excellent illustration of the interpenetration of the concepts. Used as standard measures of disability, individuals are scored on a set of physical items such as capacity for self-care or ability to climb a flight of stairs, using a set of responses indicating whether the respondent can perform the task without difficulty, with difficulty, only with help or not at all. Level of disability is

---

[10] This argument, when taken at its broadest level, is in fact coterminous with the proposal often implicit in statements about reducing the dependency of older people – that they should be cared for in the home rather than in institutions.

[11] For a review of the use of the term in the gerontological literature, incorporating reference to the range of physical, mental and social attributes which influence dependency among aged persons and a number of key measurement issues, see Rickwood (1994). For a detailed coverage of current debates concerning the definition of disability and related terms, see Madden *et al.* (1995).

thus measured in terms of need for assistance – or dependency on the services of others. In a sense this interpenetration is at the core of the definitional problems surrounding such terms as handicap, impairment and disability in both the ageing and disability fields, and there is no reason to think that such issues will be easily, or even usefully, resolved.[12]

A third area of the ageing and disability literature where dependency and related issues are discussed from a somewhat different perspective is the work on caring. This literature has been heavily influenced by feminist analyses, with a major preoccupation being the 'burden of care', and more generally the amount of unpaid work, carried out by women caring for a range of dependent persons.[13] This work began to emerge at the same time that government policies were pushing for increased home-based care, and a move away from institutional care. The essence of these earlier accounts was that care in the community meant care by the community, care by the community meant care by the family, and care by the family meant care by women (Land 1978).

Here the notion of dependency was explored largely in the private sphere, and largely in terms of its negative impact on the carer. It was a failure of public provision – or an absence of public dependency. Dependency was thus essentially conceptualised as external to the carer, but also experienced by her – it was the dependency of the other (the care recipient) which was the problem. In a later development of this literature, Fraser and Gordon (1994a, b), following Sapiro (1990), argued that the care which women provided for dependent people rendered them in turn vulnerable to dependency (i.e. the need for income support or domestic assistance in a demanding caring role). Dependency continues to be seen as inherently undesirable here, but in this sense it is undesirable not for the primarily dependent person, but for those who carry the 'burden'.

The work on caring was also influenced by researchers from a quite separate background – psychologists operating from within a modified

---

[12] It is at least arguable that one is unlikely to get consistent terminology in a research sense in fields where the politically correct usage continues to evolve. In part, the usage favoured by activists at any point in time is informed by an attempt to avoid negative stereotypes associated with a previous form of dominant usage, and also to draw attention to a particular aspect of their 'case'. While it is possible that current usage has reached a final evolutionary endpoint, and no further changes will occur, this seems unlikely. Note, for example, Morris's (1993b: x) reversion to and argument in favour of the term 'the disabled', in preference to the current emphasis on 'people with disabilities'.

[13] For early examples of this work see Ungerson (1987) and Woerness (1987), and for an overview see Gibson and Allen (1993).

stress paradigm. Again, the key factor is the 'burden of care', but this time with a particular focus on the 'coping capacity' of the individual carer. Dependency is again a characteristic of the care recipient. Only very recently, and it remains to be seen whether there is any influence on the more general field, has the relationship between the person being cared for and the carer been recognised as a key determinate of well-being and coping capacity for both caregiver and care recipient.[14]

In the early 1990s disabled feminist Jenny Morris (1993a, b) launched a strong critique of much of the feminist work on caring, arguing that this work neglected the perspective of old and disabled persons themselves – most of whom, as she pointed out, are ironically enough also women. More generally, she argued – with others such as Brisendon (1989) and Oliver (1990) – for self-determination, empowerment and more specifically the establishment of independent living arrangements for both frail aged and disabled people.

Morris argued that living independently is possible even for severely disabled persons, and leaves the reader in no doubt that independence is not merely to do with not living in an institution. The issue which emerges strongly from her work is the importance of individual control, control over what arrangements and services are required, how they are provided and by whom. In these arguments it is control over the completion of tasks, rather than being able to do them for oneself, which actually defines independence. Here, a different aspect of dependence is emerging, one which heralds a shift in focus on to the nature of the dependency relationship, and the nature of dependency itself. While notions of control and power have recurred in the literatures reviewed up to this point, they have been neither central nor explicit. In much of what follows this question of the nature of dependency, and in particular what constitutes its singularly negative aspect(s), becomes the central tenet of my argument.

Implications for reducing dependency

The ageing and the disability literatures proved to be quite fertile ground for identifying plausible structures and strategies by which dependency might be reduced. It suggests that altering aspects of the social system (and of the system of social provision) may reduce dependency among the aged; that in fact some dependency is socially created. If older people are not required to withdraw from the work force

---

[14] For prototypical examples of this work see Lawton *et al.* (1991) and Pearlin *et al.* (1990). For a critical overview of the field and the argument in favour of including dyadic aspects see Braithwaite (1994).

at a specified age, a certain amount of economic dependency on the state would doubtless disappear. If aged care services were structured in ways which provided the assistance that people needed, and not assistance which they did not need as part of an irreducible 'bundle of care', then the overall quantum of dependency could be reduced, if not the number of dependent people. Moreover, attention can be directed towards the way in which care is provided. An overly controlled environment may promote the 'decisional' dependency deplored by Baltes, just as an over-reliance on physical or chemical restraint may lead to muscle wastage and reduced capacity for both mental and physical self-care.

Dependency as a synonym for disability provides less scope, given that disability per se will continue to exist for the foreseeable future, and given that the problems addressed in this book are those encountered by disabled older people. Nonetheless, there remain some possibilities for reducing the level of disability experienced by older people, both by reducing the number of people affected, or the extent to which they are affected. Health promotion activities, medical and technological advances, and access to high quality rehabilitation services now and in the future hold out some potential direct avenues towards the overall reduction of dependency.

The feminist analyses of the negative consequences encountered by carers as a result of the dependency of the care recipient offer more limited leverage in our quest to explore ways in which the dependency of disabled older people might be reduced. Implicit in their argument is the desire to increase public dependency, thereby reducing dependency within the family, and potentially the 'flow on' or second-order dependency which family carers may experience as a result of their caring roles. In this sense, the expansion of public dependency may arguably be claimed as a way of reducing overall dependency, although not, it must be emphasised, the dependency of frail and disabled people themselves.

The writings concerning the independent living movement provide a clear indication of the association between increased community-based services, rather than institutional care, and the promotion of independence. But it is also the way in which such services are to be provided which is critical. The control of the care recipient over what is provided and by whom is paramount, as is also the need not to be reliant on the unpaid care of family members. Here, it is not the amount of care which is provided which determines dependency, but rather the circumstances under which care is provided, and the level of control held by the 'dependent' person.

Reducing dependency – the potential directions

Each of the literatures reviewed here has contributed some potential strategies for reducing dependency among frail and disabled older people. Broadly, these may be categorised as those concerned with reducing the number of dependent people, those concerned with reducing the level of dependency among dependent people, and those concerned with the transfer of dependency from one sphere to another (most commonly away from the public sphere). While the reduction of dependency among frail older people enjoys apparent universal support at both the personal and political levels, there does appear to be some potential for the rhetoric to fall short of reality. While support for the principle of maximising independence is evident in the international literature and in a range of policy and academic documents, it remains to be seen whether the more specific policy directions now occurring in many countries are consistent with that general principle.

In the concluding chapter of this book, I return to each of the international policy trends discussed in chapter 1, in order to consider their ramifications for decreasing (or perhaps increasing) levels of dependency among frail older people. For the remainder of this chapter however, the focus turns to a related but somewhat different aspect of dependency. We have considered the potential for reducing dependency per se – let us now also consider the potential for reducing the subjective negative experiences associated with dependency.

What's wrong with dependency?

Even if the overall quantum of dependency can be reduced, some dependency must remain. This is particularly the case with regard to frailty and disability in advanced old age, which shows little sign of disappearing regardless of various medical and technological advances. For those who are and must remain dependent on the care of others, the key question becomes what can be done to reduce the negative consequences and attributes of dependency. Just what is it that makes dependency undesirable, and to what extent is undesirability susceptible to change?

One broadly generalisable element evident in most discussions of dependency is that it is, one way or the other, a bad thing. While it is clear that some dependencies are more acceptable than others, there is generally a negative evaluative connotation associated with the use of the term. As a corollary, it is generally held that reducing dependency is by definition a good thing.

Occasional attempts have been made to reclaim dependency as a valued quality, in keeping with moves, for example, towards more 'woman-centred' models of feminist analysis (Pearce 1990). This is hardly, however, a dominant discourse. Even Fraser and Gordon, in arguing that some dependencies are acceptable and should be supported (i.e. AFDC (Aid to Families with Dependent Children) mothers), justify their position by setting up a distinction between 'socially necessary' and 'surplus' dependency (1994b: 23–24). Thus, theirs is a justification of the acceptability of certain unavoidable forms of dependency, rather than an attempt to reclaim dependency per se.

This dominant perspective might best be summarised as the 'maximally reducible model' of dependency, and it characterises almost all of the literature canvassed in one form or the other. There may be disagreement about how to get rid of it – transfer it from public to private, or private to public, restructure it, reinscribe it and so forth – but there is certainly agreement that generally speaking it should be got rid of. But why?

Inevitably, our social world is characterised by certain kinds and levels of dependency and interdependency. Much of it cannot be avoided, and much of it we do not wish to avoid. The question 'what is really wrong with dependency' provides the key to push the boundaries of these debates in a more productive and positive direction.

Dependency in one form or the other is in fact largely ineradicable in society as we know it – and therefore dependency as such is surely not the problem. Contemporary social debates have offered little by way of disagreement with Durkheim's observation that members of an increasingly sophisticated and integrated society will be increasingly dependent on each other – or interdependent if that terminology is preferred.

There is a danger lurking here, however, for the dependency theorist – the all too frequent tendency to accept the rather simplistic position that it is interdependence which is acceptable, and dependency which constitutes the negative face of that 'normal' pattern of social interaction. In fact, the distinction between dependence and interdependence is less important in this context than is often assumed.

There may be some initial intuitive appeal in assuming that interdependency is the acceptable face of dependency, and that where there is some form of mutually beneficial exchange the 'problem' of dependency will not arise. Yet the facts do not really fit this theory. Simply being interdependent does not preclude the possibility that one person is more dependent on the relationship than the other. And if interdependency is confined to those relations where the exchange is of exactly equal magnitude and importance to the two individuals or agents involved, it becomes relevant to such a small proportion of potential interdependencies as to render it of very limited conceptual utility.

At this point it becomes necessary to move along one of two possible paths in analysing what is wrong with dependency. The one to be followed here, in keeping with my preoccupation with the irreducible dependency of the frail aged, concerns the negative aspects of dependency as experienced by the dependent person. An alternative path would pursue the analysis of the negative aspects of dependency from the perspective of the non-dependent, from the community at large or from the perspective of those who must provide care; but that is not the task addressed here.

In fact, policies aimed at reducing the dependency of frail older people do, at least implicitly, adopt the perspective of the dependent, or potentially dependent, older person. Maintaining independence in old age is deemed to be consistent with the desires and expectations of frail older people themselves. If, however, dependency itself cannot be avoided, then the appropriate focus should be to reduce or eradicate those aspects of dependency which make it an undesirable state. Indeed, for those who are and must remain dependent, an emphasis on the reduction of dependency in policy debates inevitably assumes and reinforces the undesirability of the status 'dependent' – and thus as a necessary corollary reinforces further the negative stigma associated with being dependent.

If, as argued above, merely being interdependent is not a sufficient condition to make the circumstances of the 'more dependent' person acceptable, it follows that the question as to what makes dependency undesirable cannot be answered simply in terms of the amount or quantity of assistance exchanged. The relative importance of the exchange to each individual is more critical, and thus it becomes clear that control or power is in fact the central issue. Indeed, power has traditionally been defined in terms of asymmetry – as resting on net ability of one person to withhold rewards from and apply punishments to others.[15]

This is, however, too abstract a level of analysis for present purposes. While notions of a sense of powerlessness and lack of control may help us to understand the subjective experience of dependency and what is undesirable about it, they do not readily convert into an appraisal of potential policy directions. Earlier work has, however, established more specific criteria which underlie the degree of powerlessness

[15] See, for example, Blau (1964: 117–18).

which an individual is likely to experience in particular dependency relations, and which form a useful basis from which to review various policy developments (Gibson 1985; Goodin 1985b). These elements are:

1 The extent to which the dependent individual needs the required service or resource in order to protect his or her interests.
2 The availability of alternative sources of assistance or service.
3 The level of discretion which the resource holder or service provider has in providing the required assistance.

These three criteria define the extent to which the balance of power within a dependency relationship will be asymmetrical. And it is the asymmetry of the dependency, the lack of mutuality, which leads to the potential for exploitation. Drawing on this model, the level of vulnerability will be highest when the dependent person has the greatest need for a service, no alternative source of assistance or extremely limited alternatives, and where the provision of the service is at the discretion of the provider.

If, for example, the services which I require are available at the discretion of a service provider, and if I have no alternatives to that particular service provider, then I am inevitably in a relatively powerless (and hence dependent) position with regard to that provider – whether it be financial, domestic or physical care.[16] If the services which I require are provided by my daughter, and she can choose whether or not to provide that assistance, and no other potential source of help is available to me, I am similarly dependent on her assistance – even if she lives in my house, uses my income and has the complete use of my car. If I am bed-bound in a nursing home, and the personal care assistant on shift does not choose to give me a back rub to prevent bed-sores, or gives it in an unsatisfactory or painful way, then there is little I will be able to do even though she is paid for her services.

At some point the dependency of frail and disabled older people appears unarguable and irreducible. Assistance with mobility, or continence, or bathing, is simply an essential component of the daily routine for those individuals with certain mental or physical frailties or disabilities. But such an understanding rests on the construction of dependency as a characteristic of the individual, rather than in the interplay between that individual and the service provider. It is this

---

[16] This point is most recently exemplified in the work of Jenny Morris, when she analyses a range of possible care situations for disabled persons, emphasising the need for maximising control of those services for the disabled person.

latter construction of dependency which offers the potential, not for the absolute reduction of dependency, but rather for reducing that which renders dependency unpalatable. In the example which follows, the principles outlined above are used to examine, in some detail, a 'case study' of care in a nursing home context – and the extent to which the negative aspects of dependency might be 'maximally reducible'.

Care in a nursing home – a worked example

In taking the case of very frail older people in nursing homes, it would appear that I have taken an example where all three of the specified criteria are inevitably met. The need for assistance is great, the alternatives are tightly circumscribed and, in a variety of ways, the service provided is discretionary. Some basic level of provision will always be met, but the way in which the service is provided, the quality of care, the immediacy of response, the willingness to provide extra help – all of these are and will remain at the discretion of nursing home staff.

It would appear on this basis virtually inevitable that the institutionalised frail aged experience maximum vulnerability to exploitation. Before making that assumption, however, the susceptibility of each of those elements to structural change or modification warrants further scrutiny.

The first determinant of vulnerability, the overall level of need, is largely unresponsive to manipulation at the policy or service provision level. Both high physical and mental dependency levels are characteristic of the population in question, and will by definition remain so. However, as has been noted earlier, individual dependency levels may well be subject to modification via rehabilitation strategies, reality orientation programs and related strategies in dementia care, and generally models of care which do not themselves create further physical or psychological dependency. A culture of good nursing home care which emphasises preventive and rehabilitative strategies will undoubtedly have the capacity to reduce levels of need for certain individuals at certain points during their residence.

The second element in the model was the availability of alternative sources of assistance. Assuming that the residents do require nursing home-level care, what alternatives can be made available? One possibility is that a better resourced and managed home-based care sector could actually provide a viable alternative for many nursing home residents. Some more radical advocacy groups in the United States have argued for the replacement of all nursing home care with home-based services on the grounds that only by abolishing institutional care will the vulnerability to exploitation of the frail aged be reduced.

Unfortunately, some elements of the vulnerability which characterises institutionally based service provision are not absent from
home-based models. If access to home-based care is uncertain, then
the advantage of having an 'alternative' source of care evaporates.
Home-based care may also be more subject to discretionary provision.
If one is occupying a nursing home bed, then one is accessing a full unit
of care, however that may be defined. In home-based care, however,
hours or levels of services may be divided and redivided between
clients, with the client having little control or 'right' to a given level of
care or support. Nonetheless, an extended system of community care
capable of adequately supporting more highly dependent people
would provide one set of alternatives, and a set which, potentially at
least, could reduce the degree of powerlessness experienced by the
client group.

Another possibility is the use of market forces to ensure greater availability of alternatives at the nursing home level; that is, the option to
leave the current facility if the care provided is inappropriate or inadequate. However, there are some problems with this notion of 'market
choice' in the case of a very frail group of consumers (see Chapter 9).
Yet if such a move is known to be a viable alternative then its very availability does reduce the powerlessness of the individual.

For the move to another nursing home (say one of good quality
within the appropriate geographical area) to be viable a certain level of
over-supply is obviously a prerequisite, with subsequent implications
for cost containment. But the alternative, a shortage of vacant beds and
sizeable waiting lists into reasonable quality nursing homes, reduces
(or eradicates) the viability of relocating to another nursing home, and
the vulnerability of the resident increases accordingly.

A third and largely undiscussed policy option is that of increasing
alternative sources of service provision within the nursing home. The
issue of paid help from an alternative employer (not the nursing home)
is obviously quite a vexed one, partly due to equity considerations
among residents, partly to the regulatory considerations with a very
dependent population, and partly due to the conflict potential between
nursing home management and the alternative service provider.
Perhaps more realistically such assistance could come from volunteers
or family members.

Obviously, such assistance will not be available consistently, nor in
most cases, for core elements of the necessary care. However, if a
resident has a regular visit from family members, she or he does not
need to be entirely dependent on nursing home staff for a range of services – picking up a birthday card for a favourite grandchild, getting a
cup of tea or having an extra back rub. The nursing home staff may

provide those services, but the existence of an alternative source makes the resident less vulnerable should they choose not to do so (or be unable to do so). Of course, the vulnerability is reduced more for less immediate activities (getting the birthday card) than for others (getting a cup of tea when you feel like it). But total vulnerability is nonetheless reduced.

The third element in determining levels of vulnerability was that of the degree of discretionary control held by the service provider. Discretion is held to be at a minimum when the entitlement is determined by objective criteria and the nature of the service or benefit cannot be varied. A classic example of a non-discretionary provision is the Australian aged pension – entitlement determined by objective criteria (age and income test), available to all persons who meet those criteria via an automatically issued cheque.

Certainly, there are few parallels here to nursing home care. Private means, public provision and personal characteristics may influence access to a nursing home bed, leading to some level of discretionary control in obtaining access to the service. The key issue, however, is with the nature of the service provided to those already resident. Admittedly, regulatory requirements broadly ensure that residents are provided with beds, food, medication and so forth ('horror stories' and scandals excepted). The adequacy and quality of such provisions are, however, more open to manipulation. This is most marked at the margins, whereby the way in which a service is provided is very much at the discretion of service providers – a call bell answered promptly or not at all, or a kind smile and a brief chat or stony silence while dealing with an isolated resident. Yet, as was argued in the previous chapter, almost by its very nature, the care provided in nursing homes has significant discretionary components. Regulation of the industry or 'rights talk' may effectively reduce the extent to which certain aspects of care are regarded as discretionary, in the sense of determining what is and what is not regarded as acceptable practice. Yet ultimately discretion continues to characterise the recipient–provider relationship in this instance.

Conclusions

The nursing home case study just explored provides a detailed appraisal of how these three elements (need, alternatives and discretion) can be employed as the basis of an analysis to explore the degree of powerlessness likely to be experienced by individuals in various kinds of dependency relationships and in various kinds of service settings. While the case study itself was reasonably specific, the illustration yields a number of elements which are more broadly applicable to aged care – and indeed other service delivery contexts.

This chapter has considered the nature of dependency, the potential for its reduction, and the potential for reducing those aspects of dependency which render it an undesirable and negative state. The reduction of dependency among the aged has become a broad and continuing theme, underpinning many debates and developments in aged care policy. As such, it would seem to provide an appropriate and generalisable base from which to review contemporary trends in aged care policy – it is to that task which I now turn.

CHAPTER 11

New Problems; Old Solutions?

Introduction

This book concludes with a review of the capacity of current trends in aged care policy to support and maximise the independence of frail and disabled older people. While there may not be general agreement that this is an appropriate 'overarching goal' for aged care policies, it has nonetheless become a familiar touchstone in the political and policy rhetoric, and one which emerges in the words of older people in research spanning the decades from Townsend's *The Family Life of Older People* in 1957 to Russell's more recent foray into the ways in which older people themselves construct dependence and independence in their lives (1995). To what extent do the 'new trends' in aged care contribute to maintaining the independence of frail older people? Will our public expenditures support and maximise independence, or construct greater levels of dependency? In the words of the insistently independent old man quoted in the introduction, is public provision still starting out by 'making up their beds' and ending up by 'making up their minds'?

Home-based versus residential care

The shift in favour of providing assistance to frail and disabled older people in their homes is, as we have seen, well established both in Australia and overseas. While the balance between home-based and residential care once showed significant variation in an international context, recent trends are unequivocally in the direction of increasing home-based provision and reducing the level of nursing home care. This trend has generally been held to exemplify the growing recognition of the rights and preferences of elderly people to maintain maximum independence – in a sense, remaining at home has been taken to be synonymous with maintaining independence.

In many ways an opposing position is simply untenable. Remaining in one's own home allows a control of the environment and surroundings (including one's co-residents) which is not possible in a communal living situation. Rearranging the furniture or deciding what one feels like for dinner that night are routine activities for an individual living at home, but may well not be remotely reasonable in a nursing home accommodating 100 people. If adequate and appropriate care is provided at home, then it is highly probable that any given individual would experience a greater degree of independence there than he or she would in an institution, regardless of the quality of care available.

That having been said, there remains room for some caveats and corollaries. Where care in the home is provided it is very often the case that it assumes a large component of family care is also in place. This means, in essence, a shift from dependency on public (or privately purchased) services, towards a mixture of public (or privately purchased) and family provided care. If, as is the case of Australia, we are talking about a largely publicly funded system of provision, then the move from residential to home-based care inevitably also involves a transfer of dependency from the public to the private (family) sphere, with an associated reduction in the extent of public dependency (and the associated costs).

For some individuals, of course, there is no such family care (or to put it another way, private sphere subsidy of the public system) available, and it seems at least plausible that in many cases the individual in that situation will simply manage within the available context. In other words, their overall dependency will be reduced so that fewer of their needs will be met by the public sector, but those needs, rather than being picked up by another system, will simply remain unmet. There will, in other words, be a minimally necessary level of dependency for the individuals involved, and at a societal level a degree of what could only be termed neglect.

Of course, such an endpoint is not necessarily associated with the move from residential to home-based care – it is essentially to do with an inadequate level of provision of such care, or with people whose needs are simply inappropriate to home-based care. It is the case, however, that a home-based system lends itself to inadequate levels of provision to individual clients in a way that nursing homes do not. Modern societies do not consider it reasonable that a nursing home bed, for example, should be shared between two people in the case of scarcity of that form of service. Home-based care, however, lends itself to exactly that apportioning in times of scarcity, as available hours are stretched and divided between those deemed eligible for the service.

Rationing in the nursing home sector occurs in terms of who gains entry. Rationing in home-based care may occur with regard to who obtains the service, in terms of what kind of service and how much of it is obtained, and subsequently in terms of whether or not that service is modified to meet what will frequently be increasing levels of dependency.

Finally, there is the question of the extent to which the unpalatable aspects of dependency are reduced by the broad policy shift from residential to home-based care. As was noted above the dependent individual may have a greater sense of control in the domestic environment than is possible in an institution, always assuming an adequate level of care is available in both. On the other hand, the mixture of dependency on both family and public provision may increase a sense of 'being dependent' if the family must provide the care required, and the frail older person feels they have nothing to offer in return. If there is no alternative to a particular family member providing the required care, then the criteria for maximum dependency – a high level of need, the absence of alternatives and discretion on the part of the family member – are all met. There is no-one to see whether that particular family member turns away when help is needed, or leaves the care recipient unattended, or to take account of the fact that the frail elderly person may not want to be 'too much bother', and therefore simply not ask.

This is by no means to characterise family care as abusive and inadequate – such a reading would be a wilful misunderstanding. Rather, however, it will not do to assume that family care is necessarily adequate and appropriate, particularly in a context when alternatives such as institutional care are not available, and home-based care services are in extremely short supply.

The advantage that home-based care does offer, however, over residential care is the greater plausibility of contracting alternative service providers if the care being provided is inappropriate or of poor quality, or simply not liked. If the personal care attendant provided by the relevant local service is unsatisfactory, a change of care provider is much less disruptive than, for example, a move out of one nursing home to another. In urban regions there is the likelihood that an alternative service may be available, as well as simply an alternative care attendant. Of course, this will not be the case in all regions – and even less likely in rural ones. With the increasing shift towards contracting out now under way in the Australian context (and already more than well under way in countries such as the United Kingdom) the options of an alternative auspice may well be even less plausible on a region-by-region basis.

Assessment and targeting

The emphasis on better assessment and closer targeting of services on those most in need are manifest evidence of contemporary concerns with both cost containment and equity. Taken together, a judicious mix of both targeting and assessment is intended to ensure an effective and efficient system of aged care services.

Assessment is a key element in ensuring both an appropriate level of care to individuals, and preventing inappropriate admissions and the consequent demand-led growth of publicly funded systems. In its absence there is a likelihood that, just as happened in the Australian system in the 1970s and the British system in the 1980s, perverse financial incentives will lead to the rapid (and expensive) expansion of the residential care sector. Of course, direct rationing of public provision (supply) can prevent such an expansion, but in the absence of assessment those admitted will be less likely to be those most in need, and the likelihood of long waiting lists and public pressure to increase supply escalates. We have ample historical evidence for all of this.

The oddity driving these trends appears to be the supply-driven nature of the nursing home industry. 'Build nursing home beds and they will be filled' is the conventional wisdom, and there seems adequate evidence that this is indeed the case. Nursing home occupancy rates ran at essentially 100 per cent in Australia throughout the 'over-supply' years in the 1970s and early 1980s, and long waiting lists abounded. This characteristic also makes the industry an 'investors' dream', particularly where payment for care is essentially government guaranteed.

Given the examples of history it is not difficult to see why control over admission to nursing homes and rationing of what is quite an expensive system of care are a necessary component of contemporary aged care policies. Such a system also has the advantage of reducing the number of people in residential care, with a concurrent increase in those cared for in the community, with the consequences for increased independence (and for increased dependence in some instances) already discussed above.

On the other hand, such a system inevitably reduces the choices open to older people and their families, or in other words the alternatives available to them. If a frail elderly person elects to enter a nursing home, with or without the agreement of their family, it is the assessment team which decides whether or not they are eligible for entry. For those who do not meet the entry criteria (as determined by the assessment team), and who do not have the substantial financial means to purchase what they see as their preferred and required care option on the private market, there is no alternative but to remain in the community – whatever the difficulties or problems which led them to decide on entering institutional care. In this sense at least the emergence of a highly targeted system with fixed and formal systems of eligibility criteria may increase the negative aspects and consequences of dependency as experienced by the frail and disabled aged and their families, in that it may serve to 'enforce' family-based or home-based systems of care against the wishes of the individuals involved.

User rights

The emphasis on consumer rights or user rights is, as we have seen in earlier chapters, closely associated with ideas of independence, choice and control in the aged care literature. Promotion and recognition of user rights emerged as a vehicle to promote better quality care, but also as an attempt to ensure that the nature of that care was more closely attuned to what individual care recipients desired. Residents' committees, advocacy groups, complaints units, resident–proprietor agreements, contracts and charters in their various forms have all emerged as a result of the perceived need for greater responsiveness to the needs and desires of clients of the system and their families.

In a sense, this movement has been directly concerned with modifying the subjective experience of dependency for frail aged and disabled persons. The consumer rights strategies did not seek to reduce the dependency of the consumer per se, but rather to reduce negative consequences for the individual, attacking the powerlessness perceived to be the burden borne by the aged care service recipient. And yet the rights movement per se had little to offer by way of restructuring the system; it is more effective in modifying the rhetoric of aged care than the reality. Asserting rights among very frail and dependent populations is not a particularly viable option; in just those contexts where the assertion of rights proves most necessary, so then are the consequences for the dependent individual likely to prove most uncomfortable.

The 'normal mechanisms' of rights advocates (consumer offices, the legal courts, litigation, negotiation and so forth) have little to offer a very frail and very dependent person who must return to the care of the very person against whom he or she has so recently 'asserted' his or her rights. The pursuit of high quality and responsive care is indeed a desirable end, and one which by providing alternatives and reducing the discretionary components in the system can actively reduce the negative consequences of dependency for frail elderly people. So, for example, if a consequence of 'rights talk' and an emphasis on 'right conduct' for the carers of elderly people ensure that high quality care is a requirement, rather than a discretionary good offered by 'good and caring staff' at the 'better' aged care institutions, so too is the experience of dependency improved for those who due to physical and mental frailty must spend the remainder of their lives in a residential care facility, or maintained at home with the assistance of home-based services.

Regulation and outcomes

The shift towards a greater emphasis on regulation and accountability, on monitoring both the quality and the outcomes of aged care, has not been unrelated to the emergence of the user rights movement described above. It is not immediately clear that such a policy direction has much to do with independence, however, particularly when we think of dependency in terms of the number of people who are dependent, the level of dependency that they experience, the type of care which they require and the source from which they receive that care.

Quality of care may not initially appear to relate to dependency at all. However, when we consider the subjective experience of dependency, quality of care immediately becomes quite a pertinent issue. In particular, the issue of discretion just discussed pertains closely to the quality of the service provided. In the model of dependency discussed in the previous chapter, the notion of discretion – whether or not the service provider or caregiver could withhold the service – was a central element. What was perhaps not so clear, but needs to be emphasised here, is that this argument applies equally to providing the appropriate and desired service – not merely any service which may loosely be deemed to be appropriate.

The issue is whether or not the dependent person can obtain that required service as a matter of right or at least as one of due expectation. It makes no difference in this scenario whether the care recipient is in the physical or mental condition to specify what is good quality care; where this is no longer possible for an individual it remains perfectly possible to establish best quality principles which can guide the service provided by an individual care facility. For those who are capable of indicating their preferences, the importance of choice and control lines up with and reinforces the desirability of good quality care provided as a matter of course, rather than as a matter of discretion.

Inevitably, at a broader level the experience of dependency in a low quality facility will necessarily be much less desirable than that in a high quality facility. Imagine, if you will, the difference between having to rely on someone to hold a tepid cup of institutional brew to your lips due to physical incapacity, and having to rely on someone to hold your cappuccino (or short black) – the significance of quality of care (and quality of life) emerges quite clearly.

The concept of independence is, for many of us, inextricably bound to ideas of quality of life, of choice and control. In cases of extreme mental and physical frailty, independence may mean something other than what it is to an able-bodied person in full control of their intellectual capacities. Because it is different it does not make it less important, or less complex to define and understand. Consequently, the broad policy directions reviewed here offer mixed and conflicting possibilities for maintaining the independence of frail, disabled older people.

Some of these changes to policy and practice may potentially reduce the vulnerability of frail aged care recipients, some such modifications will inevitably have limited utility, and others may actually increase the dependency experienced by individuals. However successful one might be in restructuring systems of aged care to reduce the negative experience of dependency for frail older people, the negative consequences of dependency are unlikely to be eradicated, just as dependency itself is unlikely to be eradicated. To some extent the goal of equity of access may actually conflict with that of the promotion of independence, and indeed the increased independence of elderly people may conversely rely on the decreased independence of their family members. The issue of dependency is a complex one, and not perhaps a goal to be pursued unequivocally. It remains, nonetheless, a useful yardstick by which to measure progress in aged care policy.

APPENDIX

Timeline for the Development of Australian Aged Care Services

1954
AGED PERSONS HOMES ACT 1954
Enabled grants to be made to non-profit organisations (and local government from 1967) for the purpose of erecting or purchasing approved homes for aged persons. Subsequent policy changes meant that beds provided under this Act, while predominantly in self-contained accommodation and hostels, also included some nursing home provisions.

1956
HOME NURSING
Provided for a subsidy payable to non-profit home nursing organisations and is dependent on the number of nurses employed by the organisation.

1958
SUPPLEMENTARY ASSISTANCE
Supplementary assistance introduced for single pensioners paying rent, and who were almost entirely dependent on the pension. Eligibility criteria were subsequently extended, although the allowance was means tested from 1965, and in 1972 married pensioner couples became eligible.

1962
NURSING HOME BENEFIT
In 1962 a Commonwealth nursing home benefit was introduced, and in 1968 an additional 'intensive care' benefit was introduced for patients requiring more nursing care. Various changes occurred including the establishment of an 'additional benefit'. In 1977, the 'ordinary' and 'additional' benefits were combined, and the 'intensive' benefit replaced by an 'extensive' benefit.

1969
STATES GRANTS (DWELLINGS FOR AGE PENSIONERS) ACT 1969
Provided capital grants to the states for providing accommodation for aged pensioners eligible for supplementary assistance.

PERSONAL CARE SUBSIDY

An amendment to the *Aged Persons Homes Act* provided for a personal care subsidy to be paid to every resident aged 80 years and over in hostel-type accommodation. In 1973 the personal care subsidy was extended to residents not aged 80 years but to those who required and were receiving personal care services.

STATES GRANTS (HOME CARE) ACT 1969

Enabled grants to be made to the states on a dollar-for-dollar basis to provide home care services, establish and develop senior citizens centres and provide welfare officers in those centres. The legislation was modified in 1973 to increase the subsidy to a $2 for $1 basis.

STATES GRANTS (PARAMEDICAL SERVICES) ACT 1969

To provide paramedical services such as physiotherapy, chiropody etc. to aged persons in their own homes.

1970

DELIVERED MEALS SUBSIDY ACT 1970

To subsidise eligible organisations for the provision of meals.

1972

AGED PERSONS HOSTELS ACT 1972

Provided capital grants to a prescribed limit per person for the establishment of hostel-level accommodation; to be allocated on the basis of need and with donor contributions disallowed.

1973

COMMITTEE OF INQUIRY INTO AGED PERSONS HOUSING

To review existing provisions for aged persons housing; culminated in a more broadly based report *Care of the Aged* presented to the Social Welfare Commission in 1975.

DOMICILIARY NURSING CARE BENEFIT

Payable to persons caring for aged persons who would otherwise require nursing home care.

1974

STATES GRANTS (DWELLINGS FOR PENSIONERS) ACT 1974

Provided interest-free non-repayable grants to the state housing authorities to provide self-contained units for a range of single pensioners entitled to supplementary assistance, including aged pensioners.

AGED OR DISABLED PERSONS HOME ACT 1974

Altered the title of the *Aged Persons Homes Act* and extended its provisions to handicapped adults.

NURSING HOMES ASSISTANCE ACT 1974

Provided an alternative method of financing non-profit homes, via a subsidy equal to the home's operating deficit.

1976

HOLMES COMMITTEE ESTABLISHED

To examine the effectiveness and efficiency of existing government provisions for the care of the aged and infirm; interrelationships between levels of government and the non-government sector, and the relationship between such programs and other health and welfare programs.

1977

HOLMES COMMITTEE REPORT TABLED

Recommended consolidation of domiciliary care programs; expansion of assessment and rehabilitation provisions; review of nursing home financing; review of capital subsidies arrangements for self-contained accommodation, hostels and nursing homes; and a review of cost-sharing arrangements with the states.

STATES GRANTS (DWELLINGS FOR PENSIONERS) BILL 1977

Provided additional monies to the state housing authorities, extending the *States Grants (Dwellings for Pensioners) Act 1974* by one year.

1978

HOUSING ASSISTANCE BILL 1978

Continued grants to the states for the provision of self-contained accommodation, broadening guidelines and including married persons.

STATES GRANTS (HOME CARE) AMENDMENT BILL 1978

Modified the ratio of federal/state funding from $2 federal for every $1 state to a dollar-for-dollar ratio.

1980

SUB-COMMITTEE ON ACCOMMODATION AND HOME CARE FOR THE AGED ESTABLISHED

To examine the reasons for the continued dominance of institutional care, and to establish a framework which allows governments to make cost-effective decisions in provisions for the aged. The resulting 'McLeay Report' was presented in 1982.

1981

SENATE SELECT COMMITTEE ON PRIVATE HOSPITALS AND NURSING HOMES

Established to inquire into finance and performance, and both present and future roles.

1984

JOINT REVIEW OF HOSTEL CARE SUBSIDIES ARRANGEMENTS

The joint review was established to explore equity of access, particularly among disadvantaged groups, adequacy of services, effectiveness of administrative arrangements, the rights of residents and arrangements for respite care. The report was presented in 1985.

RESPITE CARE PROGRAM INTRODUCED

Provided subsidies to encourage the provision of respite beds in hostels.

SPECIAL BENEFIT ELIGIBILITY ALTERED

Eased eligibility requirements for elderly immigrants who were formerly not eligible for special benefit, i.e. who had migrated under the Assurance of Support Scheme which required a maintenance guarantee as a pre-condition for entry.

1985

DEMENTIA GRANTS PROGRAM

Grants were made available to hostels providing special services and facilities for dementia sufferers.

GERIATRIC ASSESSMENT PROGRAM

Established to undertake developmental work on the assessment of elderly people.

RESPITE CARE EXTENDED
Provisions were introduced to allow short-term access to respite care in nursing homes.

HOME AND COMMUNITY CARE BILL 1985
The Home and Community Care program was announced in 1984 by the federal government, and agreements were reached with most states by December 1985. Funding uptake by the states was varied over this period. The program was a cost-sharing program, intended to replace existing community care services with a comprehensive range of integrated community services.

REVIEW OF NURSING HOMES AND HOSTELS ESTABLISHED
The review was established to develop a new direction for residential care, and its report presented in 1986.

ETHNIC AGED WORKING PARTY ESTABLISHED
The working party was established to enhance the suitability and availability of aged care services for the ethnic aged. The report 'Strategies for Change' was presented in 1986.

1986
COMMUNITY OPTIONS PROGRAMS COMMENCED
Part of the initiative to trial innovative forms of community care.

1987
VETERANS' HOME HELP
The Veterans' home help program was transferred to HACC.

AGED CARE ADVISORY COMMITTEES
Aged Care Advisory Committees were established in each state to advise on the distribution of new places in hostels and nursing homes.

NURSING HOMES AND HOSTELS LEGISLATION AMENDMENT BILL 1987
Introduced specific quality of care requirements and significant changes to funding arrangements. From 1 July 1987 nursing homes began a gradual transition to a uniform national funding level for infrastructure costs, the standard aggregated module (SAM). Deficit financing of homes revoked from this date.

The outcome standards developed by the Commonwealth/State Working Party on Nursing Home Standards were published, with implementation to date from 1 July.

GUIDELINES FOR GERIATRIC ASSESSMENT TEAMS
Guidelines drawing on the experiences of pilot assessment teams published.

1988
COMMONWEALTH/STATE WORKING PARTY ON NURSING HOME STANDARDS
Final report published.

USER RIGHTS CONSULTANCY ESTABLISHED
To examine user rights in residential care, final report produced in 1989.

DATA COLLECTION ON HACC SERVICES COMMENCED
From 1988 annual collections on type and frequency of services provided to consumers commenced; data on client characteristics were collected during a sample survey in 1990.

HEALTH OF OLDER PEOPLE DECLARED A PRIORITY AREA
Under the Health for All Australians Report five priority areas were established for National Action for Better Health, including the health of older people.

1989
NEW RECURRENT FUNDING FOR NURSING HOMES AND HOSTELS

RESPITE CARE
Arrangements for nursing homes and hostels improved.

USER RIGHTS ADVOCACY SERVICE ESTABLISHED

IN-SERVICE TRAINING FOR NURSING HOME STAFF
Also in 1990, training package commissioned for HACC service providers.

FIRST TRIENNIAL REVIEW OF HACC COMPLETED

1990
STATEMENT OF RIGHTS AND RESPONSIBILITIES FOR HACC CLIENTS
Received ministerial endorsement in June 1990.

HACC ADVISORY COMMITTEES GUIDELINES REFINED
Established in all states by 1991.

CHARTER OF RESIDENTS' RIGHTS AND RESPONSIBILITIES
Legislation passed.

1991
CARING FOR FAMILY CAREGIVERS
National program aimed at caring for caregivers launched

MID-TERM REVIEW OF AGED CARE
Report presented, main recommendations included a decrease in the proposed level of hostel funding, improvements in the respite care and dementia care areas, and improved integration of residential and community care planning.

TRANSLATION
Release of videos and pamphlets translating information on HACC services for people of non-English-speaking backgrounds.

OUTCOME STANDARDS FOR AGED PERSONS HOSTELS
Introduced.

NATIONAL SERVICE STANDARDS FOR HACC
Standards launched.

STANDARDS REPORTS RELEASED
The first reports of nursing homes and hostel standards were released to the public.

COMMUNITY VISITORS SCHEMES ESTABLISHED
Established in pilot stage to provide companionship to isolated residents of nursing homes.

BACKGROUND PAPER ON AGED PERSONS HOUSING PREPARED FOR NATIONAL HOUSING STRATEGY

1992

COMMUNITY AGED CARE PACKAGES INTRODUCED

Aimed at providing high intensity community-based care to persons who might otherwise enter residential care. The residential care planning ratio was reduced to 55 hostel places and 40 nursing home beds per 1000 persons aged 70+, with 5 hostel places being reallocated to community aged care packages.

MULTI-PURPOSE CENTRES

Trialled and later expanded to allow provision in rural areas of multiple service types from one location.

FIVE-YEAR NATIONAL ACTION PLAN FOR DEMENTIA IMPLEMENTED

EXPANSION OF CARER PROVISIONS AND ENTITLEMENTS

FREEZE ON FEDERAL BENEFITS PAID TO STATE NURSING HOMES REMOVED

State homes required to meet national outcome standards and assign residents to dependency categories as part of these arrangements.

REVIEW OF NURSING HOMES FUNDING ARRANGEMENTS

Announced in 1992–93 Budget.

1993

RESIDENTIAL CARE PLANNING RATIOS REVISED

To 52.5 hostel places, 40 nursing home beds and 7.5 community aged care packages per 1000 persons aged 70+.

REVIEW OF NURSING HOMES FUNDING ARRANGEMENTS

Stage 1 report published. Capital grants made available for upgrading existing beds.

REPORT ON THE OUTCOME-BASED REGULATORY SYSTEM IN NURSING HOMES PUBLISHED

EXPANSION OF INTENSIVE HOME-BASED CARE

Transition care packages administered by aged care assessment teams implemented for post-acute care. Pilot study for nursing home options projects announced.

1994

REVIEW OF NURSING HOMES

Nursing Home Consultative Committee (Keys Committee) reports.
Stage 2 report of the Review of Nursing Home Funding Arrangements published.

MULTI-PURPOSE CENTRES EXPANDED

HOSTEL/NURSING HOME INTERMIXING PILOT SCHEME COMMENCED

Residents eligible for either nursing home or hostel services cared for within the one facility.

PSYCHO-GERIATRIC UNITS ESTABLISHED

For assessment purposes within aged care assessment teams.

ABORIGINALS AND TORRES STRAIT ISLANDERS

Special funds allocated to improve services.

1995

RESIDENTIAL CARE PLANNING RATIOS REVISED

To 50 hostel places, 40 nursing home beds and 10 community aged care packages per 1000 persons aged 70+.

TIERED SAM INTRODUCED

To better support nursing home infrastructure.

INTERMIXING AND NURSING HOME OPTIONS PROJECTS EXPANDED

RESPITE REVIEW ANNOUNCED

A national review to report on strategies for the improvement of respite care arrangements.

1996

RESPITE REVIEW REPORTS

Greater access to community-based respite care and improved co-ordination and information strategies emphasised.

RESTRUCTURING OF RESIDENTIAL CARE ANNOUNCED

The federal government announces significant intended changes to the residential care system. Hostels and nursing homes to be amalgamated into one system, federal government benefits to be subject to a means test, and entry payments (subject to an assets test) to be required of persons entering all residential care.

References

Abramovitz, Mimi. 1988. *Regulating the Lives of Women: Social Welfare Policy from Colonial Times to the Present*. Boston: South End Press.

Adelmann, Pamela K., Toni C. Antonucci and James S. Jackson. 1993. 'Retired or homemaker: how older women define their roles'. *Journal of Women & Aging* 5 (2): 67–78.

Aged Care Coalition. 1986. *If Only I'd Known: A Study of the Experiences of Elderly Residents in Boarding Homes, Hostels and Self Care Units*. Sydney.

Allen, Isobel. 1988. 'Ageing as a feminist issue'. *Policy Studies* 9 (2): 35–50.

Andersen, Margaret L. and Patricia Hill Collins. 1992. 'Reconstructing knowledge: toward inclusive thinking'. In Margaret L. Andersen and Patricia Hill Collins, eds, *Race, Class, and Gender*. Belmont, Calif.: Wadsworth.

Antonucci, Toni C. 1990. 'Social supports and social relationships'. In Robert H. Binstock and Linda K. George, eds, *Handbook of Aging and Social Sciences*. 3rd edn. San Diego, Calif.: Academic Press.

Arber, Sara and G. N. Gilbert. 1989. 'Men: the forgotten carers'. *Sociology* 18: 111–18.

Arber, Sara and Jay Ginn. 1991a. 'The invisibility of age: gender and class in later life'. *Sociological Review* 39: 260–91.

Arber, Sara and Jay Ginn. 1991b. *Gender and Later Life*. London: Sage.

Aronson, Jane. 1992. 'Women's sense of responsibility for the care of old people: "but who else is going to do it?".' *Gender and Society* 6: 8–29.

Australia. Commonwealth–State Working Party. 1987. *Living in a Nursing Home*. Canberra: Australian Government Publishing Service.

Australia. Department of Community Services. 1985. *Report of the Joint Review of Hostel Care Subsidies Arrangements*. Canberra: Australian Government Publishing Service.

Australia. Department of Community Services. 1986. *Nursing Homes and Hostels Review*. Canberra: Australian Government Publishing Service.

Australia. Department of Community Services. Office for the Aged. 1987. *Toward a Comprehensive User Rights Mechanism: A Discussion Document*. Canberra.

Australia. Department of Health, Housing and Community Services. 1991. *Report of the Mid Term Review of the Aged Care Reform Strategy*. Canberra: Australian Government Publishing Service.

226

Australia. Department of Health, Housing, Local Government and Community Services. Aged and Community Care Division. 1990. *Keeping the Quality in Hostel Life*. Canberra.

Australia. Department of Health, Housing and Community Services. 1992. *It's Your Choice: National Evaluation of Community Options Projects*. Canberra: Australian Government Publishing Service.

Australia. Department of Health, Housing, Local Government and Community Services. 1993. *Annual Report 1992–93*. Canberra: Australian Government Publishing Service.

Australia. Department of Human Services and Health. 1995. *1995–97 Agency Review and Evaluation Plan*. Canberra: Australian Government Publishing Service.

Australia. Department of Human Services and Health. Aged and Community Care Division. Office for the Aged. 1994. *Working Party on the Protection of Frail Older People in the Community*: see Working Party on the Protection of Frail Older People in the Community.

Australia. Department of Human Services and Health. Aged and Community Care Division. Office on Disability. 1996. *Towards a National Agenda for Carers: Report of the Workshop*. Aged and Community Care Service Development and Evaluation Reports, No. 21. Canberra: Australian Government Publishing Service.

Australia. Department of Human Services and Health. Aged and Community Care Division. Office on Disability. 1996. *Towards a National Agenda for Carers: Workshop Papers*. Aged and Community Care Service Development and Evaluation Reports, No. 22. Canberra: Australian Government Publishing Service.

Australia. Home and Community Care Program (HACC): see Home and Community Care (HACC).

Australia. House of Representatives. Standing Committee on Community Affairs. 1994. *Home but not Alone: A Report on the Home and Community Care Program*. Canberra: Australian Government Publishing Service.

Australia. House of Representatives. Standing Committee on Expenditure. 1982. *In a Home or At Home: Accommodation and Home Care for the Aged*. Canberra: Australian Government Publishing Service.

Australia. National Commission of Audit (Robert Officer, chair). 1996. *Report to the Commonwealth Government*. Canberra: Australian Government Publishing Service.

Australia. Office for the Aged. 1987. *Toward a Comprehensive User Rights Mechanism*. Canberra: Department of Community Services.

Australia. Senate Select Committee on Private Hospitals and Nursing Homes. 1985. *Private Nursing Homes in Australia: Their Conduct, Administration and Ownership*. Canberra: Australian Government Publishing Service.

Australian Bureau of Statistics (ABS). 1987. *Estimated Resident Population by Sex and Age: States and Territories of Australia, June 1981 to June 1987*. Cat. No. 3201.0. Canberra.

Australian Bureau of Statistics (ABS). 1988. *Disability and Handicaps*, Australia, Cat. No. 4120.0. Canberra.

Australian Bureau of Statistics (ABS). 1993a. *Disability, Ageing and Carers Australia 1993: Summary of Findings*. Cat. No. 4430.0. Canberra.

Australian Bureau of Statistics (ABS). 1993b. *Disability and Handicap, Australia 1988*. Cat. No. 4120.0. Canberra.

Australian Bureau of Statistics (ABS). 1993c. *Disability and Handicap*. Cat. No. 412.0. Canberra.

Australian Bureau of Statistics (ABS). 1993. *Estimated Resident Population By Sex and Age States and Territories of Australia*. Cat. No. 3201.0. Canberra.

Australian Bureau of Statistics (ABS). 1994. *Projections of the Population of Australia: States and Territories, 1993 to 2041*. Cat. No. 3222.0. Canberra.

Australian Council on the Ageing and Department of Community Services. 1985. *Older People at Home*. Canberra: Australian Government Publishing Service.

Australian Human Rights Commission. 1986. *Part 1 Superannuation. Superannuation and Insurance and the Sex Discrimination Act 1984*. Canberra: Australian Government Publishing Service.

Australian Institute of Health and Welfare (AIHW). 1993. *Australia's Welfare 1993: Services and Assistance*. Canberra: Australian Government Publishing Service.

Australian Institute of Health and Welfare (AIHW). 1995. *Australia's Welfare 1995: Services and Assistance*. Canberra: Australian Government Publishing Service.

Australian Institute of Health and Welfare (AIHW). 1997. *Australia's Welfare '97: Services and Assistance*. Canberra.

Australian National Audit Office (ANAO). 1981. *Commonwealth Administration of Nursing Home Programs. The Auditor-General Audit Report No. 2, Efficiency Audit*. Canberra: AGPS.

Ayres, Ian and John Braithwaite. 1992. *Responsive Regulation*. New York, Oxford University Press.

Baldock, Cora Vellekoop. 1990. *Volunteers in Welfare*. Sydney: Allen & Unwin.

Baltes, Margret. 1988. 'The etiology and maintenance of dependency in the elderly: three phases of operant research'. *Behavior Therapy* 19: 301–19.

Baltes, Paul B. and Margret M. Baltes. 1990. 'Psychological perspectives on successful aging: the model of selective optimization and compensation'. In Paul B. and Margret M. Baltes, eds, *Successful Aging*. Cambridge: Cambridge University Press.

Baltes, Margret M. and Susan B. Silverberg. 1994. 'The dynamics between dependency and autonomy: illustrations across the life span'. Vol. 12, pp. 41–90 in D. L. Featherman, R. M. Lerner and M. Perlmutter, eds, *Life-span Development and Behavior*. Hillsdale, NJ: Erlbaum.

Barrett, Michèle. 1980. *Women's Oppression Today*. London: Verso.

Barrett, Michèle and Mary McIntosh. 1982/1991. *The Anti-social Family*. 2nd edn. London: Verso; originally published 1982.

Baxter, Janeen. 1991. 'Work and the family: class and the household division of labour'. pp. 223–44 in Janeen Baxter, Michael Emmison, John Western and Mark Western, eds, *Class Analysis and Contemporary Australia*. Melbourne: Macmillan.

Baxter, Janeen and Diane Gibson, with Mark Lynch-Blosse. 1990. *Double Take: The Links Between Paid and Unpaid Work*. Canberra: Australian Government Publishing Service Press.

Beeson, Diane. 1975. 'Women in studies of aging: a critique and suggestion'. *Social Problems* 23: 52–9.

Bell, Daniel and Alice M. Rivlin. 1969. *Toward a Social Report*. Report of the Panel on Social Indicators, US Department of Health, Education and Welfare. Washington, DC: Government Printing Office.

Bennett, Fran. 1983. 'The state, welfare and women's dependence'.

pp. 190–214 in Lynne Segal, ed., *What Is To Be Done About the Family?* Harmondsworth: Penguin.

Beresford, P. and S. Croft. 1993. *Citizen Involvement: A Practical Guide for Change*. Basingstoke: Macmillan.

Bergner, M., R. A. Bobbitt, W. B. Carter, B. S. Gilson. 1981. 'The sickness impact profile: development and final revision of a health status measure'. *Medical Care* 19: 787–805.

Beveridge, William H. 1942. *Social Insurance and Allied Services*. Cmnd. 6404. London: HMSO.

Bittman, Michael. 1991. *Juggling Time: How Australian Families Use Time*. Canberra: Department of Prime Minister and Cabinet.

Blau, P. M. 1964. *Exchange and Power in Social Life*. New York: John Wiley and Sons.

Blieszner, Rosemary. 1993. 'A socialist-feminist perspective on widowhood'. *Journal of Aging Studies* 7: 171–82.

Braithwaite, J. and V. Braithwaite. 1995. 'The politics of legalism: rules versus standards in nursing home regulation'. *Social and Legal Studies* 4: 307–41.

Braithwaite, John, Valerie Braithwaite, Diane Gibson, Miriam Landau and Toni Makkai. 1991. *The Reliability and Validity of Nursing Home Standards*. Department of Health, Housing and Community Services, Aged and Community Care Service Development and Evaluation Reports, No. 4. Canberra: Australian Government Publishing Service.

Braithwaite, John, Toni Makkai, Valerie Braithwaite and Diane Gibson. 1993. *Raising the Standard: Resident Centred Nursing Home Regulation in Australia*. Canberra: Australian Government Publishing Service.

Braithwaite, John, Toni Makkai, Valerie Braithwaite, Diane Gibson and David Ermann. 1990. *The Contribution of the Standards Monitoring Process to the Quality of Nursing Home Life: A Preliminary Report*. Canberra: Department of Community Services and Health.

Braithwaite, Valerie. 1990. *Bound to Care*. Sydney: Allen & Unwin.

Braithwaite, Valerie. 1994. 'Understanding stress in informal caregiving: is burden a problem of the individual or of society?' Mimeo. Research School of Social Sciences, Australian National University. Canberra.

Brisendon, S. 1989. 'A Charter for Personal Care'. *Progress* 16.

Brody, E. M. 1981. 'Women in the middle and family help to older people'. *The Gerontologist* 21: 471–80.

Brody, E. M. and C. B. Schoonover. 1986. 'Patterns of parent care when adult daughters work and when they do not'. *The Gerontologist* 26: 373–81.

Broom, Dorothy H. 1991. *Speaking for Themselves: Consumer Issues in the Restructuring of General Practice*. NCEPH Discussion Paper No. 4. Canberra: NCEPH, Australian National University.

Brown, C. and Halladay A. 1989. 'The elderly speak for policy: perspectives on consumer involvement in policy and provision of social care services in Queensland'. *Australian Journal on Ageing*. vol. 8, No. 9, February.

Bryson, Lois. 1983. 'Women as welfare recipients: women, poverty and the state'. pp. 130–145 in Cora Baldock and Bettina Cass, eds, *Women, Social Welfare and the State*. Sydney: Allen & Unwin.

Calasanti, Toni M. 1993a. 'Bringing in diversity: toward an inclusive theory of retirement'. *Journal of Aging Studies* 7: 122–50.

Calasanti, Toni M. 1993b. 'Introduction: a socialist-feminist approach to aging'. *Journal of Aging Studies* 7: 107–10.

Calasanti, Toni M. and Anna M. Zajicek, 1993. 'A socialist-feminist approach to aging: embracing diversity'. *Journal of Aging Studies* 7: 117–32.

Clark, Margaret. 1972. 'Cultural values and dependency in later life'. pp. 263–74 in D. O. Cowgill and L. D. Holmes, eds, *Aging and Modernization*. New York: Appleton–Century Crofts.

Clarke, M. and J. Stewart. 1992. 'Empowerment: a theme for the 1990s'. *Local Government Studies* 18 (2): 18–26.

Coleman, Lisa and Sophie Watson. 1987. *Women Over Sixty*. Canberra: Australian Institute of Urban Studies.

Commonwealth–State Working Party: see Australia, Commonwealth–State Working Party.

Cox, Eva. 1983. 'Pater-patria: child-rearing and the state'. pp.186–200 in Cora Baldock and Bettina Cass, eds, *Women, Social Welfare and the State*. Sydney: Allen & Unwin.

Danigelis, Nicholas L. and Barbara R. McIntosh. 1993. 'Resources and the productive activity of elders: race and gender as contexts'. *Journal of Gerontology: Social Sciences* 48 (4): S192–S203.

David, M. and H. Land. 1983. 'Sex and social policy'. pp. 138–57 in H. Glennerster, ed., *The Future of the Welfare State*. London: Heinemann.

Davies, B. and M. J. Knapp. 1981. *Old People's Homes and the Production of Welfare*. London: Routledge & Kegan Paul.

Davison, B., H. Kendig, F. Stephens and V. Merrill. 1993. *It's My Place: Older People Talk About Their Homes*. Canberra: Australian Government Publishing Service.

Day, Alice T. 1991. *Remarkable Survivors: Insights into Successful Aging Among Women*. Washington, DC: Urban Institute Press.

Day, Patricia and Rudolf Klein. 1987. *Accountabilities: Five Public Services*. London: Tavistock.

Day, Patricia, Rudolf Klein and Sharon Redmayne. 1996. *Why Regulate? Regulating Residential Care for Elderly People*. Bristol: Policy Press, University of Bristol, for the Joseph Rowntree Foundation.

Dean, Hartley and Peter Taylor-Gooby. 1992. *Dependency Culture: the Explosion of a Myth*. Hemel Hempstead, Harts.: Harvester-Wheatsheaf.

de Beauvoir, Simone. 1972. *The Coming of Age*, trans. Patrick O'Brian. New York: Putnam; originally published 1970.

Demetrakopoulos, Stephanie. 1983. *Listening to Our Bodies: The Rebirth of Feminine Wisdom*. Boston: Beacon Press.

Dixon, Daryl and Chris Foster. 1986. 'Overview'. pp. 343–55 in Ronald Mendelsohn, ed., *Finance in Old Age*. Canberra: Centre for Research on Federal Financial Relations, Australian National University.

Donabedian, Avedis. 1966. 'Evaluating the quality of medical care'. *Milbank Memorial Fund Quarterly* 44: 166–206.

Donabedian, Avedis. 1980. *Explorations in Quality Assessment and Monitoring*. Vol. 1: *The Definitions of Quality and Approaches to Its Assessment*. Ann Arbor, Mich.: Health Administration Press.

Duckett, Stephen. 1995. Keynote Address to the Aged Care Australia 8th National Conference, Canberra, 9 November 1995. Mimeo, Office of the Secretary, Department of Human Services and Health, Canberra.

Duffy, Michael, Su Bailey, Bets Beck and Donald G. Barker. 1986. 'Preferences in nursing home design: a comparison of residents, administrators and designers'. *Environment and Behavior* 18 (2): 246–57.

Durkheim, Émile. 1952. *Suicide: A Study in Sociology*, ed. G. Simpson. London: Routledge & Kegan Paul.

Dworkin, Ronald. 1984. 'Rights as trumps'. pp. 153–67 in Jeremy Waldron, ed., *Theories of Rights*. Oxford: Oxford University Press.

Eagar, Kathy. 1995. 'Paying for health outcomes'. pp. 25–33 in *Health Outcomes and Quality of Life Measurement*, ed. Jan Sansoni. Proceedings of a conference organised by the Australian Health Outcomes Clearing House, Canberra, 14–15 August 1995. Canberra: Australian Institute of Health & Welfare.

Edwards, John N. and David L. Klemmack. 1973. 'Correlates of life satisfaction: a re-examination'. *Journal of Gerontology* 28: 437–502.

Eisenstein, Hester. 1984. *Contemporary Feminist Thought*. Sydney: Allen & Unwin.

Emerson, R. W. 1841. 'Self-reliance'. Vol. 2, pp. 25–51 in J. Slater, A. R. Ferguson and J. F. Carr, eds., *The Collected Works of Ralph Waldo Emerson*. Cambridge, Mass.: Harvard University Press.

Estes, Carroll L., Lenore E. Gerarg and Adele Clarke. 1984. 'Women and the economics of aging'. In Meredith Minkler and Carroll L. Estes, eds, *Readings in the Political Economy of Aging*. New York: Baywood Publishing.

Feinberg, Joel. 1980. 'The nature and value of rights'. In Feinberg, *Rights, Justice and the Bounds of Liberty*. Princeton, NJ: Princeton University Press.

Finch, J. and D. Groves, eds. 1983. *A Labour of Love: Women, Work and Caring*. London: Routledge & Kegan Paul.

Fine, Michael. 1995. *The Changing Mix of Welfare in Health Care and Community Support Services*. Social Policy Research Centre Discussion Papers, No. 61. Kensington, NSW: University of New South Wales.

Fine, Michael and Cathy Thompson. 1995. *Factors Affecting the Outcome of Community Care Interventions: A Literature Review*. Department of Human Services and Health Aged and Community Care Service Development and Evaluation Reports, No. 20. Canberra: Australian Government Publishing Service.

Firestone, Shulamith. 1979. *The Dialectic of Sex*. London: The Women's Press; originally published 1970.

Fraser, Nancy and Linda Gordon. 1994a. '"Dependency" demystified: inscriptions of power in a keyword of the welfare state'. *Social Politics* 1 (Spring): 4–31.

Fraser, Nancy and Linda Gordon. 1994b. 'A genealogy of dependency: tracing a keyword of the US welfare state'. *Signs: Journal of Women in Culture and Society* 19 (2): 309–336.

Freytag, K. 1986. *If Only I'd Known: A Study of the Experiences of Elderly Residents in Boarding Houses, Hostels and Self Care Units*. Canberra: Australian Consumers Association.

Friedan, Betty. 1963. *The Feminine Mystique*. New York: Norton.

Friedan, Betty. 1993. *The Fountain of Age*. New York: Simon & Schuster.

Frye, Marilyn. 1983. *The Politics of Reality: Essays in Feminist Theory*. Trumansburg, NY: Crossing Press.

Gatens, Moira. 1983. 'A critique of the sex/gender distinction'. pp. 143–62 in Judith Allen and Paul Patton, eds, *Beyond Marxism? Interventions After Marx*. Sydney: Intervention Publications.

Gee, Ellen and Meredith Kimball. 1987. *Women and Aging*. Toronto: Butterworths.

George, Linda K. 1989. 'Stress, social support, and depression over the life-course'. In S. Kyriakos, S. Markides and Charles L. Cooper, eds, *Aging, Stress and Health*. New York: Wiley.

Gewirth, Alan. 1984. 'Are there any absolute rights?' In Jeremy Waldron, ed., *Theories of Rights*. Oxford: Oxford University Press.

Gibson, Diane. 1983. 'Health status of older people'. pp. 41–68 in H. L. Kendig, D. M. Gibson, D. T. Rowland and J. M. Hemer, eds, *Health, Welfare and Family in Later Life*. Sydney: New South Wales Council on the Aging.

Gibson, Diane. 1985. 'The dormouse syndrome – restructuring the dependency of the elderly'. *Australian and New Zealand Journal of Sociology* 21: 44–63.

Gibson, Diane and Judith Allen. 1993. 'Phallocentrism and parasitism: Social provision for the aged'. *Policy Sciences* 26 (2): 79–98.

Gibson, Diane, John Braithwaite, Valerie Braithwaite and Toni Makkai. 1992. 'Evaluating quality of care in Australian nursing homes'. *Australian Journal on Ageing* 11 (4): 3–9.

Gibson, Diane, Elizabeth Butkus, Anne Jenkins, Sushma Mathur and Zhibin Liu. 1996. *The Respite Care Needs of Australians*. Prepared for the Respite Review undertaken by the Aged and Community Care Division of the Commonwealth Department of Health and Family Services. Respite Review Supporting Paper 1/Aged Care Series, No. 3. Canberra: Australian Institute of Health and Welfare.

Gibson, Diane and Zhibin Liu. 1995. 'Planning ratios and population growth: Will there be a shortfall in residential aged care by 2021?' *Australian Journal on Ageing* 14 (2): 57–62.

Gibson, Diane, Louise Harvey and Eileen Thumpkin. 1992. *Evaluation of the Gold Coast Community Options Project*. Brisbane: Department of Anthropology and Sociology, University of Queensland.

Gibson, Diane, and Stephen Mugford. 1986. 'Expressive relations and social support'. pp. 63–84 in H. L. Kendig, ed., *Ageing and Families: A Social Networks Perspective*. Sydney: Allen & Unwin.

Gibson, D. M. and D. T. Rowland. 1984. 'Community versus institutional care: the case of the Australian aged'. *Social Science and Medicine* 18: 997–1004.

Giles Report: see Australia, Senate, Select Committee on Private Hospitals and Nursing Homes (1985).

Gilman, Charlotte Perkins. 1970. *Women and Economics: A Study of the Economic Relation Between Men and Women as a Factor in Social Evolution*. New York: Harper Torchbooks; originally published 1898.

Goodin, Robert E. 1985a. 'Erring on the side of kindness in social welfare policy'. *Policy Sciences* 18: 141–56.

Goodin, Robert E. 1985b. *Protecting the Vulnerable: A Reanalysis of Our Social Responsibilities*. Chicago: University of Chicago Press.

Goodin, Robert E. 1988. *Reasons for Welfare*. Princeton, NJ: Princeton University Press.

Goodin, Robert E. and Diane Gibson. 1997. 'Rights, young and old'. *Oxford Journal of Legal Studies* 17: 185–203.

Goodin, Robert E. and Julian Le Grand *et al.* 1987. *Not Only The Poor*. London: Allen & Unwin.

Gordon, Linda. 1990. 'The new feminist scholarship on the welfare state'. pp. 9–35 in Linda Gordon, ed., *Women, the State and Welfare*. Madison: University of Wisconsin Press.

Gordon, Linda. 1992. 'Social insurance and public assistance: the influence of gender on welfare thought in the United States'. *American Historical Review* 97 (1): 19–54.

Gouldner, A. W. 1960. 'The norm of reciprocity: a preliminary statement'. *American Sociological Review* 25: 161–178.

Gouldner, A. W. 1975. *For Sociology*. London: Pelican.

Graham, Hilary. 1993. 'Social divisions in caring'. *Women's Studies International Forum* 16 (5): 461–70.

Greer, Germaine. 1970. *The Female Eunuch*. London: MacGibbon & Kee.

Greer, Germaine. 1991. *The Change: Women, Aging and the Menopause*. London: Hamish Hamilton.

Gregory, R. G. 1993. *Review of the Structure of Nursing Home Funding Arrangements Stage 1*. Department of Health, Housing, Local Government and Community Services, Aged and Community Care Service Development and Evaluation Reports, No. 11. Canberra: Australian Government Publishing Service.

Gregory, R. G. 1994. *Review of the Structure of Nursing Home Funding Arrangements Stage 2*. Department of Human Services and Health, Aged and Community Care Service Development and Evaluation Reports, No. 12. Canberra: Australian Government Publishing Service.

Griffiths, Sir Roy. 1988. *Community Care: An Agenda for Action*. London: HMSO.

Gross, Bertram M. 1966. 'The state of the nation: social systems accounting'. pp. 154–271 in Raymond A. Bauer, ed., *Social Indicators*. Cambridge, Mass.: MIT Press.

Grosz, Elizabeth. 1987. 'Feminist theory and the challenge to knowledges'. *Women's Studies International Forum* 10: 445–80.

Hardwick, Jill and Adam Graycar. 1982. *Volunteers in Non-Government Welfare Organisations in Australia*. Social Welfare Research Centre Reports and Proceedings, No. 25. Kensington, NSW: University of New South Wales.

Hart, H. L. A. 1984. 'Are there any natural rights?' pp. 77–90 in Jeremy Waldron, ed., *Theories of Rights*. Oxford: Oxford University Press.

Hatry, Harry P. 1980. 'Pitfalls of evaluation'. pp. 159–78 in Giandomenico Majone and Edward S. Quade, eds, *Pitfalls of Analysis*. Chichester: Wiley, for International Institute for Applied Systems Analysis.

Hendricks, Joh. 1993. 'Recognizing the relativity of gender in aging research'. *Journal of Aging Studies* 7: 111–6.

Herzog, A. Regula and Willard L. Rodgers. 1981. 'Age and satisfaction: data from several large surveys'. *Research on Aging* 3: 142–65.

Herzog, A. Regula, Robert L. Kahn, James N. Morgan, James S. Jackson and Toni C. Antonucci. 1989. 'Age difference in productive activities'. *Journal of Gerontology: Social Sciences* 44: S129–S138.

Hess, Beth B. 1980. 'Old women: problems, potential, and policy implications'. In E. Markson and G. Batra, eds, *Public Policies for an Aging Population*. Lexington, Mass.: Lexington Books, D. C. Heath.

Hess, Beth. 1985. 'Aging policies and old women: the hidden agenda'. In Alice S. Rossi, ed., *Gender and the Life Course*. New York: Polity.

Hockey, Jenny and Allison James. 1993. *Growing Up and Growing Old*. London: Sage.

Hohfeld, Wesley N. 1923. *Fundamental Legal Conceptions*. New Haven, Conn.: Yale University Press.

Home and Community Care Program (HACC). 1991. *Getting it Right: Guidelines for the Home and Community Care Program National Service Standards*. Canberra: Australian Government Publishing Service.

Home and Community Care Program (HACC). 1993. *Managing Complaints: A HACC National Service Standards Training Package*. Canberra: The Change Agency, for HACC, Department of Health, Housing and Community Services.

Home and Community Care Program (HACC). 1995. *The Efficiency and Effectiveness Review of the Home and Community Care Program: Final Report*. Department of Human Services and Health, Aged and Community Care Service Development and Evaluation Reports, No. 18. Canberra: Australian Government Publishing Service.

Home and Community Care Program (HACC). n.d. [circa 1991]. *Your Rights: A Guide to Help Consumers Understand and Exercise their Rights in the HACC Program*. Canberra.

House, James S. and Robert L. Kahn. 1985. 'Measures and concepts of social support'. In Sheldon Cohen and S. Leonard Syme, eds, *Social Support and Health*. Orlando, Fla.: Academic Press.

Hoyes, Lesley, Robin Means and Julian Le Grand. 1992. *Made to Measure: Performance Measurement and Community Care*. Occasional Paper 39, School for Advanced Urban Studies, University of Bristol. Bristol: SAUS for the Joseph Rowntree Foundation.

Hunt, Audrey. 1970. *The Home Help Service in England and Wales*. London: HMSO.

Hunt, S. M., S. P. McKenna, J. McEwan, J. Williams and E. Papp. 1981. 'The Nottingham Health Profile: subjective health status and medical consultations'. *Social Science and Medicine* 15A: 221–229.

Hutten, Jack B. F. and Ada Kerkstra, eds. 1996. *Home Care in Europe: A Country-Specific Guide to Its Organization and Financing*. Aldershot, Hants.: Arena/Ashgate.

Jacobs, Klaus, Martin Kohli and Martin Rein. 1991. 'The evolution of early exit: a comparative analysis of labor force participation patterns'. In Martin Kohli *et al.*, eds, *Time for Retirement*. Cambridge: Cambridge University Press.

Jamieson, Anne, ed. 1991. *Home Care for Older People in Europe: A Comparison of Policies and Practices*. Oxford: Oxford University Press.

Jencks, Christopher. 1992. *Rethinking Social Policy: Race, Poverty and the Underclass*. Cambridge, Mass.: Harvard University Press.

Joint Review of Hostel Care Subsidies Arrangements. See Australia. Department of Community Services. 1985. Report of.

Jones, Jacqueline. 1992. *The Dispossessed: America's Underclasses from the Civil War to the Present*. New York: Basic.

Kane, Rosalie A. and Robert L. Kane, with James Reinardy and Sharon Arnold. 1987. *Long-Term Care: Principles, Programs and Policies*. New York: Springer.

Keens, Carol, Frances Staden and Adam Graycar. 1983. *Options for Independence: Australian Home Help Policies for Elderly People*. Social Welfare Research Centre Reports and Proceedings, No. 35. Kensington, NSW: University of New South Wales.

Keiher, Sharon. 1991. 'Wages or welfare: compensating caregiving in two conservative social welfare states'. *Journal of Aging and Social Policy* 3 (3): 83–104.

Kendig, Hal L. 1983. 'The providers of community care'. pp. 131–53 in H. L. Kendig, D. M. Gibson, D. T. Rowland and J. M. Hemer, eds, *Health, Welfare and Family in Later Life*. Sydney: New South Wales Council on the Aging.

Kendig, Hal L. 1986. 'Intergenerational exchange'. pp. 85–109 in Hal L. Kendig, ed., *Ageing and Families: A Social Networks Perspective*. Sydney: Allen & Unwin.

Kendig, Hal L. and D. T. Rowland. 1983. 'Family support of the Australian aged: a comparison with the United States'. *The Gerontologist* 23: 643–49

Kewley, T. H. 1980. *Australian Social Security Today*. Sydney: Sydney University Press.

Keys, Sir William, chair. 1994. *Report of the Nursing Home Consultative Committee to the Hon. Brian Howe, Minister*. Mimeo., Department of Housing, Local Government and Community Services, Canberra.

Kinnear, David and Adam Graycar. 1982. *Family Care of Elderly People: Australian Perspectives*. Social Welfare Research Centre Reports and Proceedings, No. 39. Kensington, NSW: University of New South Wales.

Korpi, Walter. 1995 . 'The position of the elderly in the welfare state: comparative perspectives on old-age care in Sweden'. *Social Service Review* 69: 242–73.

Krause, Neal. 1987. 'Life stress, social support, and self-esteem in an elderly population'. *Psychology and Aging* 2: 340–56.

Laing, William. 1993. *Financing Long Term Care: The Crucial Debate*. London: Age Concern.

Lakey, Jane. 1994. *Caring about Independence: Disabled People and the Independent Living Fund*. London: Policy Studies Institute.

Land, Hilary. 1976. 'Women: supporters or supported'. pp. 108–32 in D. L. Barker and S. Allen, eds, *Sexual Divisions and Society: Process And Change*. London: Tavistock.

Land, Hilary. 1978. 'Who cares for the family?' *Journal of Social Policy* 7: 257–284.

Land, Hilary. 1985. 'The family wage'. pp. 9–29 in Clare Ungerson, ed., *Women and Social Policy: A Reader*. London: Macmillan.

Lawton, M. P., M. Moss, M. H. Kleban, A. Glicksman and M. Rovine. 1991. 'A two-factor model of caregiving appraisal and psychological well-being'. *Journal of Gerontology* 46: 181–89.

Le Grand, Julian and Will Bartlett, eds. 1993. *Quasi-markets and social policy*. London: Macmillan.

Leghorn, L. and K. Parker. 1981. *Women's Worth: Sexual Economics and the World of Women*. London: Routledge & Kegan Paul.

Leonard, Wilbert M. 1981. 'Successful aging: an elaboration of social and psychological factors'. *International Journal of Aging and Human Development* 14: 223–32.

Lewis, Jane and Howard Glennerster. 1996. *Implementing the New Community Care*. Buckingham: Open University Press.

Lewis, Myrna I. and Robert N. Butler. 1984. 'Why is women's lib ignoring old women?' pp. 199–208 in Meredith Minkler and Carroll L. Estes, eds, *Readings in the Political Economy of Aging*. New York: Baywood Publishing.

Lyons, David. 1969. 'Rights, claimants and beneficiaries'. *American Philosophical Quarterly* 6: 173–85.

Macri, Sue. 1993. *Resident Classification Instrument Documentation Consultation Report*. Mimeo., Department of Housing, Local Government and Community Services.

Macdonald, B., with C. Rich. 1985. *Look Me in the Eye: Old Women, Aging and Ageism*. London: Women's Press.

Madden, Ros, Ken Black and Xingyan Wen. 1995. *The Definition and Categorisation of Disability in Australia*. Canberra: Australian Government Publishing Service for the AIHW.

Malinowski, B. 1922. *Argonauts of the Western Pacific*. London: Routledge & Kegan Paul.

Malinowski, B. 1932. *Crime and Custom in Savage Society*. London: Paul, Trench & Turbner.

Malthus, T. R. 1826. *An Essay on the Principles of Population*. 6th edn. London: J. Murray.

March, James G. and Johan P. Olsen. 1976. *Ambiguity and Choice in Organizations*. Bergen: Universitetsforlaget.

Mathur, Sushma, Ann Evans and Diane Gibson. 1997. *Community Aged Care Packages: How do they compare?*. Department of Human Services and Health Aged and Community Care Service Development and Evaluation Reports, Canberra: Australian Government Publishing Service.

Mathur, Sushma. 1996. *Aged Care Service in Australia's States and Territories*. AIHW Aged Care Series No. 2. Canberra: Australian Institute of Health and Welfare.

McIntosh, Mary. 1978. 'The state and the oppression of women'. pp. 254–89 in A. Kuhn and A. M. Wolpe, eds, *Feminism and Materialism*. London: Routledge & Kegan Paul.

McIntosh, Mary. 1979. 'The welfare state and the needs of the dependent family'. pp. 153–172 in S. Burman, ed., *Fit Work for Women*. London: Croom Helm.

McLeay Report: see Australia, House of Representatives, Standing Committee on Expenditure.

Mead, Lawrence M. 1986. *Beyond Entitlement: the Social Obligations of Citizenship*. New York: Free Press.

Mead, Lawrence M. 1992. *The New Politics of Poverty: the Nonworking Poor in America*. New York: Basic Books.

Means, Robin and Randall Smith. 1994. *Community Care: Policy and Practice*. London: Macmillan.

Meenan, R. F., P. M. Gertman and J. H. Mason. 1980. 'Measuring health status in arthritis: the Arthritis Impact Measurement Scale'. *Arthritis Rheumatism* 23 (2): 146–152.

Melden, A. I. 1959. *Rights and Right Conduct*. Oxford: Blackwell.

Mendelson, Mary A. 1974. *Tender Loving Greed: How the Incredibly Lucrative Nursing Home 'Industry' is Exploiting America's Old People and Defrauding Us All*. New York: Knopf.

Mendes de Leon, Carlos F., Stanislav V. Kasl and Selby Jacobs. 1993. 'Widowhood and mortality risk in a community sample of the elderly'. *Journal of Clinical Epidemiology* 46 (6): 519–27.

Mill, John Stuart. 1848. *Principles of Political Economy*. London: Parker & Son.

Mills, C. Wright. 1959. *The Sociological Imagination*. New York: Oxford University Press.

Minkler, Meredith and Robyn Stone. 1985. 'The feminization of poverty and older women'. *The Gerontologist* 25 (4): 351–7.

Monk, Abraham, Lenard W. Kaye and Howard Litwin. 1984. *Resolving Grievances in the Nursing Home: A Study of the Ombudsman Program*. New York: Columbia University Press.

Montague, Meg. 1982. *Ageing and Autonomy*. Melbourne: Brotherhood of St Laurence.

Morris, Jenny. 1993a. 'Feminism and disability'. *Feminist Review* 43: 57–70.

Morris, Jenny. 1993b. *Independent Lives: Community Care and Disabled People*. London: Macmillan.

Moynihan, Daniel Patrick. 1973. *The Politics of a Guaranteed National Income*. New York: Random House.

Murray, Charles A. 1984. *Losing Ground: American Social Policy, 1950–1980*. New York: Basic Books.

Myrdal, Gunnar. 1944. *An American Dilemma: The Negro Problem and Modern Democracy*. New York: Harper.

National Citizens' Coalition for Nursing Home Reform. 1987. *The Rights of Nursing Home Residents*. Washington, DC: NCCNHR.

Nelson, Barbara J. 1990. 'The origins of the two-channel welfare state: workmen's compensation and mother's aid'. pp. 123–51 in Linda Gordon, ed., *Women, the State and Welfare*. Madison: University of Wisconsin Press.

Nelson, Martha A. 1993. 'Race, gender, and the effect of social supports on the use of health services by elderly individuals'. *International Journal of Aging and Human Development* 37: 227–46.

Nemschoff, H. L. 1981. 'Women as volunteers: long history, new roles'. *Generations* 5: 35–48.

Nicholas, Michael K. and Timothy J. Sharp. 1995. 'Assessment of outcomes in a pain management service'. pp. 81–3 in Jan Sansoni, ed., *Health Outcomes and Quality of Life Measurement*. Proceedings of a conference organised by the Australian Health Outcomes Clearing House, Canberra, 14–15 August 1995. Canberra: Australian Institute of Health & Welfare.

Nursing Homes and Hostels Review. See Australia. Department of Community Services. 1986. Nursing Homes and Hostels Review.

Oakley, Ann. 1974. *The Sociology of Housework*. New York: Pantheon.

Offe, Claus and Rolf G. Heinze. 1992. *Beyond Employment: Time, Work and the Informal Economy*. Oxford: Polity.

Oliver, Michael. 1990. *The Politics of Disablement*. Basingstoke: Macmillan.

Pateman, Carole. 1988. 'The patriarchal welfare state'. pp. 231–60 in Amy Gutmann, ed., *Democracy and the Welfare State*. Princeton: Princeton University Press.

Paterson, H. M. 1982. 'Voluntary work in Australia'. *Australian Bulletin of Labour* 8 (2): 95–103.

Payne, Barbara and Frank Whittington. 1976. 'Older women: an examination of popular stereotypes and research evidence'. *Social Problems* 23: 488–504.

Peace, Sheila. 1986. 'The forgotten female: social policy and older women'. pp. 61–86 in C. Phillipson and A. Walker, eds, *Ageing and Social Policy: A Critical Assessment*. Aldershott: Gower.

Pearce, Diana. 1990. 'Welfare is not *for* women: why the war on poverty cannot conquer the feminisation of poverty'. pp. 265–279 in Linda Gordon, ed., *Women, the State and Welfare*. Madison: University of Wisconsin Press.

Pearlin, L. I., T. Mullian, S. J. Semple and M. M. Skaff. 1990. 'Caregiving and the stress process: an overview of concepts and their measures'. *The Gerontologist* 30: 583–94.

Peat, Marwick, Mitchell. 1986. *Services, Quality, Staffing and Standards: Commonwealth Subsidised Hostels for Aged Persons*. Canberra: Australian Government Publishing Service.

Piven, Frances Fox. 1990. 'Ideology and the state: women, power and the welfare state'. pp. 250–64 in Linda Gordon, ed., *Women, the State and Welfare*. Madison: University of Wisconsin Press.

Piven, Frances Fox. 1994. 'Social entitlements'. Paper presented to the Sixteenth World Congress of the International Political Science Association, Berlin.

Power, Michael. 1994. *The Audit Explosion*. London: Demos.

Preston, G. and B. O'Connell. 1985. *Report on a Census of Aged and Extended Care Populations in Institutions in Victoria*. Melbourne: Health Commission of Australia.

Pynos, Jon and Phoebe Liebig, eds. 1995. *Housing Frail Elders: International Policies, Perspectives and Prospects*. Baltimore, Md.: Johns Hopkins University Press.

Rein, Martin, 1970. *Social Policy Issues of Choice and Change*. New York: Random House.

Reinharz, S. 1986. 'Friends or foes: gerontological and feminist theory'. *Women's Studies International Forum* 9 (5): 503–14.

Rickwood, Debra. 1994. 'Dependency in the Aged: Measurement and Client Profiles for Aged Care'. Welfare Division Working Paper No. 5. Canberra: Australian Institute of Health and Welfare.

Rivlin, Alice M. 1971. *Systematic Thinking for Social Action*. Washington, DC: Brookings Institution.

Rivlin, Alice M. and Joshua M. Wiener, with Raymond J. Hanley and Denise A. Spence. 1988. *Caring for the Disabled Elderly: Who Will Pay?* Washington DC: Brookings Institution.

Roberts, Helen. 1981. 'Some of the boys won't play any more: the impact of feminism on sociology'. In Dale Spender, ed., *Men's Studies Modified: The Impact of Feminism on the Academic Disciplines*. Oxford: Pergamon.

Robine, J., C. Mathers, and N. Brouard. 1993. 'Trends and differentials in disability-free life expectancy'. In *Health and Mortality Trends among Elderly Populations: Determinants and Implications*. Vol. 1. Proceedings of the UN–WHO–IUSSP (International Union for the Scientific Study of Populations) Conference on Health and Mortality among Elderly Populations, held at Sendai, Japan, June 1993.

Rodeheaver, Dean. 1987. 'When old age became a social problem, women were left behind'. *The Gerontologist* 27: 741–6.

Ronalds, Chris. 1988. *I'm Still an Individual*. Canberra: Department of Community Services and Health.

Ronalds, Chris, with Philippa Godwin and Jeff Fiebig. 1989. *Residents' Rights in Nursing Homes and Hostels: Final Report*. Canberra: AGPS.

Rose, Hilary. 1981. 'Rereading Titmuss: the sexual division of welfare'. *Journal of Social Policy* 16: 477–502.

Rose, Richard. 1985. 'Getting by in three economies: the resources of the official, unofficial and domestic economies'. pp. 103–4 in Jan-Erik Lane, ed., *State and Market*. London: Sage.

Rosenman, Linda. 1982. *Widowhood and Social Welfare Policy in Australia*. Social Welfare Research Centre Reports and Proceedings, No. 16. Kensington, NSW: University of New South Wales.

Rosenman, Linda. 1986. 'Women and retirement age income security'. pp. 251–63 in Ronald Mendelsohn, ed., *Finance in Old Age*. Canberra: Centre for Research on Federal Financial Relations, Australian National University.

Rosenman, Linda. 1995. 'Restructuring retirement policies: changing patterns of work and retirement in later life'. Paper presented at the International Sociological Association Research on Ageing Intercongress Meeting, Melbourne, May 1995.

Rossi, Alice. 1986. 'Sex and gender in an aging society'. *Daedalus* 111 (1): 141–69.

Rossiter, Chris. 1984. *Family Care of Elderly People: Policy Issues*. Social Welfare Research Centre Reports and Proceedings, No. 50. Kensington, NSW: University of New South Wales.

Rowland, Don. 1991. *Aging in Australia*. Melbourne: Longman Cheshire.

Rudinger, Georg and Hans Thomae. 1990. 'The Bonn longitudinal study of aging: coping, life adjustment and life satisfaction'. In Paul B. and Margret M. Baltes, eds, *Successful Aging*. Cambridge: Cambridge University Press.

Russell, Cherry. 1987. 'Aging as a feminist issue'. *Women's Studies International Forum* 10 (2): 125–132.

Russell, Cherry. 1995. 'Older people's constructions of dependency: some implications for aged care policy'. pp. 85–106 in Sarah Graham, ed., *Dependency, the Life Course and Social Policy*. Social Policy Research Centre, Reports and Proceedings, No. 118. Kensington, NSW: University of New South Wales.

Sainfort, François, James D. Ramsay and Hermes Monato, Jr. 1995. 'Conceptual and methodological sources of variation in the measurement of nursing facility quality: an evaluation of 24 models and an empirical study'. *Medical Care Research and Review* 52 (1): 60–87.

Sansoni, Jan. 1995. 'Quality of life: measure for measure'. pp. 84–106 in Jan Sansoni, ed., *Health Outcomes and Quality of Life Measurement*. Proceedings of a conference organised by the Australian Health Outcomes Clearing House, Canberra, 14–15 August 1995. Australian Institute of Health & Welfare.

Sapiro, Virginia. 1990. 'The gender basis of American social policy'. pp. 36–54 in Linda Gordon, ed., *Women, the State and Welfare*. Madison: University of Wisconsin Press.

Schreiner, Olive. 1977. *Women and Labour*. London: Virago; originally published 1911.

Scott, H. 1984. *Working Your Way to the Bottom: The Feminisation of Poverty*. London: Pandora Press.

Scott, Rose. 1903. 'Why women need a vote'. Unpublished speech, Scott family papers, Mitchell Library Manuscripts 38/36, Sydney.

Segal, Lynne. 1983. 'No turning back: Thatcherism, the family and the future'. pp. 190–214 in Lynne Segal, ed., *What is to be Done About the Family?* Harmondsworth: Penguin.

Shaver, Sheila and Michael Fine. 1996. 'Social policy and personal life: changes in state, family and community in the support of informal care'. pp. 19–36 in *Towards a National Agenda for Carers: Workshop Papers*. Aged and Community Care Service Development and Evaluation Reports, No. 22. Canberra: Australian Government Publishing Service.

Smith, Dorothy E. 1987. *The Everyday World as Problematic: A Feminist Sociology*. Boston: Northeastern University Press.

Smith, Peter, ed. 1996. *Measuring Outcomes in the Public Sector*. London: Taylor & Francis.

Smith, Steven Rathgeb and Michael Lipsky. 1993. *Non-profits for Hire: The Welfare State in the Age of Contracting*. Cambridge, Mass.: Harvard University Press.

Social Welfare Commission. 1975. *Report of the Committee of Inquiry into Aged Persons Housing*. Canberra: Australian Government Publishing Service.

Sommers, Tish. 1978. 'The compounding impact of age on sex'. In R. Gross, B. Gross and S. Seidman, eds, *The New Old: Struggling for Decent Aging*. New York: Anchor Press.

Sontag, Susan. 1975. 'The double standard of aging'. pp. 479–94 in E. Lasky, ed., *Humanness: An Exploration into the Mythologies about Women and Men*. New York: MSS Information.

Spencer, Herbert. 1894. *The Study of Sociology*. London: Williams & Norgate.

Stacey, Judith and Barrie Thorne. 1985. 'The missing feminist revolution in sociology'. *Social Problems* 32: 301–17.

Stone, Robyn and Meredith Minkler. 1984. 'The sociopolitical context of women's retirement'. pp. 225–38 in Meredith Minkler and Carroll L. Estes, eds, *Readings in the Political Economy of Aging*. New York: Baywood.

Streib, G. F. and R. W. Beck. 1980. 'Older families: a decade review'. *Journal of Marriage and the Family* 42: 937–56.

Sundström, Gerdt. 1994. 'Care by families: an overview of trends'. pp. 15–56 in Patrick Hennessy, ed., *Caring for Frail Elderly People: New Directions in Care*. Social Policy Studies, No. 14. Paris: Organisation for Economic Co-operation and Development.

Thornton, Patricia and Rosemary Tozer. 1994. 'Involving older people in planning and evaluating community care: A review of initiatives'. The University of York: Social Policy Research Unit.

Tinker, Anthea. 1994. 'The role of housing policies in the care of elderly people'. pp. 57–82 in Patrick Hennessy, ed., *Caring for Frail Elderly People: New Directions in Care*. Social Policy Studies, No. 14. Paris: Organisation for Economic Co-operation and Development.

Titmuss, R. M. 1958/1976. *Essays on 'The welfare state'*. 3rd edn. London: Allen & Unwin.

Titmuss, R. M. 1968. *Commitment to Welfare*. London: Allen & Unwin.

Townsend, Peter. 1957. *The Family Life of Old People*. London: Routledge & Kegan Paul. 2nd edn. 1963. Harmondsworth: Penguin.

Townsend, Peter. 1981. 'The structural dependency of the elderly: a creation of social policy in the twentieth century'. *Ageing and Society* 1: 5–28.

Tulloch, Patricia. 1984. 'Gender and dependency'. pp. 19–37 in Dorothy H. Broom, ed., *Unfinished Business*. Sydney: Allen & Unwin.

Ungerson, Clare. 1987. *Policy is Personal: Sex, Gender and Informal Care*. London: Tavistock.

United Kingdom. Department of Health. 1989. *Caring for People: Community Care in the Next Decade and Beyond*. Cmnd. London: HMSO.

United Nations. 1989. *Demographic Yearbook 1987*. New York: United Nations.

United Nations. 1993a. *The Sex and Age Distribution of the World Population: The 1992 Revision*. New York: United Nations.

United Nations. 1993b. *World Population Projections: The 1992 Revision*. New York: United Nations.

United Nations. 1995. *Demographic Yearbook 1993*. New York: United Nations.

United States. Department of Health, Education and Welfare; Panel on Social Indicators: *see* Bell and Rivlin 1969.

Victoria. Department of Health and Community Services. Office of the Deputy Secretary for Community Services. Industry Analysis Unit. 1994. *A Guide to Output-based Funding*. Melbourne: DHCS.

Waldron, Jeremy. 1984. 'Introduction'. In J. Waldron, ed., *Theories of Rights*. Oxford: Oxford University Press.

Walker, Alan. 1980. 'The social creation of poverty and dependency in old age'. *Journal of Social Policy* 9 (1): 49–75.

Walker, Alan. 1982. 'Dependency and old age'. *Social Policy & Administration* 16: 115–35.

Walker, Alan, Anne-Marie Guillemard and Jens Alber. 1993. *Older People in Europe*. Brussels: Commission of the European Community.

Walker, Alan and Lorna Warren. 1996. *Changing Services for Older People*. Buckingham: Open University Press.

Ware, John E. and C. D. Sherbourne. 1992. 'The MOS 36-item short form health status survey (SF-36): I. Conceptual framework and item selection'. *Medical Care* 30: 473–83.

Waring, Marilyn. 1988. *Counting for Nothing*. Wellington, NZ: Allen & Unwin. Also published under the title *If Women Counted: A New Feminist Economics*. New York: Harper & Row.

Wildavsky, Aaron. 1979. *Speaking the Truth to Power: The Art and Craft of Policy Analysis*. Boston: Little, Brown.

Wiles, D. 1987. *Living on the Aged Pension: A Survey Report*. Social Welfare Research Centre Reports and Proceedings, No. 64. Kensington, NSW: University of New South Wales.

Wilson, Elizabeth. 1977. *Women and the Welfare State*. London: Tavistock.

Wilson, William Julius. 1987. *The Truly Disadvantaged: The Inner City, the Underclass and Public Policy*. Chicago: University of Chicago Press.

Wistow, Gerald, Martin Knapp, Brian Hardy and Caroline Allan. 1994. *Social Care in a Mixed Economy*. Buckingham: Open University Press.

Woerness, Kari. 1987. 'A feminist perspective on the new ideology of "community care" for the elderly'. *Acta Sociologica* 30: 133–50.

Woolf, Virginia. 1997. *A Room of One's Own*. London: Granada; originally published 1929.

Working Party on the Protection of Frail Older People in the Community. 1994. *Report*. Office for the Aged, Aged and Community Care Division, Department of Human Services and Health. Aged and Community Care Service Development and Evaluation Reports, No. 14. Canberra: Australian Government Publishing Service.

Wright, F. 1983. 'Single carers: employment, housework and caring'. In J. Finch and D. Groves, eds, *A Labour of Love*. London: Routledge & Kegan Paul.

Young, Michael and Tom Schuller. 1991. *Life after Work: The Arrival of the Ageless Society*. London: HarperCollins.

Zimmerman, David R., Sarita L. Karon, Greg Arling, Brenda Ryther Clark, Ted Collins, Richard Ross and François Sainfort. 1995. *Health Care Financing Review* 16 (1): 107–29.

Zinn, Deborah K. 1984. 'Turning back the clock on public welfare'. *Signs: Journal of Women in Culture and Society* 10 (2): 355–70.

Index

Abramovitz, M. 193
accountability of service providers 148, 149
Activities of Daily Living (ADL) scales 200
Adelmann, P. K. 139
advocacy services 48, 116–17, 118, 167, 208, 216
  see also carers' advocacy and support groups
age- and sex-specific handicap rates 54, 55
aged care
  outcome measures 147–65
  policy history, Australia 29–35
  responsibility for 5
Aged Care Advisory Committees 35, 44, 119
aged care assessment teams 18, 42, 43
  and targeting 215–16
  user rights issues 127–8
aged care programs, outcome evaluation 19
Aged Care Reform Strategy 33, 37–8, 44
  and deinstitutionalisation 51–69
aged care services
  and consumer rights 179–81
  and dependency needs 200
  Australian regulatory system 20
  delivery and funding 6
  government expenditure 65–6
  planning base changes 34
  provision 6
  reviews, Australia 33
  timeline, Australia 219–25
Aged Consumer Forums 117, 118, 119
aged pension 40, 210
aged persons, home care preference 12–13, 15

Aged Persons Homes Act 1954 29
Aged Persons Hostels Act 1972 31
aged population
  and health-related quality of life measures 158–60
  country comparison 7, 8
  home help service use 10, 11–12
  projected annual growth rates 9–10
  recent annual growth rates 8–9
  residential care use 10, 11–12
  structural changes, Australia 34
  trends, Australia 54–5
ageing
  as a male problem 24–5
  as public issue 4, 5
  as social problem 4
  see also feminisation of ageing; older men; older women
ageing and disability literatures
  implications for reducing dependency 202–4
  reducing dependency 199–202
Allen, I. 25, 71, 76, 80, 81, 133, 144, 201
Andersen, M. L. 142
Antonucci, T. C. 138, 139
Arber, S. 70, 73, 74, 133, 143, 144
Aronson, J. 78
assessment and targeting 215–16
Australia
  aged population 7–10, 34
  funding and service arrangements 28
  home care policy 12, 13
  outcome standards monitoring system 21, 22
  policy developments 28–47
  policy history (1954–1984) 29–35
  residential regulatory system 20–1
  system reform 33–5

242